Reel Education

minding the media

CRITICAL ISSUES FOR LEARNING AND TEACHING

Shirley R. Steinberg
General Editor

Vol. 17

The Minding the Media series is part of both the Peter Lang Education list and the Media and Communication list. Every volume is peer reviewed and meets the highest quality standards for content and production.

PETER LANG
New York • Bern • Frankfurt • Berlin
Brussels • Vienna • Oxford • Warsaw

Jacqueline Bach

Reel Education

Documentaries, Biopics, and Reality Television

PETER LANG
New York • Bern • Frankfurt • Berlin
Brussels • Vienna • Oxford • Warsaw

Library of Congress Cataloging-in-Publication Data

Names: Bach, Jacqueline, author.
Title: Reel education: documentaries, biopics, and reality television / Jacqueline Bach.
Description: New York: Peter Lang, 2016.
Series: Minding the media: critical issues for learning and teaching; vol. 17 | ISSN 2151-2949
Includes bibliographical references.
Identifiers: LCCN 2016015262 | ISBN 978-1-4331-2916-2 (hardcover: alk. paper)
ISBN 978-1-4331-2915-5 (paperback: alk. paper) | ISBN 978-1-4539-1880-7 (ebook pdf)
ISBN 978-1-4331-3630-6 (epub) | ISBN 978-1-4331-3631-3 (mobi)
Subjects: LCSH: Audio-visual education.
Classification: LCC LB1043 .B28 2016 | DDC 371.33/5—dc23
LC record available at https://lccn.loc.gov/2016015262

Bibliographic information published by **Die Deutsche Nationalbibliothek.**
Die Deutsche Nationalbibliothek lists this publication in the "Deutsche Nationalbibliografie"; detailed bibliographic data are available on the Internet at http://dnb.d-nb.de/.

29 Broadway, 18th floor, New York, NY 10006
www.peterlang.com

CONTENTS

ACKNOWLEDGMENTS AND INTRODUCTION

As I was writing this book there were two films titled *Teacher of the Year*: one came out in 2014 (Strouse), and the other was scheduled to be released in 2015. Strouse's was a motion picture film starring Keegan-Michael Key as a principal and Matt Letscher, who has just become "teacher of the year;" the other stars Angie Scioli as herself, a former "teacher of the year." While Letscher's is a fictional film pretending to be a documentary (a mockumentary) and Scioli's is a documentary, both feature teachers who are not new to the profession and who are facing similar experiences. These depictions are a departure from the new-to-the-classroom idealistic teachers that dominate the genre of school films, which I define for the purposes of this book as a film that focuses on teachers, students, parents, and administrators. Films like these that are focused on similar issues—in this case, honoring two excellent teachers who are struggling to balance the demands of their teaching jobs and everything else—always catch my attention.

It wasn't until I was preparing my materials for promotion and tenure that I realized so many of my publications and presentations had been in the field of school films. I thought that I had been writing about more "important" issues in education: young adult literature, teacher preparation, and English language arts. Looking back, however, and specifically at my first publication about a school film, *Napoleon Dynamite* (Hess & Hess, 2004), I realized that I had always been taken with the relationship between the schools found on the screen and the schools in which I had taught high school English. In the education courses I currently teach, many of my students and I include references to these films in our class discussions. Combined with a fascination with Žižek and then Lacan through Žižek, I realized that reality can never be accessed but that wouldn't stop filmmakers who claim to capture reality, represent reality, or base their films on reality to depict what really goes on in schools. I wanted to know what prevented them from capturing the reality that I believe audiences so desperately need to see.

Before I introduce this work, I'd like to thank the many parties involved with the creation of this book. First, I must thank my students, who know of my obsession with school films and send me recommendations all of the time. A tremendous thank you to Elena and Albert LeBlanc, whose financial gift to Louisiana State University's School of Education supported this project. And, thanks to LSU for that sabbatical. Thanks to Carol Schanche for her fine editing skills and to Sue Weinstein for the countless conversations on the early (and late) drafts of this book. A dear thanks to the members of my writing group, Laura Choate and Petra Hendry, whose contributions and support are impossible to put into words. Thanks to Yvette Hyde, Heather Johnston Durham, Veta Parker and the student workers who helped me with the finishing touches. To the pioneers in this field, Mary Dalton, Robert Bulman, James Trier, John Weaver, Cameron McCarthy, and the late Greg Dimitriadis, thank you for your scholarship, collegiality, and support. And, of course, thanks to my family, Victor and Emery Gischler—Emery, unlike your dad's books, you can actually read this one.

This entire book is concerned with the concept of what is real about education in school films. While I acknowledge there is no such thing as reality nor is it possible to have just one notion of reality, each of these three genres relates to the real, intersects with the real, claims to be real, or markets itself with the phrase "based on a real story." Given the increasing attention these films and television shows are receiving in multiple disciplines, new theoretical frameworks are needed to understand the complicated relationship these texts have with educational policy and public conversations about education. *Reel Education: Documentaries, Biopics, and Reality Television* opens with an overview of these three genres and examines their relationship representing aspects of education. *Reel Teaching* also examines the implications of incorporating documentaries, biopics, and reality television shows into humanities and education courses. Working through the lens of media studies, the book reveals the ways in which cinematic texts with realistic claims challenge, perpetuate, upend, and complicate audiences' understanding of education. When audiences comprehend the relationship between these cinematic texts and larger contemporary conversations about education, viewing these films, television shows, and those found on the Internet, becomes a more enriching experience. This book serves as a resource for analyzing and discussing that relationship.

Overview of Book

This book is divided into three sections, each focusing on one genre, with three chapters in each. The first chapter in each section situates the genre and contextualizes landmark texts from that genre within contemporary conversations about educational issues. The second chapter in each section focuses on an exemplar in each genre—one that often challenges other works through the blending of previous narratives and the codes and conventions associated with that genre. Each section concludes with a chapter on the pedagogical implications associated with each genre, highlighting teaching strategies for each genre found in a variety of disciplines.

The first section, "Race to Represent First: Documentaries," examines the genre of documentaries set in schools. In Chapter 1 I consider the relationship between documentaries about schools and educational reform and policy. Beginning with the 1983 report, *A Nation at Risk*, these documentaries often reflect the contemporary reforms and policies regarding schools. The second chapter in this section, "'But No One Taught Me': An Educational Mockumentary," examines the film *Chalk* (Akel & Mass, 2006), which pulls codes from the documentary and fictional film genres, such as interviews, a narrative structure, and unscripted scenes in order to distance the film from the audience's expectations for both genres—namely, to present the objective truth as well as to sustain a traditional narrative structure. Promoting itself with the slogan "Real Teaching Leaves Its Mark," the film engages conventions from both fictional and nonfictional genres in order to uncover, perhaps facetiously, why 50% of teachers quit within the first three years. Given the privileged status documentaries have acquired through their claims of representing reality and the ways audiences read these films as reflecting reality, Chapter 3 considers how educators and their students might negotiate what is presented to them as fact by this genre. In this chapter, I examine how we might teach documentaries about education through a close reading of them, through careful examination of their ideological claims, and through the activist approach many of these filmmakers take in promoting their films.

In Section 2, "Based on Actual Events: Biopics," I discuss the history of biopics set in schools and the reasons for the lasting popularity of this genre. Functioning primarily in an emotional register, biopics attempt to capture the personal and professional aspects of teaching. Such films often distort the stories on which they are based to the point of absurdity, perpetuating the "teacher as savior" myth. While these films do not claim to be real, they are often based on real stories from recorded memoirs, television talk shows, and newspaper interviews. In an attempt to understand the complicated process that unfolds when a story based on actual events is adapted for film, this chapter examines three biopics that not only received some degree of box office success but that comprise much of the conversation surrounding representations of good and bad teachers, and good and bad teaching, in school films. These are: *Dangerous Minds* (Smith, 1995), *Freedom Writers* (LaGravenese, 2007), and *Stand and Deliver* (Menendez, 1988). This chapter weaves together the reception of these films by film critics and scholars and the reactions from subjects of the biopics themselves in response to seeing their stories adapted for the screen. This analysis uncovers the aspects of teachers' narratives that have been silenced to fit the Hollywood model for biopics and how those stories represent particular narratives to the public about schools.

Chapter 5 is a close reading of the French film *The Class* (Cantet, 2009), which won the Palme d'Or at Cannes. Based on François Bégaudeau's book *Entre Les Murs* (2006) (which translates into *Between these Walls*), which many scholars consider an autobiographical novel or semi-autobiographical novel, the film is about the relationship between a French teacher and his students, who are an ethnically diverse group, many of whom are from immigrant families from Africa, Asia, and the Caribbean. *The Class* is technically not a fictional or nonfictional film although it employs the codes and conventions of both, such as creating fictional characters and employing documentary styles of filming. The film was praised for many reasons, but perhaps the most frequent compliment was how it represented the realities of the urban classroom.

I have a problem with those critics and scholars who praise it for its reality, and use it as a way to talk about contemporary education problems. They are trapped in a conversation in which they must acknowledge that while they believe it reflects the contemporary real classroom, it is also a movie with fictional elements. Some of those elements, which I will discuss in this chapter, possibly reinforce stereotypes and assumptions about schools, teachers, and students. In other words, while Bégaudeau's story may contain elements of truth, it is a story told through a genre (memoir) that is often criticized for its representation of past events based on the author's memory and interpretation of them.

Since biopics, arguably, wield the most attention out of all the genres of films and television shows about education, Chapter 6 explores the possibilities of teaching them as between the worlds of the real and not real, or based on reality. Since many of these narratives are based on memoirs and real-life stories, how should educators approach this genre in their courses? In this chapter, I outline the questions raised by scholars who research biopics and suggest that educators use these questions as a way to teach biopics about teachers. I then go on to examine how instructors from communication studies, sociology, and teacher education incorporate school biopics into their courses. Finally, I offer two approaches to teaching biopics that reflect the conventions of the biopic genre.

Section 3, "Real Worlds: Reality Television," examines the world of reality television and its intersections with education and pedagogy. Whether it's a look into the daily activities of housewives or the competitive world of dance, reality television shows provide an insider's view to various professions and lifestyles and offers audiences ideas about improving their own lives. Section 3 considers the genre of reality television. The first chapter in this section, Chapter 7, is an overview of the genre, as I consider how its roots are somewhat set in a pedagogical basis. Reality television informs, teaches, and supports various lifestyles and ways of being. It remains a contested genre, criticized for its artificiality and inexpensive paths to production. The chapter begins with an overview of the growth of reality television and a discussion of the different types of shows that have developed over the years and their intended purposes. It concludes with a consideration of the educative aspects located in this genre through audiences' fascination and interactions with these lives caught on film.

Chapter 8 provides an analysis of how the reality television genre distorts the elements found in television shows to create representations of education that focus the audience's attention on the boundary between real and contrived. Using a case study approach to examine the first reality television show to feature a teacher, *Teach: Tony Danza* (Grief & Reed, 2010), this chapter reveals how a reality show featuring a questionably qualified celebrity teacher was unable to escape the mundane aspects of teaching that essentially led to its being canceled. In Chapter 9, I examine how scholars look to the structure of these shows to create a sense of real-world application and engagement for their course material. This chapter focuses on educators who are using reality television shows to teach their students about their professions by interrogating and critiquing representations of professionals found in such shows.

References

Akel, M., & Mass, C. (Writers & Directors). (2006). *Chalk* [Motion picture]. San Francisco, CA: Someday Soon Productions.

Cantet, L. (Director). (2008). *The class* [DVD]. France: Haut et Court.

Greif, L., & Reed, A. (Producers). (2010). *Teach: Tony Danza*. Philadelphia, PA: A&E.

Hess, J. (Co-Writer/Director) & Hess, J. (Co-writer). (2004). *Napoleon Dynamite*. [Motion picture]. United States: Universal Pictures.

LaGravenese, R. (Director). (2007). *Freedom writers* [Motion picture]. United States: Paramount.

Menendez, R. (Director). (1988). *Stand and deliver* [Motion picture]. United States: Warner Bros.

Philips, R., & Korreck, J. (Directors). (2016). *Teacher of the Year*. [Motion Picture]. United States: At Large Productions.

Smith, J. N. (Director). (1995). *Dangerous minds* [Motion picture]. United States: Don Simpson/Jerry Bruckheimer Films/Hollywood Pictures.

Strouse, J. (Writer & Director). (2015). *Teacher of the Year*. [Motion Picture]. United States: Lower Marion Films.

United States. National Commission on Excellence in Education. (1983). *A nation at risk: The imperative for educational reform: A report to the Nation and the Secretary of Education, United States Department of Education*. Washington, DC: The Commission.

SECTION I

RACE TO REPRESENT FIRST: DOCUMENTARIES

· 1 ·

"SOMETHING IS WRONG IN THE EDUCATION SYSTEM"

Manufacturing a Crisis in the School Documentary

In her book, *Reign of Error: The Hoax of the Privatization Movement and the Danger to America's Public Schools* (2013), education historian and former assistant secretary of education in George H. W. Bush's administration Diane Ravitch argues that the real crisis in the United States' public schools is not what the public has been led to believe. It is not, she argues, the result of poor urban schools. The real problem is the result of decades of misguided educational reform that was meant to deal with the poverty and racial segregation that created those urban schools and that resulted in today's "market-based" reforms. Part of that narrative, she argues, can be found in the films about schools from the last twenty years. She writes:

> In Hollywood films and television documentaries, the battle lines are clearly drawn. Traditional public schools are bad; their supporters are apologists for the unions. Those who advocate for charter schools, virtual schooling, and "school choice" are reformers; their supporters insist they are championing the rights of minorities. They say they are leaders of the civil rights movement of our day.
>
> It is a compelling narrative, one that gives us easy villains and ready-made solutions. It appeals to values Americans have traditionally cherished—choice, freedom, optimism, and a latent distrust of government.
>
> There is only one problem with this narrative.
>
> It is wrong. (Ravitch, 2013, p. 4)

Those, like Ravitch, who refer to the messages sent to audiences in movie theaters tend to lump fictional and nonfictional films together. But, given the scholarship on the field of documentaries, one can argue that they wield more power to sway audiences to a particular cause. According to Nichols (1991), audiences tend to be more invested with real lives than with the fictional ones they see on screen: "We are less engaged by fictional characters and their destiny than by social actors and destiny itself" (p. 5). It's hard for me not to be moved by a documentary about a school. As I watched the 27 film and television documentaries that would form the basis for this chapter, I empathized with the teachers who were just trying to do their job, the parents who just wanted the best for their children, and the students who possessed amazing abilities and wonderful dreams. At the same time, I was appalled by the documentaries that suggested simple solutions to the educational woes of the United States: hire better teachers, privatize education, and challenge students academically.

My purpose in this chapter is not to prove or disprove the claims made in these films and television shows (in this chapter, I will use documentaries made both for the theater and television) but instead to demonstrate how they intersect with the educational issues and policies of their time. The problem with documentaries is similar to the other genres discussed in this book that claim to have a connection to reality—in sticking to the codes and conventions of the genre, they are unable to capture the realities of education.

In this chapter, I first contextualize these documentaries within the larger educational conversation that dominated public discourse at the time they were produced. Because my analysis relies on actual scenes of classroom practice, I consider documentaries that capture scenes of students learning in schools. This narrowing is essential in order to locate documentaries that reflect educational topics in K–12 schools, such as reform and policy; however, this decision leaves out influential documentaries about schools, such as Michael Moore's examination of the potential causes of school violence in *Bowling for Columbine* (Moore, 2002) and Andrew Rossi's *The Ivory Tower* (2014), which is about the rising costs of a college degree. While both of these films (and others) have scenes in schools, they lack pedagogical moments that show teachers and students engaged in the act of schooling in a traditional sense, such as teachers delivering lessons and students working on assignments. Furthermore, while there are several documentaries set in schools that are about sports teams, I have, for the most part, not included them in this study because they both lack pedagogical scenes and their purposes are fundamentally different. (Documentaries about school sports could comprise an additional chapter in which we might examine their relationship to fictional films about school sports.) Finally, there are a number of high-quality, interesting documentaries produced by countries other than the United States, but the focus of this chapter is on educational issues in the United States, so I have chosen to focus only on those produced in this country.

Next, I constructed a list of 27 documentaries produced for the theater and television between the years 1993 and 2015 (please refer to the filmography at the end of this chapter for the list). Among those filmed for television are several that appeared on Public Broadcasting Service (PBS) stations. I include made-for-television documentaries because they share some of the same conventions as those made for the theater, although they have the flexibility to air over a longer period of time or in hour-long segments. In the end, they still contribute to this notion of "discourses of sobriety" (Nichols, 2010). Hill (2005) argues that these texts share some of the modes of documentaries filmed for the theater, but believes that "most television documentary has undergone a dramatic restyling, often using a variety of techniques to tell fact-based stories" (p. 103). The documentaries that are made for television exhibit a wide range of approaches. At one end of the spectrum is the journalistic approach in which a journalist reports the show's narrative through his or her own investigative efforts, e.g., the "Stupid in America" special that aired on ABC. Alternatively, many take a more theater-type approach, as in the *180 Days* series that aired on PBS; this series had less noticeable involvement from the filmmaker and constructed a story that was told in a chronological manner.

In this chapter, I also address the most frequent educational issues and themes represented by documentaries about education. For example, during my analysis of 27 documentaries produced since 1993, I noted that in order to convey a strong message, these films focus on outliers or extremes—e.g., students and their families who are trying to leave their failing school systems by entering a lottery for a chance to attend a charter school in *Waiting for Superman* (2010) and *The Lottery* (2010); overworked students who are stressed out by homework in *Race to Nowhere* (2010); and a group of students from inner city Baltimore who attend a boarding school in Kenya in *The Boys of Baraka* (Ewing & Grady, 2005). While Ravitch's observation in this chapter's opening suggests that fictional and nonfictional films equally contribute to this narrative and that the solutions to fixing public education can only be found in alternative spaces, like charter schools, I argue that the documentary filmmaker puts forth "truth claims" (the claim to represent the real, not fictional, world) that set documentaries apart from the fictional film. A documentary's apparent relationship to truth, built through the filmic strategies it employs, conveys to audience members that its representation of education is more truthful than a fictional one, and they should take it seriously. That narrative of identifying problems and proposing solutions is built through a body of work that uses the conventions of the genre. In other words, documentaries invite viewers to presume a particularly close relationship to the truth, or the real, when in fact, they are just as conventional as any other genre of film in terms of the ways that narratives are shaped and manipulated to fit the norms of the genre (in terms of dramatic tension, etc.) in order to support the particular stance the filmmaker is taking toward the subject matter.

Documentary

> For me, the making of a documentary film is in some ways the reverse of making a fiction film. With fiction, the idea for the film is transformed into a script by the imagination and work of the writer and/or director, which obviously precedes the shooting of the film. In my documentaries the reverse is true: The film is finished when, after editing, I have found its "script."
>
> —Wiseman's Foreword in Grant (2006, p. xi)

In 1964, there were two notable documentaries about schools: one was a contemporary commentary, the other a historical one. Wiseman's *High School* (1964) was a look into a high school during the 1960s. Filmed at Northeast High School in Philadelphia, Pennsylvania, *High School* consisted of several scenes of teachers, students, and administrators going through their school day (Wiseman shot the footage over the course of several weeks). Interestingly, Northeast High School would serve in 2009 as the host school for the A&E reality television show, *Teach: Tony Danza*, which featured actor Tony Danza teaching a high school English class. (I analyze this show in Chapter 8.) In that same year, Charles Guggenheim's *Nine from Little Rock* (1964) won several awards for its retelling of the story about the first black students to attend an all-white school in Arkansas. Unlike Wiseman, Guggenheim's documentary was told from the point of view of one of the students and relies heavily on stock footage.

In *High School*, Wiseman attempted to capture the culture of the institution audiences know as a high school and most likely have attended themselves. In building his narrative, Wiseman relied on the juxtaposition of scenes in the classroom, interactions among students, teachers, and administrators, and scenes of various spaces in the school. The story he found after the editing process represented the high school as a lonely, alienating space (Grant, 2006). This message was conveyed through the observational style that obscures the filmmaker's role in the film—he or she is merely presenting what the camera recorded. There is no intrusion by the filmmaker during the production process, and there are no additions of a soundtrack, voiceover, or other notable influences from Wiseman other than the finished edited project.

Also notable is that *High School* stands as a commentary not on a particular person or group of people, not on an issue or historical event, but rather on an institution. Schools are often viewed as institutions, and their spaces serve many functions other than just the learning of skills and content knowledge. In *Discipline and Punish* (1975/1995), Foucault noted that in order for discipline to occur, individuals must be distributed in some kind of "enclosed" space; secondary schools are one example of a place where discipline and punishment can occur. Wiseman defines an institution as a "place that has certain kinds of geographical limitations and where at least some of the people have well-established roles" (Grant, 2006, p. 3). Grant notes that Wiseman's work on institutions, the people who represent them, and the people they are "supposed to serve" (p. 3) is "dynamic" because Wiseman does not limit himself to following a particular person/subject. As institutions, schools have clearly defined roles for individuals and spaces—such as students, teachers, parents, administrators, classrooms, and playgrounds—that are generally not to be crossed or chaos would ensue. But the members of this institution, like the other ones Wiseman explores, are marked by their transience—in this case, students, teachers, and administrators who transfer, drop out, or graduate, as new ones take their places. Meanwhile, the institutional spaces remain largely the same.

Today, documentaries about schools continue to look at the space as an institution; however, I have found that for the most part, their messages are not as subtly conveyed as Wiseman's work. As the genre has employed filmmaking strategies that became available with technological advances, new approaches permeate the field of school documentaries. For example, filmmakers today tend to present their messages in modes other than observational, although there are a few notable exceptions. Another reason for the difference in subtlety might have to do with a different relationship between the filmmaker and the subject of the film. Wiseman simply wanted to capture the inner workings of a high school; Guggenheim, who made *Waiting for Superman*, opened with a story about deciding where to send his children to school.

In this section, I offer a definition of the documentary, the structure of a school documentary, the different documentary modes, and how those approaches shape school documentaries. The consideration of a film's mode becomes important when analyzing the drastic shift in the field of the school documentary around the time No Child Left Behind was passed in 2002; that shift accounts for the ways certain documentaries represent some version of a *crisis* in public education, mirroring the rhetoric of crisis that has followed public education in the public sphere almost since the inception of public schools.

Just as with the other two genres I will discuss in this book (biopics and reality television), defining terms is always a problem for scholars of documentary film, especially given the changing nature and the continual blurring of boundaries in nonfiction texts. First, the overall body of work that falls under the category of nonfictional texts is referred to in a variety of ways, including *nonfiction texts*, *factual television*, *documentaries*, *mock documentaries*, *docudramas*, and *reality television*. While I do not find these terms to be interchangeable, they do share some characteristics, such as onscreen interviews with participants and experts, stock footage, and onscreen narrative subtitles. This blurring makes it difficult to settle on one definition for each of them. In defining what documentaries are, scholars tend to describe the conventions used by them and how they differ from other genres. In doing so, they acknowledge that documentaries are obviously constructed but differentiate themselves from other ostensibly "true" genres, like television news, mainly for their reliance on creating a narrative or a piecing together of fragments into a narrative (Ellis, 2000).

However, documentaries tend to include one or more of the following elements:

- Unscripted filmed scenes of events that are edited into a narrative structure.
- The imposition of some sort of order, such as chronological.
- Interviews with experts, the filmmaker(s), or with particular subjects of the documentary.
- Scenes filmed with inexpensive, lightweight equipment.
- Stock footage, soundtracks, and archival footage.

An additional characteristic of documentaries is their relationship with reality. They possess, according to Cowie (2011), the ability to "enable reality to 'speak' at the same time as it 'speaks about reality'" (p. 1). Audiences are aware of this relationship and the ways the genre represents reality though the genre's conventions (Corner, 2002). Buckland (2008) gives three characteristics of documentaries before acknowledging that all three have been contested by scholars: 1) the events that are filmed must be unstaged, 2) audiences understand that the world represented in the film is real, "not imaginary," and 3) the filmmaker is attempting to "make an objective record of real events" (p. 138).

Cowie (2011) offers a definition of a documentary that further explores the genre's relationship with reality and the way the film's reality is presented to audiences. She writes that the documentary "as a cinematic project ... seeks to enable the citizen-spectator to know and experience reality through recorded images and sounds of reality" and is "characterized by a dual assertion of the objective knowableness of the world and its claim that it gives us access to this knowledge" (p. 1). In doing so, however, the documentary "becomes prey to a loss of the reality in its narratives of reality" (Cowie, p. 1). In other words, the documentary loses its claim to the real when it brings "forth a new reality" (p. 2). Golden (2006), too, considers audience's expectations of documentaries and their relationship to reality. He writes that documentaries are based on audience's expectations for the truth, and that nonfiction films can "*expand our beliefs* in what is possible [author's emphasis]," while fictional films ask audiences to "*suspend their beliefs* [author's emphasis]" (p. 16).

Documentary filmmakers often rely on creating a narrative through the piecing together of fragments of footage (Ellis, 2000). Wiseman, who directed two films on high schools, explains that fictional films start with scripts, but that his documentaries end when he has found the story, or script, through the process of editing. Another way to distinguish a documentary is through the mode the filmmaker takes to (re)present the story. The documentary usually falls into one of six modes:

- the observational, which minimally uses a soundtrack, narrative voice, or interviews with experts;
- the participatory, which includes interviews with subjects of the film, voiceover, and a soundtrack;
- the expository, which is the presentation of often abstract ideas or concepts with a purpose or argument;
- the poetic, which is a film that attempts to represent ideas in new ways;
- the reflexive, in which the filmmaker interacts with the audience in such a way as to expose the genre's constructed nature; and
- the performative, which attempts to involve the audience in experiencing what the subjects of the film experience. (Nichols, 2010)

The mode or modes adopted by the filmmaker are important to consider when trying to understand how the genre of the school documentary has built up a narrative over the past few decades that attempts to convey the filmmaker's (or producers') messages about education.

Bill Nichols's notion of the "discourse of sobriety" is one way to examine how the documentary always serves as a diversion of reality, "because it draws us away from something we ought to behold more directly" (1991, p. 3). He explains that the documentary is not unlike other systems, such as science and education, in that they "can and should alter the world itself, they can effect action and entail consequences" (p. 3) because they claim to be a direct link to the real. However, given the mechanisms of the cinema, documentaries remain unequal with these other systems, in part because their messages are mediated through images. His observation is especially important when considering educational documentaries for two reasons. First, if they can only be a diversion of reality, then how are audiences to react and/or engage with the filmmaker's message? Second, because they do wield so much power through their claim to knowledge and reality, they will (and maybe should) always produce an amount of skepticism.

Scholars and most audiences recognize that documentaries make some claim to reality and employ the genre's codes and conventions to support their purpose. The relationship, then, between the film and the audience is negotiated by this indirect representation of reality mediated through the sounds and images that appear on the screen. According to Hill (2007), "a documentary's truth claims need to be trusted if it is to function as a genre," and in order to trust those truth claims, "most viewers have to suspend disbelief in order to foreground its referential integrity" (pp. 137–138). This idea is what leads to much of the genre's critique by viewers. Corner (2008) explains, "A longstanding issue in documentary analysis has been the kind of truth-claim that documentaries make and the frequent overstatement or over-projection of these claims, producing a consequent requirement to challenge them" (p. 24). One of the ways documentary studies can uncover how educational documentaries are manufacturing a crisis is an examination of the modes they employ and the "truth-claims" they make.

Mapping the "Discourse of Sobriety" in Education

As Nichols (1991) notes, systems like education have a claim on being connected to the real (the important issues associated with a discipline, for example) that can result in change and transformation (one hopes in a positive way) because they can entice action and enact consequences for failure to do so. The public conversations about education conducted by legislators, educators, and other stakeholders during the past several decades have referred to test score data as a way to support the contention that students in the United States are falling behind their global peers. The resulting legislation has affected the field of education in a sobering way. In fact, the reforms and policies that occurred between 1983 and 2015 have led to the increased amount of school accountability. Ravitch and others argue that these reforms that are often tied to money have resulted in the privatization of education we have today. In this next section, I highlight the larger conversation about education that was occurring during a particular era and discuss three or four of the documentaries that were released around the same time.

1983–1993

I start with *A Nation at Risk*, a 1983 report on the state of education in the United States. This report is notable for its strong discourse and recommendations about the state of education during this time. Commissioned by President Ronald Reagan's National Commission on Excellence in Education, the report found that in the preceding 50 years, there had been a decline in test scores, thereby jeopardizing the United States' ability to compete on a global scale:

> Our Nation is at risk. Our once unchallenged preeminence in commerce, industry, science, and technological innovation is being overtaken by competitors throughout the world. This report is concerned with only one of the many causes and dimensions of the problem, but it is the one that undergirds American prosperity, security, and civility. … What was unimaginable a generation ago has begun to occur—others are matching and surpassing our educational attainments.

These opening lines of *A Nation at Risk* position United States students as victims whose scores on international tests do not measure up. It also claims that there is now a crisis that did not exist a generation ago. Our students need better teachers, better schools, and higher expectations. Many of the Committee's recommendations can be found in public schools today, including a suggested set curriculum, a school day of at least seven hours, and teachers knowledgeable in their content areas. The report has been studied many times since its publication and the veracity of the data it used scrutinized, but the discourse forms the basis of educational reforms that would follow.

On the publication of the report, President Reagan remarked:

> Your Commission was asked to assess the quality of teaching and learning in America compared with our own educational tradition and the rising competition from other industrial nations. You've taken a long, hard look at America's educational system and found that quality is lacking, but not because today's students are any less capable than their predecessors. You've found that our educational system is in the grip of a crisis caused by low standards, lack of purpose, ineffective use of resources, and a failure to challenge students to push performance to the boundaries of individual ability—and that is to strive for excellence.

The report and the crisis in the educational system it found, while impacting educational reform tremendously, were reflected in different ways in the documentaries about education filmed during the 1980s. One film in particular, *High Schools* (Guggenheim, 1983), examined the crisis located in the United States educational system. This film was based on Boyer's book *High School*, which was a study of the contemporary high school. Boyer's team's findings (which were funded by the Carnegie Corporation) suggested that high schools encouraged mediocrity through a menu-style approach to education that did not challenge most students.

Two other documentaries about education produced during this time focused on elementary school. One film was the 1993 documentary, *I Am a Promise: The Children of Stanton Elementary School* (Raymond, 1993). This documentary followed the day-to-day activities of Stanton's principal, several of her initiatives, and a few of the students. Located in perhaps the poorest section of Philadelphia, the faculty and staff at Stanton do their best to prepare their students for the demands of middle school. *Educating Peter* (Wurzburg, 1992) is the story of a boy who has Down syndrome who must navigate inclusion in a third grade classroom at a public school. The story resulted from the Individuals with Disabilities Act (IDEA), which means students should not be removed from a regular classroom unless necessary, and they must be educated in the least restrictive environment possible. *Educating Peter* was followed by *Graduating Peter* (Wurzburg, 2003) several years later on HBO and continued tracking his progress through middle and high school. Overall, these three documentaries did engage with current legislation and research conducted during this time period. The crises in these three films are adolescence, poverty, and special education, and the films approach these topics through three lenses: an examination of several schools, one school, and one student.

1994–2001

Two notable documentaries of this period spotlight individual schools but move away from issues of legislation. This period begins with a sequel. Wiseman's 1994 *High School II*, a follow up to his *High School* (1968), continued in the tradition of observational style. The narrative was created through the juxtaposition of dialogue from inside and outside the classroom, and this second film, set in Central Park East Secondary School in New York City, became more of a reflection of relationships and social issues as students and faculty discussed the Rodney King shooting in Los Angeles.

In *Chain Camera* (Dick, 2001), a crew gave each of 10 students at John Marshall High School in California a camera and asked them to record a week in their lives. They were then to give those cameras to 10 more students, who would pass them on to 10 more students, until the end of the school year. This footage was then paired down to focus on 16 students and their stories. Those students showed their personal lives as they discussed their experiences with eating disorders, sexual orientation, running away, and suicide. Their overwhelming desire, however, was just for companionship.

During this time, one documentary that featured an unconventional school is *Boot Camp High* (Braverman, 2000), an examination of Eagle Academy, a military-type boarding school in Palm Beach County, Florida. This film followed the experiences of several recruits who attended the high school program. At this school, many students found not only friendship, but also a pedagogical approach that enabled them to succeed in school academically. Their parents were also required to attend weekly parenting sessions. The DVD extras feature follow-ups with several of the former cadets. Altogether, these documentaries about education seem unencumbered by educational policy and reform as they focus on the students' experiences, yet they still send a strong message of one way to address a problem found in education—the juvenile delinquent.

These three documentaries send the message that the issue most pressing to education during this era is understanding the students and their developmental needs. They continued Wiseman's tradition of presenting schools as being unable to meet the needs of students or, as in the case of *Chain Camera*, of just being another thing an adolescent must tolerate and/or navigate. The solution to educating well-adjusted students is understanding them and providing structure and support.

2002–2009

The number of documentaries about education increased during this era. This time, President Bush's legislation, No Child Left Behind (NCLB) (2001), which picked up on the themes of both the Democratic and Republican parties to improve education, shifted direct accountability to schools. This legislation built upon President Clinton's act Goals 2000: Educate America, which placed responsibility for improved student performance directly on the schools. As President Bush stated in a speech:

> The first principle is accountability. Every school has a job to do. And that's to teach the basics and teach them well. If we want to make sure no child is left behind, every child must learn to read. And every child must learn to add and subtract. So in return for federal dollars, we are asking states to design accountability systems to show parents and teachers whether or not children can read and write and add and subtract in grades three through eight. (Bush, 2002)

In regards to NCLB, historian of education and bestselling author Diane Ravitch simply states, "In retrospect, NCLB was the worst education legislation ever passed by Congress" (p. 244) because it became a deliberate attempt to eradicate public education. She argues that the government is not set up to run schools, that test scores are not the end result of a good education, the consequences for schools failing based on student test scores is unfair and punitive, and its implementation would narrow the curriculum and encourage teaching to the test.

Educational reforms appear to have had little influence on school documentaries in the early 2000s. Instead, documentaries filmed during this time focused on students, schools, and their special projects. Furthermore, there were several films that employed the observational techniques of Wiseman (including his own work) to profile high school students rather than schools, their teachers, or their parents.

Paper Clips, filmed in 2004 (Fab), examined a school's ongoing project to collect enough paperclips to represent each person who died during the Holocaust in an effort to understand the magnitude of those deaths. *American Teen* (Burnstein, 2008), which won an award at the Sundance Film Festival for direction of a documentary, focused on the different "categories" of students found in high school cliques—the rebel, the geek, the heartthrob, and the princess. The film followed five students through their everyday lives. The poster mimicked the promotional poster for John Hughes's

The Breakfast Club (1985), and the film's trailer suggested neat and tidy storylines that resemble those found in films from Hughes.

For the most part, the documentaries of this time were interested in a variety of topics, and were focused on students rather than on policy, schools, or teachers. That would change over the next few years, however. In 2005, a filmmaker who had done his student teaching in New York set out to learn whether or not NCLB was successful. In his film *No Child Left Behind* (Wilson, 2005), Wilson traveled to several different large cities in the northeastern US to interview experts in the educational field. Ultimately, the answer his film put forth was an ambiguous one: it's likely that NCLB is doing good by improving standards for students, but that it is also doing harm. This last film would foreshadow many of the documentaries in the next few years that did not focus as overtly on educational reform policy, but instead on the potential changes that it would encompass.

2009–2010

The next educational reform that followed NCLB actually built upon many of the tenets found in the bipartisan bill. The reform, called Race to the Top, was established in 2009 by President Obama and Secretary of Education Arne Duncan. President Obama introduced it to the public as a competition in which states and school districts would work to come up with a winning plan that would earn them a part of the four billion dollars set aside for reform:

> That's how we can incentivize excellence and spur reform and launch a race to the top in America's public schools.
>
> That race starts today. I'm issuing a challenge to our nation's governors, to school boards and principals and teachers, to businesses and not-for-profit, to parents and students: if you set and enforce rigorous and challenging standards and assessments; if you put outstanding teachers at the front of the classroom; if you turn around failing schools, your state can win a Race to the Top grant that will not only help students outcompete workers around the world, but let them fulfill their God-given potential.
>
> ... We will use the best evidence available to determine whether a state can meet a few key benchmarks for reform—and states that outperform the rest will be rewarded with a grant. Not every state will win and not every school district will be happy with the results. But America's children, America's economy, and America itself will be better for it. (Obama, 2009)

Race to the Top maintained NCLB's punitive measures while encouraging states to privatize education (note the language that includes businesses and not-for-profits). States were encouraged to use test scores (assessments) to evaluate schools. The award for winning the competition, then, would be great sums of money for those states that created plans that met the goals stated in Race to the Top. Tenets from this piece of legislation were to appear several times over the next few years in many school documentaries.

The period encompassing 2009 and 2010 needs to be discussed apart from the other documentaries of this time. While there were some documentaries that did not directly reference school reform—including *Ten9Eight: Shoot for the Moon* (Mazzio, 2009) that followed a group of students through an entrepreneurial competition (this was filmed before Race to the Top was announced), others such as *Race to Nowhere* (Abeles & Congdon, 2010), which examined overworked students who are stressed out by homework—considered the themes found in *Waiting for Superman* and *The Lottery* such as the lack of student openings in quality schools, the negative influence of standardized testing, and teacher accountability. Perhaps the most scathing examination was the ABC *20/20* episode titled "Stupid in America" (Stossel, 2006), which championed school choice, especially charter schools, and lamented the state of public education. Likewise, *The Cartel* (Bowdon, 2009) also enacted a discourse of sobriety—an attempt to bring attention to and transform a system—by championing charter schools and educational reform. Furthermore, three more films supporting school choice followed a similar format: *Nursery University* (Simon & Maker, 2009), which followed five families in New York trying to get their students into elite New York preschools; *The Lottery* (Sackler, 2010), which followed four families trying to get their children into a charter school in Harlem, New York; and *Waiting for Superman* (Guggenheim, 2010), which followed five families trying to win their children spots in charter schools.

Even *Race to Nowhere* resembled these films in discussing the relationship of high-stakes testing to earning spots in schools, only in this case, students were trying to earn spots in prestigious universities. Within its message of student stress from homework and testing culture was a discussion of educational reform and policy. The filmmaker's personal concerns in *Race to Nowhere*, which had affected her own family, resulted in the DVD version of the film, including a 245–page "facilitation guide and companion resource" to bring awareness and enact change regarding this issue.

In addition to following five families' journeys through the school lottery, *Waiting for Superman* explored the promise of charter schools, the role teacher unions play in keeping incompetent teachers, and educational leaders with new ideas. These messages were structured around the students' experiences and contained interviews with experts, stock footage, undercover unedited footage, and animated segments to illustrate various educational concepts and practices. Ravitch (2010) argues that *Waiting for Superman* "was a fairy tale, based on half-truths, exaggerations, and misrepresentations" before she goes on to refute many of the claims made by the documentary. In the year following *Waiting for Superman*, two teachers from New York City produced the documentary, *The Inconvenient Truth behind* Waiting for Superman (Bruhn, Cavanaugh, Donlan, & Scott, 2011). In it, they attempted to refute some of the claims made in *Waiting for Superman* and included facts that were left out of the film, including the advent of charter schools being housed inside of public schools. At the end, the filmmakers, both teachers in the New York system, proposed their own solutions to the educational woes of the country.

The Lottery ends with the plea, "Find out how you can support great schools in your community. Mentor. Teach. Donate. Vote. Visit thelotteryfilm.com to find opportunities near you." In an interview with Reasontv, Sackler (2010) says news footage of families attending the lottery to win a spot in Harlem Academy was one of the reasons behind making the film. When she saw so many involved parents, she saw the debunking of the myth that parents don't care about their children's education. Ultimately, she blames the educational system's problems on politicians and unions.

2011–2015

In the years after *Waiting for Superman*, the focus of the school film turned to profiling schools that were trying to address the dropout problem and the achievement gap. *Brooklyn Castle* (Dellamaggiore, 2012), for instance, followed the extremely successful school chess club at a school in Brooklyn, New York, that was in danger of losing funding for its chess program due to budget cuts. During the 2012–2013 television season, an episode of *Spurlock: Inside Man* for CNN featured Spurlock teaching a lesson to students in Finland and the United States in order to gain a better understanding of why Finland's students perform better on international tests than students in the US. *180 Days: A Year in an American High School* profiled a public high school in Washington, DC. At the end of the film, the principal was let go and several of the students who were profiled had dropped out or transferred from the school. An audience member could interpret this film's message in either of two ways: as supporting the need for better schools and bringing in strong leaders, or as a picture of unfunded and unsupported programs within a system that lags behind the rest of the world.

Recent documentaries are incorporating new technologies and modes of delivery in order to represent different aspects of education. One player in the realm of factual television and documentaries is YouTube. A fairly recent example of this genre is *Last Chance High* (Renaud, C., & Renaud, B., 2014). *Last Chance High* consists of eight episodes set in and around Moses Montefiore Academy, an alternative high school in Chicago, Illinois. Most of MMA's students have behavioral and/or emotional disorders, and several scenes are of fights among students on the school bus or teachers attempting to calm down students who have lost control of their emotions. Each episode follows a different student, such as one who set a sibling on fire or the two who attacked teachers at their previous school. There are no voiceovers or words on the screen, and storylines are left unfinished. Shows like this one, which are low budget, lightly edited, and set inside schools that camera crews may have found somewhat intimidating, highlight aspects of "extreme" schooling. Coining itself "news for a new generation," Vice News, the corporate producer of *Last Chance High*, makes documentaries for the digital generation through platforms found on the Internet, including YouTube.

In an effort to answer the questions *What makes a good teacher?* and *How should teaching be measured?*, the forthcoming documentary *Teacher of the Year* (Philips, R., & Korreck, J., 2016) profiles a social studies teacher from North Carolina who was Wake County's first teacher of the year in 1994. Based on the promotional trailer and clips from the film, this documentary's subject sets herself apart from most of the teachers found in fictional and nonfictional films (Coincidentally, an exception is the fictional film that came out the previous year with the same title): she is not fresh out of a certification program, she clearly has been successful, and her personal life is shown on-screen in ways that are not often seen. (See Trier's [2006] research for an example of how teachers' personal lives are represented on screen.)

Teacher of the Year (2016) is being produced by two teachers who are raising money online to help with production; their topic is the crisis of teacher accountability and evaluation, and their main character is a social studies teacher juggling the demands of teaching and raising a family. The promotional shots for the documentary include scenes of the teacher, Angie Scioli,

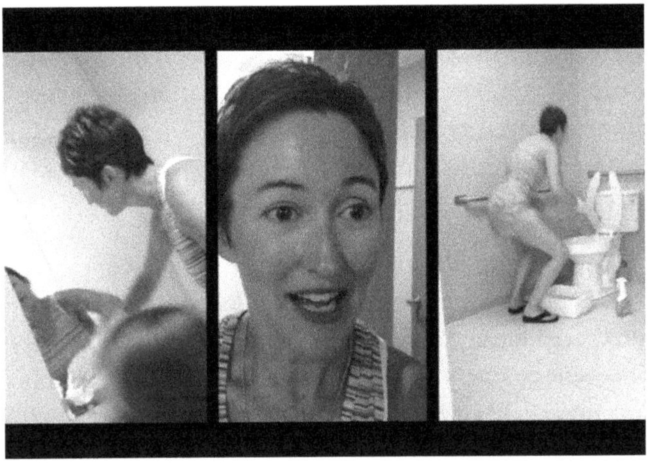

Figure 1.1. Angie Scioli. Source: Jason Korreck and Robert Phillips (At Large Productions).

cleaning the toilet in her classroom and juggling the demands of teaching while raising children.

This film exemplifies releases from the last few years that seem to model earlier documentaries (featuring a school, a teacher, or a policy) while taking advantage of the multiple paths to production and publishing available today. Notably, these more recent efforts seem less secure in their recommendations for the future of education. As we wait for a new administration and presumably new legislation, these documentaries are forces meant to inform rather than transform.

Methods

Documentaries about schools take many approaches and employ various modes; however, in my sample of 27, I found they tend to follow a similar narrative structure intended to position the film as uncovering, examining, or analyzing an element of schools and/or education. They are not as self-reflexive or as performative as other documentaries can be, and they generally approach their message without humor. They often begin with an opening montage followed by a startling statistic. Here are some of those opening statistics from this sample:

- 1 kid every 9 seconds will drop out of high school. (*Ten9Eight: Shoot for the Moon*, 2009)

- The number of children under the age of five in New York City has increased by 30% since 2000. Competition for admission to the city's best preschools is fierce, with over 15 applications for every available slot. (*Nursery University*, 2009)
- Education's hidden crisis: hundreds of thousands of students fail to complete school each year. (*Dropout Nation*, 2012)

After such an opening, the film usually gives the audience a glimpse of the current state of the city in which the school, students, community, or teachers is shown. Often these images are generic shots of a run-down neighborhood, a dilapidated school, or teachers and students getting ready for school.

The documentary will often then turn to the subject of its representation: a school, a group of teachers, a few students—someone or something that is trying to challenge the status quo, trying to succeed, trying to counteract the alarming statistic that opened the film. What follows in the documentary, then, is a portrayal of this group's efforts. The narrative may or may not include testimonies from experts in the field, interviews with stakeholders (such as parents or students), or stock footage of related events, such as notable historical events or public meetings with school boards. The endings often take one of several approaches, depending on the narrative structure used in the documentary: some choose to update the viewer on the subjects, others offer recommendations for improving the educational system, and still others point audiences toward resources or organizations they can choose to support if they are interested.

In preparation for this study, I watched each of the 27 documentaries multiple times, noting their themes, their settings, their subject(s), and the documentary mode(s) they employed. Using a qualitative approach to content analysis (Altheide, 1996) and with some guidance from Trier (2006), I coded the 27 films according to the answers to the following questions:

1. What is the film's setting (a single school, multiple schools, urban, elite, etc.)?
2. What/who is the subject of the narrative (teacher, school, student, policy, or program)?
3. How does this film employ one of the six modes of documentaries (Nichols, 2010): expository, observational, participatory, reflexive, poetic, or performative?
4. What issues/themes are considered by these documentaries?

Results

I was only able to locate a few documentaries about schools that were filmed before the year 1993. Of the list I compiled from after 1993, an overall pattern emerged among those films made after 2002, where many considered similar educational policies and reforms that were taking place in the United States. For example, over the years 2009–2010, there were three films that dealt directly with the issue of school choice. While school choice had appeared briefly in a couple other documentaries ("Stupid in America" for example), three films in a row suggest a growing awareness of this concept as part of the current discussion in education. Finally, the most recent documentaries in my list deal with school accountability, as opposed to earlier documentaries (pre-2002) that dealt with more diverse topics and issues.

1. What is the film's setting?
For this category, I sorted the films into different settings depending on where they were set (rural, suburban, and urban) and in what type of school (charter, public, private, independent). Nine films that focused on a single school were set in urban schools, two in rural schools, and two in suburban schools. The rest (14) were set in multiple settings: two films featured urban, suburban, and elite schools; three featured urban and elite schools; and nine featured multiple schools in urban cities. What is interesting to note is what is missing from this list and what that omission suggests about the educational system in the United States: out of 27 films, only four feature suburban schools (a deduction, since the films did not identify them as urban, as was done in other films). The lack of representation of suburban schools or schools with middle-class socioeconomic status could either suggest that these schools do not have a crisis, they have nothing to offer the educational field, or they are not interesting enough to make the subject of a documentary. It might also suggest something about the audience's expectations and commonly held beliefs about schools. As Nichols (1991) notes, this lack contributes to the documentary's natural tendency to divert audience's attention from other issues peripheral to the main theme of the documentary.

2. On what element of education does the film focus (teacher, school, student, policy, or educational program)?
The results from this question were difficult to separate, as many films focused on one or more of these elements. Therefore, I categorized the films according to their *primary* focus. Two films focus primarily on teachers' lives inside and

outside of the classroom. Eight focus primarily on a particular school's culture. Three films explore students' and/or their parents' experiences with an aspect of education, such as trying to win a spot in a charter school. Five specifically focus on an educational policy or legislation, such as *No Child Left Behind* (Wilson, 2005), and 9 feature educational programs such as debate, entrepreneurial competitions, and mentorship. It should be noted that 15 out of these 27 films use the stories of students to create a narrative structure in which to explore the specific element of education on which the film focuses.

3. Which of the six modes of documentaries (Nichols, 2010)—expository, observational, participatory, reflexive, poetic, or performative—does the filmmaker employ?

Filmmakers employ different modes to convey truth claims, and those modes are influenced by the larger approaches taken by documentary filmmakers of their time. For example, Wiseman's 1968 *High School* employed the observational mode. Observational documentaries, according to Ellis (2000) are those that "assembl[e] fragments of evidence from the world, from observations of actions to the testimonies of witnesses and the commentaries of experts, the combinatory documentary attempts to organize a coherent explanatory or investigative structure" (p. 117), but he goes on to say there is something in this assemblage that calls attention to the problem that is probably not directly stated in the documentary.

The filmmaker's choice of mode(s) highlights the differences among *Nursery University*, *The Lottery*, and *Waiting for Superman*. Watching families try to get their children into schools is the main narrative for all three films; however, *Waiting for Superman* is the only one that employs a participatory mode—a mode in which the narrator has a strong presence. The opening scene is of the narrator driving by a number of public schools on the way to drop his children off at a private school. His narrative voice, combined with a suspenseful storyline, interviews with experts, stock footage, hidden cameras, and performative scenes that make abstract concepts more concrete for the audience create a more compelling work than the other two films that incorporate fewer modes.

The Lottery and *Nursery University* both take place in New York City. *The Lottery* uses the expository mode by featuring scenes that just contain text to present facts, such as, "In the United States, 365,000 students are on waitlists for charters." This strategy works to reinforce and connect the parts of the film in order to highlight the urgency for better teachers, more charters, and more support from communities. *Nursery University* employs a similar formula and like *The Lottery*, uses the suspense of parents waiting to hear the results of their application to keep viewers on the edges of their seats until the very end. These three documentaries, filmed during 2009–2010, use a combination of the performative (scenes that are reenacted) and expository modes to explore the crisis of too few spots for children in quality schools in large cities. They weave messages about the lack of spaces within charter and "quality" preschools by constructing narratives that are based on parents' and guardians' efforts to "win" spaces in these select schools through the winning of a lottery.

The findings for both this question and question number two show that there was a tendency for a certain time period to employ the expository mode coupled with the performative mode in order to explore the issue of school choice. For these filmmakers, it was just not enough to say there are not enough spots in quality schools; they wanted the audience to feel what it might be like to be in a similar position, and each filmmaker adopted a mode or a combination of modes to capture the families' experiences. For example, when asked about her inspiration for making *The Lottery*, filmmaker Shackler referred to seeing a news report about a lottery for those trying to get into a charter school located in Harlem, New York. She was moved by the large number of parents vying for so few slots and wanted to tell their story (Gillespie, 2010).

On the other hand, documentaries like *The Inconvenient Truth behind* Waiting for Superman (Bruhn, Cavanaugh, Donlan, & Scott, 2011) (whose title is a combination of two documentaries made by the same filmmaker, *An Inconvenient Truth* and *Waiting for Superman*), in which two public school teachers from New York City attempt to share some of the facts *Waiting for Superman* left out (such as the co-location of charter schools within public schools) do not create a narrative story to frame their message—a decision that might have encouraged an audience member to sympathize more with a cause when confronted with a family's struggle with it. The difference in approaches means that some films rely more on the facts that they present and the relationship of the documentary to the "discourse of sobriety" to contribute to the overall conversation about education in the United States. In the end, I found *Waiting for Superman* to be more compelling—not right or wrong, just a more engaging film overall.

4. What themes do these documentaries cover?
Here is a list of themes covered by these 27 documentaries. They were derived both from key words found in descriptions for each film and from the reflections of the researcher.

Themes

School choice	Educational history
Supporting at-risk students	Accountability
Best practices/programs	Inequity
Successful students	School culture
Teachers	International approaches to education
Policy	Competition
Charter schools	

The four most frequent themes found in these documentaries are school choice, best practices/programs, supporting at-risk students, and school culture. As the years move forward, some issues are covered more often, such as charter schools, but the focus on at-risk students remains constant.

Taken together, the issues and settings for the majority of these films support the notion that since suburban schools are absent from this body of work, they must be doing fine. For example, some of the films that deal with suburban and elite schools are *Paper Clips* (Fab & Berlin, 2004), which looks at a school project to collect a paper clip for every victim who died during the Holocaust; *Race to Nowhere* (2010), which examines the stress students feel at the amount of schoolwork they must complete in order to get into good colleges; *Country Schools* (Rundle & Rundle, 2010), which examines the history of rural schools and their role in small-town and immigrant education; and *American Promise* (Brewster & Stephenson, 2013), which examines the experiences of two African American boys in New York who enter an elite school's program to diversify its school population. The idea that more successful educational experiences exist outside of the United States is demonstrated in *Boys of Baraka* (Kenya) and *Spurlock: Inside Man* (Finland).

Conclusion

Today, recent documentaries continue to cite the language of educational policy and reform in their scripts. Charter schools are fighting a system that is against them, public schools are just trying to survive in a time of accountability, and students are all potential dropouts. The language found in legislation and the media is bound to trickle down (or up) into the school documentary. But it is a limited picture, one driven by the interests and agenda of the filmmakers and those who support them.

Given the nature of the genre to focus on the problems and issues with education (struggling schools, underserved students) and the need to represent things "as they are" according to the filmmaker's agenda, how are audiences to gain insight into other aspects of education—the mundane, day-to-day, unglamorous, even sometimes trivial demands? If documentaries are limited in their ability to capture the realities of schooling because they focus on outliers and extremes rather than the status quo, then what type of nonfictional text holds hope for the profession? Perhaps it can be found in an offshoot of the genre—the mockumentary, which is explored in the next chapter.

References

Altheide, D. L. (1996). *Qualitative media analysis.* Thousand Oaks, CA: Sage.

Bowdon, B. (Director). (2009). *The cartel.* [Motion picture]. United States: Bowdon Media.

Buckland, W. (2008). *Teach yourself: Film studies.* Blacklick, OH: McGraw-Hill.

Burnstein, N. (Director). (2008). *American teen* [Motion picture]. United States: Paramount Vantage.

Bush, G. (2002). President signs landmark No Child Left Behind education bill. Retrieved from http://georgewbush-whitehouse.archives.gov/news/releases/2002/01/20020108-1.html

Corner, J. (2002). Performing the real: Documentary diversions. *Television and New Media, 3,* 255–269.

Corner, J. (2008). Documentary studies: Dimensions of transition and continuity. Retrieved from http://www.johncorner.com/wp-content/uploads/2014/08/documentary_studies.pdf

Cowie, E. (2011). *Recording reality: Desiring the real.* Minneapolis, MN: University of Minnesota Press.

Ellis, J. (2000). *Seeing things: Television in the age of uncertainty.* London, UK: I. B. Tauris.

Foucault, M. (1995). *Discipline & punish: The birth of the prison* (A. Sheridan, Trans.). New York, NY: Second Vintage Books. (Original work published 1975)

Gillespie, N. (2010). Interview with the director of the school choice documentary *The lottery* Madeline Sackler. Retrieved from https://reason.com/reasontv/2010/08/10/director-of-school-choice-docu

Golden, J. (2006). *Reading in the reel world: Teaching documentaries and other nonfiction texts.* Urbana, IL: National Council of Teachers of English.

Grant, B. K. (2006). Five films by Frederick Wiseman: *Titicut follies, High school, Welfare, High school II, Public housing.* Berkley, CA: University of California Press.

Guggenheim, C. (Director). (1964). *Nine from Little Rock* [Motion picture]. United States: United States Information Agency.

Guggenheim, C. (Director). (1983). *High schools* [Motion picture]. United States: Guggenheim Productions, Inc.

Hill, A. (2005). *Reality TV: Audiences and popular factual television.* Abingdon/New York, NY: Routledge.

Hill, A. (2007). *Restyling factual TV: Audiences and news, documentary and reality genres*. New York, NY: Routledge.

Hughes, J. (Director). (1985). *The breakfast club*. [Motion picture]. United States: Universal Pictures.

Moore, M. (Director). (2002). *Bowling for Columbine*. [Motion picture]. United States: Alliance Atlantis.

Nichols, B. (1991). *Representing reality: Issues and concepts in documentary*. Bloomington, IN: Indiana University Press.

Nichols, B. (2010). *Introduction to documentary* (2nd ed.). Bloomington, IN: Indiana University Press.

No Child Left Behind Act of 2001, 20 U.S. U.S.C. § 6319.

Obama, B. (2009). Remarks by the president on education. Retrieved from https://www.whitehouse.gov/the_press_office/Remarks-by-the-President-at-the-Department-of-Education/

Phillips, R., & Korreck, J. (Directors). (2016). *Teacher of the Year*. [Motion picture]. United States: At Large Productions.

Ravitch, D. (2010). *The death and life of the great American school system: How testing and choice are undermining education*. New York: Basic Books.

Ravitch, D. (2013). *Reign of error: The hoax of the privatization movement and the danger to America's public schools*. New York: Vintage Books.

Rossi, A. (Director). (2014). *The ivory tower* [Motion picture]. United States: Participant Media.

Trier, J. (2006). Exemplary introductory critical media literacy documentaries. *Journal of Adolescent and Adult Literacy*, 50(1), 68–71.

United States. National Commission on Excellence in Education. (1983). *A nation at risk: The imperative for educational reform: A report to the Nation and the Secretary of Education, United States Department of Education*. Washington, DC: The Commission. United States. Goals 2000: Educate America Act (P.L. 103–227).

Wiseman, F. (Director). (1968). *High school*. [Motion picture]. United States: Osti Productions.

Wiseman, F. (Director). (1994). *High school II*. [Motion picture]. United States: Zipporah Films.

Wurzburg, G. (Director). (1992). *Educating Peter* [Motion picture]. United States: Direct Cinema Limited.

Wurzburg, G. (Director). (2003). *Graduating Peter* [Motion picture made for television]. United States: HBO.

Filmography for Content Analysis (Chronological Order by Release Date)

Raymond, S. (Director). (1993). *I am a promise: The children of Stanton Elementary School*. [Motion picture]. United States: Video Verité LLC.

Fadiman, D. (Director). (1999). *Why do these kids love school?* [Motion picture]. United States: Fadiman Productions.

Braverman, C. (Director). (2000). *High school boot camp* [Motion picture]. United States: Braverman Productions, Inc.
Dick, K. (Director). (2001). *Chain camera.* [Motion picture]. United States: Chain Camera Pictures.
Fab, J., and Berlin, E. (Directors). (2004). *Paper clips.* [Motion picture]. United States: Miramax Films.
Stuart, M. (Director). (2005). *The Hobart Shakespeareans.* [Motion picture made for television]. United States: PBS.
Wilson, L. (Director). (2005). *No child left behind.* [Motion picture]. United States: Boondoogle Films.
Ewing, H., and Grady, R. (Directors). (2005). *Boys of Baraka.* [Motion picture]. United States: Loki Films.
Kalin, A. (Director). (2006). *The pact.* [Motion picture]. United States: Duke Media.
Stossel, J. (Host). (2006). *Stupid in America: A 20/20 special* [Television special]. United States: ABC.
Eisenhardt, B. (Director). (2007). *Small steps: Creating the high school for contemporary arts* [Motion picture made for television]. United States: PBS.
Whiteley, G. (Director). (2007). *Resolved* [Motion picture]. United States: One Potato Productions.
Mazzio, M. (Director). (2009). *Ten9Eight: Shoot for the moon.* [Motion picture]. United States: 50 Eggs Films.
Simon, M. H., & Makar, M. (Directors). (2009). *Nursery university* [Motion picture]. United States: Variance Films.
Guggenheim, D. (Director). (2010). *Waiting for Superman.* [Motion picture]. United States: Participant Media.
Sackler, M. (Director). (2010). *The lottery.* [Motion picture]. United States: Great Curve Films.
Abeles, V., & Congdon, J. (Directors). (2010). *Race to nowhere.* [Motion picture]. United States: Reel Link Films.
Rundle, K., & Rundle, T. (Directors). (2010). *Country school: One room–one nation* [DVD]. United States: Fourth Wall Films.
Bruhn, M., Cavanaugh, J., Donlan, L., & Scott, N. (Directors). (2011). *The inconvenient truth behind Waiting for Superman.* [Motion picture]. United States: Real Reform Studios.
Roth, V. (Directors). (2011). *American teacher.* [Motion picture]. United States: Warner Brothers.
Dellamagiore, K. (Director). (2012). *Brooklyn castle* [Motion picture]. United States: Chicken and Egg Pictures.
Koughan, F. (Writer). (2012). *Frontline: Dropout nation.* [Television special]. United States: PBS.
Brewster, J., and Stephenson, M. (Directors). (2013). *American promise* [Motion picture made for television]. United States: Rada Film Group.
Jones, J., & McLaurin, G. (Directors). (2013). *180 days: A year inside an American high school.* [Motion picture]. United States: National Black Programming Consortium.

Spurlock, M., & Chilnick, J. (Writers). (2013). *Morgan Spurlock: Inside man, education.* [Television episode]. United States: CNN.

Renaud, B., & Renaud, C. (Directors). (2014). *Last chance high.* [Motion picture]. United States: Vice News.

Jones, J., & McLaurin, G. (Directors). (2015). *180 days: Hartsville.* [Television series]. United States: National Black Programming Consortium.

· 2 ·

"BUT NO ONE TAUGHT ME"

An Educational Mockumentary*

I am sometimes asked at conferences what genre has the best hope of capturing the realities of teaching if the documentary genre cannot. I answer that mockumentaries might offer the best representations of what it is like to be a teacher. Mockumentaries, which pull codes from the documentary and fictional film genres, such as interviews, a narrative structure, and unscripted scenes, distance themselves from the audience's expectations for both genres—namely, to present the objective truth as well as to sustain a traditional narrative structure. Promoting itself with the slogan "Real Teaching Leaves Its Mark," the 2006 mockumentary *Chalk* (Akel & Mass, 2006) engaged conventions from both genres in order to uncover, perhaps facetiously, why 50% of teachers quit within the first three years.

Chalk, whose storyline follows three teachers and an administrator over the course of a school year, employs the postmodern strategies of the mockumentary to challenge the notion that teachers in the cinematic world quit, are fired, or persevere in the profession because of one, or a series of, life-changing event(s). Just as postmodern curriculum theory tries to dislodge

*This chapter is 95% reprinted from Bach, J., and Jolly, J. L. (2011). Chalking the profession: Unintended lessons about teaching. *Journal of Curriculum Teaching*, 27(1): 87–98. Reprinted by permission.

education's adherence to modernist teaching strategies (such as the tendency for desks to be arranged in rows facing the teacher, for teachers to deliver only whole-group lectures, or for strict implementation of a mandated curriculum), a mockumentary relies on postmodern cinematic strategies, such as the use of professional actors in scenes with non-actors, to subvert the status associated with documentaries. Intended to mock the "real" teaching profession, this film also mocks the educators portrayed in many Hollywood films—the alternatively certified teacher, the female physical education teacher, the overworked administrator. This chapter examines *Chalk*'s engagement with mockumentary strategies—especially in blurring the lines between real and reel by using actual students and teachers as actors without adhering to an actual script—and offers an alternative answer to the statistic that 50% of teachers quit in their first three years of teaching.

The numbers surrounding teacher attrition vary, but one report places that number as within the first five years. In 2003, Ingersoll published a report on teacher attrition that some credit with first publicizing the statistic that half of all teachers quit within the first five years of teaching. Upon closer examination, however, details of his research revealed the unevenness of that statistic: the numbers are probably closer to 40–50% (so somewhat less than half), more teachers quit in lower-socioeconomic areas, and some teachers leave and come back (Ingersoll, 2003). In the 2005 Report from the National Center for Education Statistics (NCES), Provasnik, Dorfman, and the Education Statistics Services Institute cited some of the reasons that teachers gave for leaving the profession:

> Both teachers who left teaching and teachers who transferred at the end of 1999–2000 reported a lack of planning time, too heavy a workload, too low a salary, and problematic student behavior among their top five sources of dissatisfaction with the school they left. (p. 24)

These are just two of the reports that were shaping the public's conversation about teachers when Mike Akel and Chris Mass co-wrote and directed the film (Mass also acted in the film). It posits that educators who are new to the profession do not necessarily suffer the traumatic events often portrayed in fictional films and documentaries about teaching. In fact, as teachers themselves, they were in a position to have experienced similar conditions and to have observed how Hollywood portrayed the downtrodden teacher. *Chalk* maintains that teachers' hardships may also be a result of the culminating effects of a mundane, absurd, even humorous job. *Chalk* became their response to the discourse on teacher attrition in the mid-2000s.

The premise of the film is simple: a documentary crew follows three teachers and one newly appointed assistant principal throughout a year at a Texas high school. Two of the teachers are male history teachers: Mr. Stroope is in his third year and Mr. Lowrey, an alternatively certified teacher, is in his first year. The other two protagonists are female: Coach Webb, a second-year physical education teacher, and Mrs. Reddell, a former choir teacher who is in her first year as an assistant principal. All four are white. The film incorporates the teachers' interviews with the documentary crew, the teachers' Web diaries, and, at times, rough footage of the school and its students.

Before *Chalk*, the body of high school films never truly captured the complexities of teaching, particularly from the teacher's point of view. Instead, cinematic portrayals of schools generally featured prescribed paths for teachers. Teachers in movies tend to be male (Beyerbach, 2005), are successful when they are charismatic (Ellsmore, 2005), and serve as educator-heroes who follow the prescribed curriculum, which is almost overwhelmingly Eurocentric (Ayers, 1994). The type of school setting also delineates the film's plot: urban schools are portrayed as run-down, graffiti-riddled institutions (Beyerbach, 2005), while suburban schools are as beautifully appointed as the characters portrayed in them (Bulman, 2005). White teachers can usually transcend both urban and suburban settings; teachers of color are generally relegated to working in urban schools (Beyerbach, 2005). Finally, teachers in many films transform into change agents for their schools or communities (Paietta, 2007).

While these films tend to focus on the extreme situations teachers may face, very rarely do they suggest that teachers might be troubled in their professions by ordinary tasks, such as grading papers, getting evaluations, and attending faculty meetings. They choose to focus on rogue teachers, those who challenge the educational system (Giroux, 1997). However, nobody even *thinks* to challenge this system in *Chalk*; no one has the time.

The Mockumentary Tradition

The term *mockumentary* (*mock-documentary* or *pseudo-documentary* are other terms used to describe this type of film), which "is commonly associated with films that are formally constructed as documentaries, but whose subject is utterly fictional; they are usually satires or, at least, parodies" (Rascaroli, 2005, p. 188). In their book *Faking It: Mock-documentary and the Subversion of Factuality*, Roscoe and Hight (2001) are careful not to characterize a mock-documentary as a separate genre but as a way of using discourse. In other words, mockumentaries rely on similar strategies as documentaries; however, the ways in which they portray their subjects engage different types of humor.

Roscoe and Hight define mock-documentaries (their preferred term as it reflects and retains both the "mock" and the "doc" aspects) as "*fictional* [their emphasis] texts; those which make a partial or concerted effort to appropriate documentary codes and conventions in order to represent a fictional subject" (p. 2). Rascaroli (2005) credits one of the first uses of "mockumentary" to Rob Reiner, who used the term to describe his film *This Is Spinal Tap* (1984). Other noteworthy mockumentaries include satirical works from Christopher Guest, such as *Waiting for Guffman* (1996) and *A Mighty Wind* (2003), and, arguably, Daniel Myrick's *The Blair Witch Project* (1999). These fictional texts, which employ nonfictional elements (such as in *Chalk* where actual students and teachers mix with professional actors) are compelling because they gain an authenticity not found in fictional films or, perhaps, even documentaries. *Chalk* achieves authenticity by providing its cast of both actors and real students and teachers with loose direction and scripts in order to portray exacting situations without the extraneous detractors of real life or the need to dramatize situations to please audience's expectations.

Mockumentaries challenge not only the "privileged status" of documentaries, but also the "tensions within the genre, in particular where different codes and conventions appeal to competing, often contradictory, cultural understandings of how 'reality' can be represented" (Roscoe & Hight, 2001, p. 4). Roscoe and Hight identify three degrees of mockumentaries that reflect the intentions of the filmmakers(s), the construction of the text, and the role constructed for the audience. The first two degrees are parody films that mimic other types of film, such as horror films—and critique and hoax—films that critique either culture or the genre itself or serve as hoaxes that generate a reflexive stance on the genre.

Chalk falls under their third degree of "deconstruction." At this degree, a mock-documentary "examine[s], subvert[s] and deconstruct[s] factual discourse and its relationship with documentary codes and conventions" (p. 73). Mock-documentaries at this degree also feature a reflexive stance toward "factual discourse" and suggest "the *potential* [their emphasis] of the mock-documentary form to serve as a site for the active subversion of factual discourse" (p. 161). *Chalk* deconstructs the "factual discourse" of the school documentary genre through its attention to the unexamined aspects of teaching (the little acts of resistance from students rather than traumatic altercations or academic successes), its portrayal of what it is like to teach in a school without major funding or academic issues, and most important, its discourse surrounding teacher attrition. Paramount to mockumentaries is playing with conventions, even within its own tradition.

Juhasz (2006) argues that fake docs "copy, mock, mimic, and gimmick documentary style" (p. 7) and "are a special breed of parody in that they accomplish something different, something extra; they do manage a 'link to the real'" (p. 2). Akel and Mass, who were teaching during the writing of this film, intended for *Chalk* to portray another side of their profession. "We wanted to tell a story from inside the world of teaching," reflect the writers on their collaboration. In their role as directors, Akel and Mass also adopted many of the strategies employed by mockumentaries and heavily based their direction on the improvisation tradition. The film's press kit describes several techniques they use to recreate this "realistic" examination, including actors improvising based on narrative arcs rather than a completed script—a strategy that accumulated over 60 hours of footage. From this footage, they mined new narratives and situations, which they admit resemble the reality show *Cops* and go against the documentary tradition. However, in this film, the characters are not caricatures of actual types of teachers, as one might expect to find. In actuality, their decision to "mock" teachers turned them into more realistic representations.

Chalk never claims to provide the answer to the statistic that opens the film, but the answers it does provide are antithetical to some of the other "answers" found in school films.

Furthermore, Akel and Mass choose to represent the marking of time by counting down the days left in the school year rather than celebrating accomplishments, like scoring well on high-stakes tests as seen in some fictional films about teachers. In order to be convincing, Akel and Mass choose to depict what other school films, particularly those that focus on teachers, neglect or oversimplify. *Chalk* not only "mocks" the types of teachers in school films identified by Ayers (1994), Trier (2001), and Dalton (2004) as the "teacher hero," but also the conclusions audiences may make about the challenges of teaching based on the representations of the profession found in other films, including documentaries.

Mocking the Act of Teaching

In the school film narrative, whether they are fictional or nonfictional, pedagogical scenes tend to remain teacher-centered. That is, lessons are teacher-led and designed, even if those lessons are inspired by the students. Benton

(2013) argues that there are two pedagogical approaches in the teacher film narrative that are determined by the type of curriculum in place. First, if the curriculum is bureaucratic and heartless, then the teacher will be caring (as in the case of *Freedom Writers*). However, if the approach is "ineffectual complacency," the teacher will be aggressive (as in *Blackboard Jungle*) (p. 99). A notable exception is *History Boys*, which gives audiences a glimpse of the kind of vibrant intellectual life that can develop in a classroom in which teaching is a collective enterprise and disagreement between professionals is emphasized instead of hidden (p. 103). It is rare to find examples of great teaching in school films, and even in this example, the teaching comes from the teachers.

In spite of its many transformative possibilities for the high school movie genre (because of its reliance on the mockumentary format), *Chalk* includes teaching strategies that are disappointing and portray a more modernist approach to teaching. More often than not, the students at Harrison High School sit in desks, in rows, facing the front of the classroom (with the exception of Stroope's class in which the classroom is divided to provide a "cat walk" for him to walk up and down)

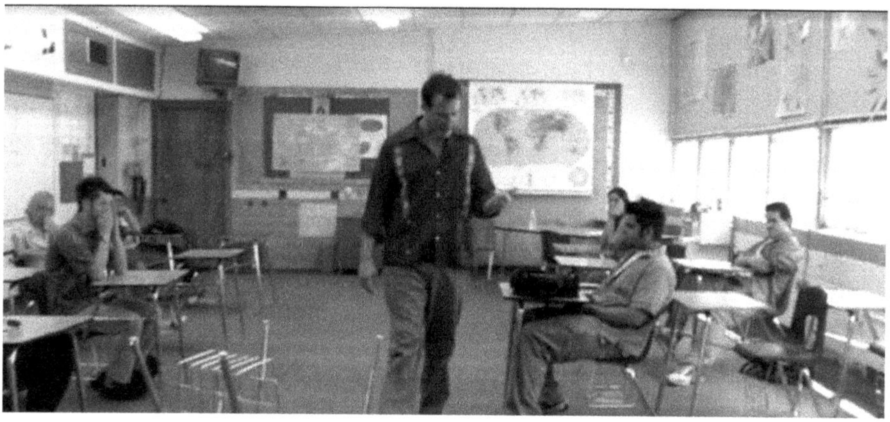

Figure 2.1. Mr. Stroope's classroom arrangement. Source: Akel & Mass. *Chalk*. Virgil Films. 2006. Reprinted by permission of Virgil Films. All rights reserved.

There is an unspoken contract between students and teachers wherein students outwardly accede to each teacher's approach in the classroom while privately serving as a panel of judges for their various pedagogical approaches. We watch as they shake their heads at Lowrey's ineptitude or laugh at the absurd activities they willingly participate in during Webb's class. Mrs.

Reddell longs to return to the kind of teaching that has students bent over books, busily working quietly on their own, while she circulates the room offering individual help. Mr. Lowrey's own attempts to improve his pedagogy consist of relating history to his students and their lives (a practice educational research supports), telling jokes (entertaining but questionable), and checking out a book on classroom management from the school's library. The teachers engage in swapping classroom stories, but scenes such as the one Benton (2013) describes are not present.

The best teaching in *Chalk* comes from two unconventional sources. First, Coach Webb incorporates her and her students' interests (however awkward and embarrassing at times for her students) into her physical education lessons. She individualizes and varies her instruction and partakes in the assigned activities in a way that her cinematic counterparts fail to do (perhaps because of her discipline). The second example comes from the students themselves, who coach Mr. Lowrey to victory at the Spelling Hornet. One illustration of how students are able to see what their teachers cannot about what makes good teaching occurs when Meeka, one of Lowrey's students, introduces the concept of a Spelling Hornet to Lowrey. In a twist on the traditional "Spelling Bee," a Spelling Hornet requires students to coach a teacher in the spelling of slang words. She explains that in the Hornet, the teacher must spell contemporary slang words used by the students and offers the word *whoadie* as an example:

Lowery: How do you spell it?
Meeka: W ... H ... O ... How do you think it's spelled? That's the point of a Spelling Hornet.

It is disappointing when a film that so eloquently explores an important issue in a postmodern way still portrays the modernist mechanisms our educational system embodies.

Another curriculum found in school films refers to the course of study created through multiple versions of schooling and education. For Chennault (2006), a film's "curriculum" is more than just the "images and sounds emerging from the screen ... it is constructed through the manner in which these elements are configured by the film's writer, director, and producers (and performers) to create the final product" (p. 151). Similarly, for curriculum theorist Doll, a postmodern "curriculum is a process—not of transmitting what is (absolutely) known but of exploring what is unknown; and through exploration," students and teachers "transform both the land and themselves" (1993, p. 155).

Because *Chalk* begins with a statistic (50% of teachers quit within the first three years of teaching) and turns that fact into a question to explore (not necessarily answer), this work can potentially transform the genre of high school films in a number of ways. As one of the ubiquitous posters (in this film and in "real life" classrooms) proclaim, "Life—it's a journey, not a destination."

Meet the Teachers

"But Nobody Taught Me": Mr. Lowrey

In high school films, the teachers who face the most problems tend to be those who choose teaching as a second profession. For example, Lowrey, the newest addition to the history faculty, represents those brand new teachers who face a difficult beginning at the start of the film. Lowrey is having a hard time adjusting from his career in computer engineering. He confesses that he became a teacher after he took two aptitude tests that suggested he should either teach or practice veterinary medicine. During the first semester, Mr. Lowrey loses control of his classroom, his chalk, and his temper. While there are many similarities between Mr. Lowrey and his cinematic counterparts (think Sydney Poitier as Mark Thackeray in *To Sir, With Love*; Michelle Pfeiffer as Lou Ann Johnson in *Dangerous Minds*; and Richard Dadier in *Blackboard Jungle*), he differs from these educator-heroes in a number of noticeable ways, the first being that he begins his career with relatively "benign" students. At the beginning of the film, we see Mr. Lowrey, chalk in hand, tie neatly tied, with his back to a chalkboard divided into well-organized sections. He begins his lesson in this manner:

> I'm just going to start. You're going to say your name and then I want you to tell me what comes to your mind with history, right? And I'd like you to start. [He points to a boy in the middle of the class, who remains silent, mouth open, as the girl next to him snickers from behind her hand.] Anything? [He pauses for a brief moment.] Okay, well, that's why we're here.

About 10 minutes into his lesson, the female student from the opening shot timidly raises her hand and asks Lowrey how long he has been teaching. After stumbling through the non-teaching experiences he has had in computer engineering, which he claims have prepared him for this position, Lowrey admits that it's been about 12 minutes. Lowrey is reminiscent of another cinematic engineer-turned-teacher, Mark Thackeray (played by Sydney Poitier). Lowrey shares with Thackeray a similar experience in his first year of teaching; however, his troubles are minimal when compared to Thackeray's in that Lowrey's students only steal his chalk and argue in class. Lowrey's character at once reincarnates and renews Thackeray's to demonstrate the ongoing experience of alternatively "trained" teachers. Lowrey's students, with the exception of one, are all actual students, not professional actors, and their behavior seems mild when compared to other students' behaviors found in school films. They, too, challenge the real and reel notion that they might be the primary reason for teachers wishing to leave the profession.

When a new teacher makes mistakes early, students typically take advantage of the ineptness, and that teacher's performance in the classroom quickly spirals downward as they lose confidence in themselves. However, students in *Chalk* treat their teachers with respect and often restrain their laughter at the naivety or quirks of these teachers. Unlike Thackeray, who "saves" his students, Lowrey's students "save" him many times throughout the film. By the middle of the year, Lowrey's students "save" him when they invite him to represent them in the annual "Spelling Hornet." When Lowrey wins by spelling "shawty," the slang word for shorty (or an attractive woman), he pumps the air with his fist—an action that signifies to the audience a turning point in his teaching experience.

However, Lowrey's victory does not seem to instill enough confidence in his perceptions of his own skill as a teacher. In one Web diary entry, Lowrey announces that teaching is a gift and that maybe it is something that can be taught, but "No one taught me." During a faculty lunch, Lowrey is asked by Reddell if he plans to resign his contract. He responds in one of the most painfully honest confessions from a cinematic teacher, "I don't know if I like [teaching] that much—to be honest." Mr. G., another teacher, follows Lowrey's comment with his own confession, "I wish I had the guts to leave." The revelation of these two nearly neutral reflections about teaching contradicts the public's expectations of teachers committed to their jobs and, more important, to their students.

Both *To Sir, With Love* and *Chalk* pay homage to those who become alternatively certified to teach, and both teachers face a difficult decision at the end of the school year. At the end of *To Sir, With Love*, after submitting several applications for engineering jobs, Thackeray has been offered one. After two students who are scheduled to be in his class next year run in and disrupt a pensive moment, Thackeray rips the piece of paper containing the offer. Similarly, at the end of *Chalk*, Lowrey also contemplates a piece of paper; however, it is a contract to continue in his position at Harrison High School. The final scene shows Lowrey pondering whether to sign a teaching contract for the next year and then leaving his classroom, carrying his framed poster of Sitting Bull. The inconclusive scene invites viewers to replay his final exit several times to determine for themselves whether he signed the contract. As in a postmodern curriculum, there is never a fixed or "right" answer.

"Mr. Stroope Is My Name, History's My Game": Mr. Stroope

If Mr. Lowrey is a tribute to those teachers who learn the importance of respecting one's students and a nod to all of those cinematic teachers who grow into their professions, Mr. Stroope (a name that conjures Mr. Shoope—the young, hip, laid-back English teacher from *Summer School*) represents those teachers who persevere through non-growth. Stroope's character resists the assumptions of what it means to be a good teacher, and he misdirects his good intentions onto a contest rather than his classroom practice.

On the first day of school, Stroope addresses his students with the line "Mr. Stroope's my name, and history is my game," a line that positions Stroope as teacher-as-performer. Stroope visits with his mentor teacher, who tries to refocus him on the three goals he set for himself last year (less sarcasm, cleanliness/organization, and timely submission of lesson plans). However, it's clear that his mind is on the "Teacher of the Year" competition, and he spends more time enlisting the help of his students (who paint campaign posters for him) and the winner from last year than actually addressing the goals he had previously set. This character fulfills what Bulman (2005) sees as the normal expression of good teaching in Hollywood's high school films. Good teachers in these films, argues Bulman, are mainly white, middle-class people who portray a teaching style rooted in "autonomy, a capitalist work ethic, personal ambition, faith in meritocracy, and free expression" as normal (p. 166). *Chalk* demonstrates that these characteristics do not necessarily result in outstanding teachers, especially in the case of Stroope.

Mr. Stroope sees teaching as more of a corporate-type job in which hard work, determination, and even underhanded tactics can mean success. Stroope's strategies for winning Harrison High School's Teacher of the Year contest demonstrate his misplaced dedication and determination. He seems to enjoy his job, but it is not because of the students. In order to prepare for the Teacher of the Year competition, Stroope interrogates last year's winner, who tells him it's all about the students. He tells her, "That's the biggest bunch of crap I've ever heard." All of these actions point to Stroope's misguided idea of what it means to be a successful teacher.

He also brings into question what it means to be a "good" teacher in that he takes to extremes what it means to be interested in students' lives, how to design student-centered discussions and activities, and how to be seen as an outstanding professional. Dalton (2004) contends that Hollywood's "good" teachers are often portrayed as "radical," but that in reality, they "challenge the system while they are, in fact, not in the least bit radical and win only the occasional symbolic victory, while effectively changing nothing" (p. 25). This certainly fits Stroope's role in the film. On the other hand, the outstanding teachers in this film are the "real" ones—his opponent, the previous winner, and a math teacher who bends the rules according to her students' needs.

Another example of Stroope focusing on the political aspect of the Teacher of the Year competition occurs in his interactions with his colleagues. Stroope offers to speak during a faculty meeting in an effort to win support from his colleagues. During this meeting, Stroope once again displays a misguided assumption about teaching ethics. He begins by jokingly asking how many of them have used the copier machine for personal business or "borrowed" money from a club's treasury for happy hour. After eliciting a few laughs and a few hands, Stroope announces, "Well, that's gotta stop." Stroope's actions demonstrate that he cannot move beyond the notion that hard work and honesty are enough to ensure a successful career; however, his willingness to bend the rules in order to win the Teacher of the Year contest reifies that for Stroope, teaching is not about the students but rather himself. During the candidates' Teacher of the Year debate, Stroope adopts politician-style hand gestures and microphone techniques. Not unlike those cinematic students who run for class president, he makes outrageous promises, like giving every teacher their own copy machine for their classrooms with their own codes. In his final Web diary, Stroope confesses that he "wouldn't follow someone like me"—a statement he seems to direct not at his students but his colleagues.

According to Ellsmore (2005), the teaching profession faces a consumer-oriented society in which discourses of competition and pay do not seem as suspicious as they would have in earlier times. In her discussion of British and American teacher films, Ellsmore observes: "Because in postmodern society money talks louder than service and status, the idea of teaching as a vocation rewarded by societal respect has been replaced by being just a job with an emphasis on pay" (p. 26). Stroope, perhaps believing in status more than pay, is not ready to function in this postmodern paradigm, and his archaic beliefs result in a ridiculous attempt to win what has become an almost meaningless award in a society that equates teacher success with students' scores on tests.

"I'm an AP, I'm Not a Teacher Anymore": Mrs. Reddell

Reddell, who has recently accepted the position of assistant principal, finds that her new position requires her to relate to her colleagues, students, and family in new ways. In her opening interview with the documentary crew, Reddell reveals that the position for which she was recommended opened after Mr. Fletcher was "found guilty," and even though she had not really considered becoming part of the administration so soon, she accepted the offer anyway. The newly appointed Reddell's first day finds her, ironically, in the principal's office, seeking advice for handling a rude student. She assumes the position of the troublemaker student sitting across the desk from the principal. Reddell avoids the two stereotypical paths available to most cinematic administrators who are cast either as bumbling fools who are unaware of what goes on in a classroom or as figures who lead their schools to triumph over adversity (Dalton 2004; Scull & Peltier, 2007). Instead, she embodies the complex relationships that administrators who have served as teachers endure.

Chalk's administrators, like their real and cinematic counterparts, are overworked and break up the occasional fight; however, Reddell emphasizes the differences between being a teacher and administrator and how that knowledge informs her feelings about leaving the classroom. Reddell learns that being an administrator means facing long hours at school away from her husband and dealing with the "less desirable" students nearly all of the time. As an administrator, disciplinary issues consume most of her time, and her relationships with students and teachers are now skewed. No longer a teacher herself, she is once removed from her students and acts as a mediator between teachers and students. In one of her Web diaries, she chronicles the number of times she has come home after ten o'clock at night, that she neglects her family, and that she ultimately doubts her decision to move out of the classroom. At one point in the film, she confides the realities of her job to the documentary crew:

> The toughest part of this job right now is dealing with teachers constantly complaining about other teachers. Being a teacher before, I mean, the teachers are my peers, my friends—now I still, of course, have those friendships, but now I'm in a position of power and so I feel that they are trying to manipulate that a bit.

Reddell does spend quite a bit of time managing an unruly faculty, including her best friend, Coach Webb. Tired of Webb asking her for help and then having to defend her from the other teachers who think she is a little rigid, Reddell blows up. She tells Webb that she *is* "pushy" and that she is the "only one willing to tell [her]." Blurring the line between her responsibilities as boss and friend, Reddell also tries to mediate teachers' personal relationships.

An aspect of life as an educator that is often overlooked in high school films, but covered frequently in research on teachers' identities, is the separation between professional and personal identities (Alsup, 2006; Atwell-Vasey, 1998; Trier, 2001). In *Chalk*, teachers muse on how the profession often stagnates their personal relationships.

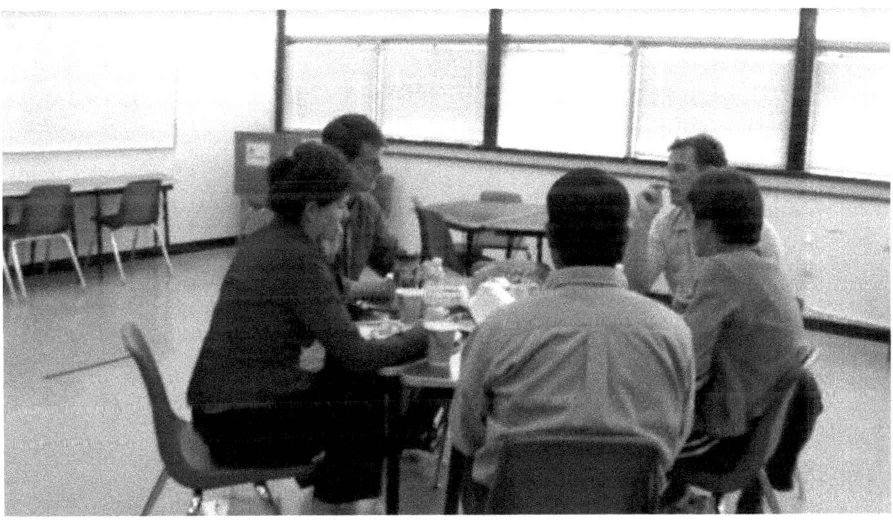

Figure 2.2. In *Chalk*, teachers often bond over meals. In this scene, Lowrey's colleagues try to convince him to come back next year. Source: Akel & Mass. *Chalk*. Virgil Films. 2006. Reprinted by by permission of Virgil Films.

Not only is Reddell's marriage strained, Lowrey, who becomes aware of Webb's attraction to him, meditates on how little time teaching leaves for a personal life. Lowrey reveals in a Web diary entry:

> I've been divorced for almost two years now, and uh, I find that, you know, uh, the subject of dating, the idea of going out with someone, keeps coming up at work.

> I mean, teaching's hard enough for me right now; it's taking all my life. I can't imagine having time for a personal life.

Reddell is the one character who pulls together all of the other teachers' and students' experiences and rearranges them in a way that makes sense. When she does so, she realizes the absence of relations with students' home lives. At the end of the film, Mrs. Reddell once again engages in the process of "doing" and then "reflecting on doing" (Doll, 1993, p. 179) and concludes that "we [teachers, the school] can only do so much" and that the home plays the largest role in the success of a student.

"Not All PE Teachers Are Gay": Coach Webb

Chalk continues to interrogate the stereotypical representations of teachers in many Hollywood films, including the female physical education teacher. Webb, like Lowrey and Stroope, continues her relationship with real and reel (Ellsmore, 2005) counterparts. For example, female PE teachers in films are often portrayed in extremes—either as sexy females or females with masculine attributes (Duncan, Nolan, & Wood, 2002; McCullick, Belcher, Hardin, & Hardin, 2003). Webb openly addresses the popular narrative represented by Hollywood and held by much of the public (Cahn, 1998), who hypothesize that female PE teachers are lesbians. Webb, aware of this belief, seeks to challenge it as well as complicate it.

In her opening interview with the documentary crew, Webb, who refers to the myth that female gym teachers are lesbians (as perpetuated by high school films like *Clueless*), both addresses and separates herself from this notion, explaining that it is this assumption that possibly keeps men from asking her out:

> I find that as a PE teacher … I've had a few instances where students or, uh, teachers have assumed I was gay and I, uh, think it's a mixture of I'm a PE teacher [and] my hair's short. I don't know if that, uh, affects the way, uh, guys see me—I don't know … but not all PE teachers are gay.

Webb feels the need to claim her sexual orientation because she believes that men assume she is a lesbian, which must be the reason they, including Lowrey to whom she is attracted, are not asking her out on dates. In reality, the lack of interest is probably because, like her colleagues, they find her confrontational and somewhat pushy—off-putting behavior that is atypical of female teachers.

According to Dalton, "Hollywood has long been reluctant to give women teachers, whether lesbian or straight, stories in which they can act out their sexuality without being punished" (2004, p. 199). Webb does not wind up in Lowrey's arms at the end of the film, even though he fantasizes about the two of them dancing together.

Chalk's underlying commentary seems to be that it would be all right for Webb to be gay, if she were, but she is not. What is missing from the film are answers to two questions: who else other than Webb actually makes that assumption and on what are they basing their generalizations about PE teachers? To the viewer, only Webb seems to consider how others regard her sexual orientation. In her final Web diary, she confides that "teachers are extra sensitive," but it is unclear as to whether she identifies with her conclusion. Webb's character shows how powerful normative assumptions can be and the ways in which a mockumentary can both parody and leave questions unanswered.

"Well, That's Why We're Here": Conclusion

Just as this country's educational system continues to rely on modernist teaching strategies, so too does the mainstream high school film continue to dominate national theaters. According to Bulman (2005), high school movies that "break the Hollywood mode do not often have wide audiences" (p. 66). Rejected by the major independent film festivals like Sundance, *Chalk* received a lukewarm reception from critics, mainly because of its failure to make a "stronger" commentary on this staggering statistic that serves as the inspiration for the film. In one of the most critical reviews of the film, Sarris (2007) accuses it of not "begin[ning] to address the literal life-and-death issues of education in the schools of the nation's inner cities" (¶3). However, these movies, often set in inner-city schools, perpetuate the problematic "teacher-as-hero, students-need-saving" narrative that distorts the public's narrow perceptions of what can "save" our educational system.

By far the most frequent criticism concerns *Chalk*'s subtlety. In the DVD version of *Chalk*, Morgan Spurlock—known for his documentary, *Supersize Me*—introduces his admiration of the film by referring to members of his own family who were teachers. Kennedy (2007), referring to the "Morgan Spurlock Presents" banner, comments, "But it's hardly supersized. Instead, the movie offers some modest, amusing and true lessons about an honorable profession" (¶14). Referring to the unique performance by a real-life administrator, Burr (2007) notes that the movie "might have been funnier and more penetrating as a real documentary." On the other hand, Wiegand (2007) observes, "[M] ost of these people [the teachers] are ready to go over the edge at any minute. Maybe if they did, the film would be more interesting" (¶7). These critics seem to long for the hyper-reality of fiction, whereas *Chalk* clings to the ordinary of reality. Indeed, it seems as if *Chalk* is destined to become just a "cult classic among educators" (Weitzman, 2007, ¶1).

Observing secondary teachers as audiences of teacher films, Ellsmore (2005) notes that "according to their experience and construction of reality, there will be differences in how each person receives a text, and how they perceive the overlap between the real and *reel* life" (p. xiv). She then argues that real-life teachers are better positioned to assess the *realism* of their cinematic counterparts. Ellsmore, who analyzes the responses of two focus groups of teachers who watch school films, reports that her participants felt that these films did not portray the monotonous, mundane aspects of teaching as well as the importance of stamina. More tellingly, one of her participants observes, "Who would watch the truth?" (2005, p. 130). Ellsmore concludes that "film is a poor medium through which to portray the work of a teacher" (2005, p. 130). However, this depiction is exactly what *Chalk* tries to capture.

Chalk's use of the mockumentary to comment on real teachers and "reel" teachers has not gone unnoticed by film critics. For critic Katey Rich (2008), *Chalk*'s "willingness to view teachers as more than wage slaves or Hollywoodized heroes is practically revolutionary" (¶7). The preservice teachers who view this film in our classes appreciate the focus on the seemingly mundane: the eternally broken copy machine, the happy hours on Thursdays. What *Chalk* does address is the vast number of mediocre teachers we do have in our classrooms and the mediocrity of the profession rather than its superstar or truly awful teachers. *Chalk* might be too real because it does not mock teachers enough. Our students do not have enough experience to recognize the difference between reel and real—at least as crafted in *Chalk*'s subtle representations. *Chalk*'s reliance on the mockumentary form, which blurs the line between fiction and reality, presents an alternative viewpoint on the hardships of teaching—one not found in Hollywood or in documentary films about teachers.

The final scene of *Chalk* leaves the audience with a sense of ambiguity as to the fate of Mr. Lowrey's teaching career. Will he decide to return to Harrison High School or will he leave the profession altogether? This ambiguity is similar to what real teachers feel when their students leave at the end of the school year. Students are evolving as learners, and what they learn with a particular teacher may not be realized until years later. Postmodernists would argue that accepting this ambiguity is necessary in order to continue as a teacher. The same approach is found in the ambiguous construction of a mockumentary: Lowrey becomes that student for the audience, who must accept that they will never know what his future holds for sure. *Chalk* represents the unknowable answer for the school film.

References

Akel, M., & Mass, C. (Writers & Directors). (2006). *Chalk* [Motion picture]. San Francisco, CA: Someday Soon Productions.

Alsup, J. (2006). *Teacher identity discourses: Negotiating personal and professional spaces.* Mahwah, NJ: Lawrence Erlbaum Associates.

Atwell-Vasey, W. (1998). *Nourishing words: Bridging private reading and public teaching.* Albany, NY: SUNY Press.

Ayers, W. (1994). A teacher ain't nothin' but a hero: Teachers and teaching in film. In P. Joseph & G. Burnaford (Eds.), *Images of schoolteachers in twentieth-century America* (pp. 147–156). New York: St. Martin's Press.

Benton, S. (2013). Two heads are better than one (and three are better than two): Challenging the individualist ethos of the educator-hero film. *Journal of Popular Film and Television, 41*, 98–108.

Beyerbach, B. (2005). The Social Foundations Classroom: Themes in sixty years of teachers in film: Fast times, dangerous minds, and stand on me. *Educational Studies, 37*, 267–285.

Bulman, R. (2005). *Hollywood goes to high school: Cinema, schools, and American culture.* New York, NY: Worth.

Burr, T. (2007, September 14). School mockumentary gets credit for effort. *The Boston Globe.* Retrieved from http://www.boston.com/ae/movies/articles/2007/09/14/school_mockumentary_gets_credit_for_effort/

Cahn, S. K. (1998). *Coming on strong: Gender and sexuality in 20th century women's sports.* Boston, MA: Harvard University Press.

Chennault, R. (2006). *Hollywood films about schools: Where race, politics, and education intersect.* New York, NY: Palgrave.

Dalton, M. (2004). *The Hollywood curriculum: Teachers in the movies* (2nd ed.). New York, NY: Peter Lang.

Doll, W. E., Jr. (1993). *A postmodern perspective on curriculum.* New York, NY: Teachers College Press.

Duncan, C., Nolan, J., & Wood, R. (2002). See you in the movies? We hope not! *Journal of Physical Education, Recreation & Dance, 73*, 38–44.

Ellsmore, S. (2005). *Carry on, teachers!: Representations of the teaching profession in screen culture.* Stoke on Trent, UK: Trentham Books.

Giroux, H. (1997). Race, pedagogy, and whiteness in *Dangerous minds. Cineaste, 22*(4), 46–49.

Guest, C. (Director). (1996) *Waiting for Guffman* [Motion picture]. United States: Sony Pictures Classic.

Guest, C. (Director). (2003). *A mighty wind* [Motion picture]. United States: Castle Rock Entertainment.

Ingersoll, R. M. (2003). *Is there really a teacher shortage?* (Document R-03-4). Seattle, WA: Center for the Study of Teaching and Policy and The Consortium for Policy Research in Education. Retrieved from http://depts.washington.edu/ctpmail/PDFs/Shortage-RI-09-2003.pdf

Juhasz, A. (2006). Introduction: Phony definitions and troubling taxonomies of the fake documentary. In A. Juhasz & J. Lerner (Eds.), *F is for phony: Fake documentary and truth's undoing* (pp. 1–38). Minneapolis, MN: U of Minnesota P.

Kennedy, L. (2007, July 19). Teachers get a mockumentary moment. *Denver Post*, F-09 Retrieved from http://www.denverpost.com/movies/ci_6407786

McCullick, B., Belcher, D., Hardin, B., & Hardin, M. (2003). Butches, bullies and buffoons: Images of physical education teachers in the movies. *Sport, Education and Society*, 8, 3–16.

Myrick, D. (Director). (1999). *The Blair witch project* [Motion picture]. United States: Artisan Entertainment.

National Center for Education Statistics. (2005). *The Condition of Education* (NCES 2005-094). Washington, DC: U.S. Department of Education, Institute of Education Sciences. http://nces.ed.gov/pubs2005/2005094.pdf

Paietta, A. C. (2007). *Teachers in the movies: A filmography of depictions of grade school, Preschool, and day care educators*. Jefferson, NC: McFarland.

Provasnik, S., Dorfman, S., & Education Statistics Services Institute. (2005). Mobility in the Teacher Workforce: Findings from the Condition of Education. Washington, DC: National Center for Education Statistics.

Rascaroli, L. (2005). Home and away: Nanni Moretti's *The last customer* and the ground zero of transnational identities. *Cinemas: Journal of Contemporary Film*, 3, 187–200.

Reiner, R. (Director). (1984). *This is spinal tap* [Motion picture]. United States: Embassy Pictures.

Rich, K. (2007). *Chalk* [Review]. *Film Journal International.* Retrieved from http://www.filmjournal.com/filmjournal/reviews/article_display.jsp?vnu_content_id=1003594615

Roscoe, J., & Hight, C. (2001). *Faking it: Mock-documentary and the subversion of factuality*. Manchester, UK: Manchester U P.

Sarris, A. (2007, June 12). *Blackboard jungle* '07: School crisis spelled out in *Chalk*. *New York Observer*. Retrieved from http://www.observer.com/2007/blackboard-jungle-07-school-crisis-spelled-out-chalk

Scull, R. W., & Peltier, G. (2007). Star power and the schools: Studying popular films' portrayal of educators. *The Clearing House*, *81*, 13–18.

Spurlock, M. (Director, Writer, & Producer). (2004). *Supersize me* [Motion picture]. United States: Samuel Goldwyn Films, Roadside Attractions.

Trier, J. (2001). The cinematic representation of the personal and professional lives of teachers. *Teacher Education Quarterly*, *28*, 127–142.

Wiegand, D. (2007, September 7). Review of *Chalk*. *San Francisco Chronicle*. Retrieved from http://www.sfgate.com/entertainment/article/FILM-CLIPS-Also-opening-today-2504815.php

Weitzman, E. (2007, June 8). *Chalk*. *New York Daily News*. Retrieved from http://www.nydailynews.com/entertainment/tv-movies/short-takes-article-1.221338

· 3 ·

"YOU KNOW THAT KIDS ARE GETTING A REALLY CRAPPY EDUCATION NOW"

Teaching Documentaries through Interpretive, Ideological, and Activist Approaches

For the past three summers, I've shown the documentary *Waiting for Superman* (Guggenheim, 2010) in my secondary school curriculum course as a way to expand our discussion of school choice and teacher accountability, both of which have been "hot" topics in education for the past several years. The quotation in the title for this chapter comes from that documentary; the words were spoken by Michelle Rhee, who is featured in this film as the chancellor of Washington, DC, schools. Her statement, "You wake up every morning and you know that kids are getting a really crappy education now," refers to the state of public schools in Washington, DC. The filmmakers, in order to show her as an agent of change, feature her for approximately 10 minutes of the film, following her from schools to her office to her car as she makes what appear to be harsh decisions that are designed to significantly improve the schools in DC. The camera captures her firing principals, closing schools, and battling with teacher unions. The highlighting of these decisions suggests that the filmmakers believe they will improve the "crappy education" students will get. Because documentaries about schools imply ways to improve education, those of us who use them in the classroom should consider how our university students might interrogate the ways those suggestions are conveyed.

My approach to incorporating documentaries about education into my curriculum depends on the objectives for a particular course, but I usually try to avoid showing films that have received quite a bit of attention, since my students, most of whom are middle and high school teachers, have probably seen them already. For example, in my secondary school curriculum course—a course in which we read much of Diane Ravitch's work tracing educational history (2010, 2013)—I like to show documentaries that deal with school choice, charter schools, and teacher accountability. However, given the three documentaries concerning school choice that were released in the years 2009 and 2010, I always choose to show *Waiting for Superman* over films like *The Lottery* (Sackler, 2010) and *The Cartel* (Bowdon, 2009). I make this decision, in part, because the multiple modes the filmmaker employs in *Waiting for Superman*, as discussed in the first chapter, encourage more critical discussion among my students. This film's references to specific people and events also enable me to connect it with other nonfictional texts. For example, I pair the film with Michelle Rhee's memoir, *Radical: Fighting to Put Students First* (2013), and we watch her TEDx Wall Street talk on YouTube (2012).

This past summer, I was especially fortunate in that our local public library's book club had read Michelle Rhee's memoir and arranged for a public Skype session with her. Our class met at the library that night to participate in the discussion and get an opportunity to meet the "real" Rhee. In the course of that one summer, then, we were presented with at least four representations of Rhee, and each time we wondered which one was the real "Rhee." These experiences required us to return to our first contact with her in *Waiting for Superman*, and then consider how her representation in that film might have been manipulated for the filmmaker's own purposes.

Given the privileged status documentaries have acquired through their claims of representing reality and the ways audiences read these films as reflecting reality, how should educators and their students negotiate what is presented to them as factual by this genre? How might we address the multiple "real" representations of people and issues found in other nonfictional texts? How should we treat documentaries that come with intentions to teach the public about an issue and/or how to take action? In this chapter, I examine how we might teach documentaries about education through a close reading of them, through careful examination of their ideological claims, and through the activist approach many of these filmmakers take in promoting their films.

Teaching Documentaries

With documentaries about education, it is important to keep in mind Nichols's (1998) notion of the sobriety of discourse and how documentaries share with other fields, like science and education, the potential and/or desire to enact change. Documentaries about education often contain a message, a discourse, for transformation. Even if the film may seem purely informational, as in the documentary *Country School: One Room–One Nation* (Rundle & Rundle, 2010), which traces the role of one-room schools in the United States, that filmmaker still incorporated contemporary discourse found in other educational conversations about immigration, teacher quality, and standardized assessments.

It's important to recognize the power inherent in teaching with a documentary—with its claim to reality, its use of primary sources, and its authoritative approaches such as interviews with experts in a given field. Sometimes it's hard not to see a documentary as an objective voice for important issues such as education. What also sets documentaries about education apart from other documentaries is that education is something all audiences, including our students, will have shared. They may have been in a public school, private school, charter school, homeschooled, or unschooled, but they will be able to relate to what it means for someone to take charge of their education. This positions all audiences of documentaries about education as potential experts—a stance that, whatever approach an educator takes in teaching a documentary about school, must be interrogated.

While there are undoubtedly myriad ways to teach a documentary about education, I have chosen to discuss the three ways I believe are accessible to educators, no matter what their experience with documentaries in this field. By narrowing these approaches to just three, I have left out others that may be more pertinent to other fields. In marketing and business, for instance, the focus may be more on audience reaction and sales, and in the field of critical media literacy, educators often advocate that students create their own texts as one way to understand how genres function. I've also left out approaches to reading these works alongside critical theories, such as critical race theory, feminism, and postmodernism; these approaches are extremely productive, of course, and I encourage readers to explore them through the references I've supplied. I also encourage readers to explore approaches to teaching documentaries through their own disciplines.

The three ways to teach documentaries that I will discuss in this chapter allow for educators to approach them through one of three objectives: to inform, to interrogate, or to act on issues related to education. As with all of the strategies I present in this book, however, they start by asking the viewer to consider the genre's relationship to reality; in this case, I want students to ask *How real are the issues presented in each film? How real are the solutions these filmmakers often present—whether covertly, as in* Country School: One Room-One School, *or overtly, as in* Waiting for Superman?

The Close-Reading Approach

The close-reading approach to teaching documentaries about education focuses mainly on analyzing a film and/or the genre. It is an approach that one might find in a literature course, where students and their instructor focus on one novel at a time, unpacking its symbolism, themes, and characters. They may take note of the historical time period in which the plot is set or examine how the text is an example of a particular genre, but their main focus is on the novel and what meaning readers may take from it. This approach to documentaries might begin with introducing students to the genre—e.g., examining what characteristics (codes and conventions, such as using a narrative voiceover as a way to establish authority) they employ and what their purpose might be. Students go on to analyze the genre's structure and the ways filmmakers employ other filmic elements, like soundtracks, the arrangement of scenes, and the narrative structure. A course in humanities that includes documentaries, for example, might focus more on discourse and the rhetorical strategies of a film, whereas a course in film studies might focus more on camera angles and blocking.

An interpretive approach to teaching documentaries is based on a close reading and often does not look beyond what is represented on the screen. In fact, one could teach *Waiting for Superman* just by asking students how the filmmaker creates a documentary that supports, through sounds and images, Rhee's contention that "Students are getting a really crappy education." This approach should begin with understanding a genre and how filmmakers employ the codes and conventions to construct the final product. That objective might be accomplished by watching various scenes from a documentary and asking students to identify common elements found in those scenes. Students might then work together to construct their own definition of the genre, to determine the relationship of their definition with the purpose of the genre, and to theorize about the audience's expectations of documentary films.

A close-reading approach to teaching documentaries can begin in any number of ways; however, there are some general steps that work with almost all films in this genre that can be applied to documentaries about education. In his book on teaching documentaries, Golden (2006) provides a number of strategies that apply to both seasoned professionals and novices to the genre. His book is filled with useful ideas, examples, and handouts that ask students to interrogate the genre and its tenuous relationship to reality. He offers the following suggestions to educators; rather than explain Golden's approach to each suggestion in detail, I offer a question he uses with his students to address each one:

1. Define nonfiction film by introducing students to the similarities and differences between fiction films and documentaries (p. 3). For example, what is the literary equivalent of a documentary film (p. 17)?
2. Teach students about the three main elements in the genre: visual, sound, and text [the words that appear or don't appear on the screen] tracks (p. 3). For example, why did he or she [the director] not identify the newspaper from which the article was taken on the text track (p. 22)?
3. Present the role of editing in nonfiction film (p. 3). For example, why does this scene make an effective opening to the film (p. 30)?
4. Introduce students to the various modes found in documentaries (p. 3). For example, why does the observational mode somehow feel more "real" to us (p. 39)?
5. Address the ethical considerations of nonfiction film (p. 3). For example, can someone outside of a culture accurately and ethically depict that culture (p. 46)?

Covering all of these approaches may present a challenge for those instructors who wish to limit their use of a documentary to one or two weeks of a course. However, any one of these suggestions can be used alone or in combination when teaching a documentary about education.

For example, it is possible to begin with the second approach, as Philips and Teasley (2010) suggest in their work on teaching about the uses of sound tracks in documentaries using Golden's framework. These educators have their students focus specifically on the way sound is used in documentaries, and they explore documentaries featuring young adults (many of those films include issues of schooling).

Before viewing a documentary, they go over with their students the different ways an audio track functions in documentaries. They then split their students into small groups. Each group focuses on a different way sound functions in a documentary: as diegetic (the on-screen music or sound effects), the non-diegetic music (off-screen music or sound effects), and any narration done by voiceover. Students then consider how these audio elements work together in relation to the overall film's message or theme(s) and share their group's findings with the rest of the class. Another variation of that strategy would be to have students analyze the text track through a series of questions—What words appear on the screen? Is there a pattern to them? What message is the filmmaker sending? Golden's book is essential for anyone thinking about using documentaries about schools, although his main audience is the middle and high school English language arts teacher. Many of the films he uses as examples are set in schools or are about school children, and his graphic organizers, such as the one on character development, are easily adapted to any documentary.

The approach discussed in this section means that students work together to understand the parts of a documentary; it depends on a close reading that can be 1) completed with or without additional texts, 2) adjusted for time, and 3) tied into course content easily. Additional activities could include examining critics' reviews of the documentary (especially conflicting ones); this activity might be further extended by asking students to write their own reviews. However, a close-reading approach lacks the benefit of considering the role of the documentary within a larger context and connecting its contribution to a larger form of discourse. For example, Guggenheim's earlier documentary on five first-year teachers, *The First Year* (2001), was shown in Baltimore, followed by comments from a panel that included the director, David Guggenheim; his wife, actress Elisabeth Shue; Maryland's Teacher of the Year; and the superintendent of Maryland's schools. The conversation that followed the film went back and forth between how the documentary was put together, what the director's hopes for it were, and the lack of financial resources in Baltimore for its students that are in most need (Lanier, 2012). For Teach for America educator Heather Kirn Lanier (2012), this documentary put forth a dangerous message for first-year teachers—that they must work obscene hours, and if they don't make tremendous gains, they are not as successful as these on-screen, real, teachers.

Finally, because these are documentaries about education, it's important to keep in mind the discourse of education, the milestones, the images often associated with the field, and the potential stereotypical representations of the institution; always keep in mind these questions: *Who are the teachers? What are the schools? Who are the stakeholders?* An ideological approach can help uncover some of the answers.

The Ideological Approach

A second approach to teaching documentaries about education is examining the ideologies inherent in their representation of the profession as well as our own ideas concerning education. As Stoddard (2009) points out, educators who want their students to become good citizens and those who opt to use documentaries to inspire their students to take action choose media texts like documentaries that reflect their ideas about society. Stoddard defines ideology as "the set of ideas, beliefs, and values used to make and legitimize decisions" (p. 408). Those ideas are subjective, which means that we as educators must carefully interrogate not only the decisions made in the making of the documentary but also our own for choosing them. For Phillips and Teasley (2010), reading documentaries for their hidden or overt ideologies "helps students to ask and answer the following questions: What is the filmmaker's point? How is it being made? Am I convinced? Am I being manipulated fairly?" (p. 52). Students and educators should examine their own ideologies as well by asking, *Why am I choosing this documentary? What does it say about my own beliefs about education? How can I share my ideologies with my students in an overt way?*

In the case of using documentaries about schools, we can apply these questions to curricular decisions, as when we consider whether using a documentary is the right genre to incorporate into our course to begin with. For example, if a teacher wants to teach about the lotteries used by charter schools to admit students, the decision to use a segment featured on a local news station, an amateur video published on YouTube, or *Waiting for Superman* will reflect an educator's own ideology, whether or not he or she is conscious of that influence. A news segment will be shorter and more informative, while the amateur video might be perceived as more "real," though possibly less relatable than the narrative structure used in *Waiting for Superman*. The type of nonfictional text will probably also determine how obvious the ideology that shaped them is to students. In his review of scholarship on using documentaries in the classroom, Stoddard (2009) suggests that audiences are less likely to critique documentaries that are less commercial because they view them as more objective. On the other hand, commercial nonfictional films are more likely to engage students in critical pedagogy. In other words, the representation of a charter school lottery from *Waiting for Superman* is more likely to be interrogated than the one featured on the YouTube video.

Another approach to teaching about the ideologies inherent in the making of a documentary about education would be to research those who contributed to the project and their relation to education. Because documentaries are not always produced by large film companies such as Warner Bros. or distributed by companies such as TriStar, who most likely choose projects based on entertainment value and potential box office success, the funding sources behind documentaries are important. Likewise, a PBS documentary might have a different message and access to audiences than a documentary funded by a group of teachers. There are several points of departure that educators can use to lead their students away from just a close reading of the film, including finding more information on the filmmaker and the producer, watching a film while researching the issues mentioned in it, and categorizing the film according to the issue and/or theme examined therein.

Teaching documentaries within a larger historical approach to education is another way to understand ideology. Studying particular important pieces of legislation and how those can serve as inspiration for documentaries is an excellent way to clarify what can seem like abstract policies and reforms to those who are not immediately involved in them. *Educating Peter* (Wurzburg, 1992), a film sometimes used in courses on children with special needs, can be watched after learning about the Individuals with Disabilities Education Act (IDEA). One of IDEA's mandates is to provide all children "a free and appropriate public education in the least restrictive environment appropriate for the students' specific learning needs." Students could consider if that mandate is met for Peter, his teacher, and his classmates.

A final suggestion for teaching documentaries about education through an ideological lens is to pull in educational theory. For example, Reid (2011) proposes a way for students in a foundations of education course to apply Paulo Freire's (1970/2000) scholarship, specifically the banking theory, to the school documentary *Resolved* (Whiteley, 2007). *Resolved* follows several policy debaters, including one team who uses Paulo Freire's theories to argue that the field of policy debate is racist and prohibitive to all those who cannot afford the time or access to resources to become successful in the competitions. Furthermore, they see the process of preparing and responding to arguments using research as a regurgitative practice instead of an educational experience. Part of Freire's problem with education is this difference that forms the basis of his banking theory: that students are treated as banks for information into which teachers deposit and from which tests withdraw.

Reid's (2011) pedagogical objective is to have students reconceptualize their views of pedagogy (p. 112). He offers a number of steps to lead students to reflect and challenge these views—from interrogating images of teaching frequently found in various forms of media to reading excerpts from Freire's *Pedagogy of the Oppressed* (1970/2000) to finally having students read and analyze a particular scene from the documentary with Freire's theories in mind.

One might expand on how an image is repeated in documentaries about education. For example, Reid (2011) discusses an animated scene in *Resolved* that relates to Freire's banking system:

> In this scene, the image of a student having his head literally opened and filled with random ideas by a teacher appears as the narrator discusses the idea of students sitting "passively as teachers deposited information" (from *Resolved*, 2007). The entire scene is cleverly constructed with images directly related to the narrator's discussion. For students who may still be struggling to grasp the concepts found in the text, this entire scene serves as a basic introduction for some of his larger ideas. It does so by articulating ideas directly from Freire's (1970/2000) seminal writing. (p. 125)

A similar scene appears in *Waiting for Superman*; however, there is no mention of Freire. In this animated scene, a voiceover says the following: "It should be simple: a teacher in a schoolhouse, filling her students with knowledge, and sending them on their way. But we've made it complicated," while a cartoon teacher stands behind her students, heads flipped open on a hinge as she pours in what appears to be a soup consisting of alphabet letters, numbers, and symbols (Guggenheim, 2010). What has complicated this ideal process of teaching filling students' heads with content is the subject of the documentary: the teachers' union preventing a teacher from being fired, and the different testing expectations for each state. The different ideas toward similar images regarding how students learn are startling to those familiar with Freire's work and can serve as ways to illustrate his theories.

The ideological approach to teaching documentaries about education is a useful way to apply and extend course content. In addition, it helps to approach these films through the theoretical lens found in one's academic discipline. While it may take more time to prepare for and then include these approaches in a course than a close-reading approach might, it does align with

Reid's objectives—to transform the way his students think about education. That does not mean they know how to take action, however. Teaching viewers to involve themselves in the causes examined by many of these documentaries is explored in the next section.

Activism

A third approach to teaching documentaries about education happens not in the classroom, but outside of a formal educational setting. And the teachers are not classroom teachers, per se, but those involved with the making of the film. These are documentaries that urge viewers to act to support their cause. By the filmmakers (not teachers) teaching viewers to act, these documentaries come closest to Nichols's (1998) "sobriety of discourse." Documentaries that not only inform audiences about a cause but also encourage them to become involved in that cause tend to either direct audiences to support their cause or provide a participant guide on how to take action. Sometimes that call to action is a simple invitation to an informational website; other times, the filmmakers have published guides for viewers interested in becoming more involved with the cause. One of the most thorough guides is the one that accompanies the documentary, *Race to Nowhere: The Dark Side of America's Achievement Culture* (Abeles, 2010).

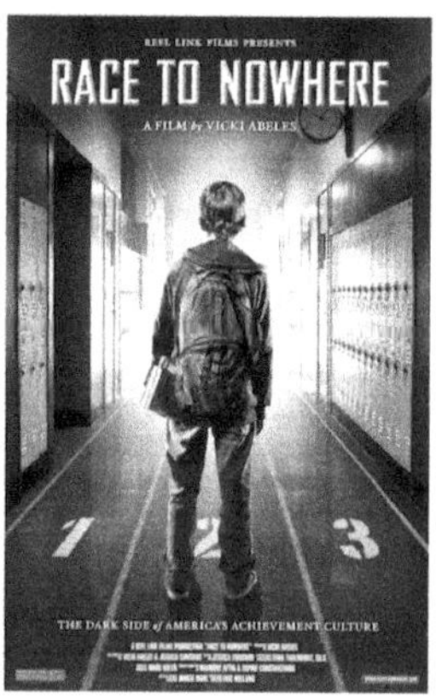

Figure 3.1. While *Race to Nowhere* (2010) focuses on the stress students endure from excessive homework and standardized testing, Abeles's latest documentary, *Beyond Measure* (2015), examines schools that are challenging what it means to educate children. Source: Abeles, *Race to Nowhere*. Lafayette, CA: Reel Link Films. 2010. Reprinted by permission of the publisher.

Race to Nowhere is a compelling commentary on the stress many students in the United States experience because of the extremely competitive nature of getting accepted into a select college or earning a scholarship (yes, one might argue that this film focuses on a problem that only affects a small percentage of students). The filmmaker includes stories told by students and their parents, including her own children, about the pressure they feel school exerts on them, especially in this culture of high-stakes testing. Some of those stories show pictures of younger, happier students; in one case, the film features a rail-thin student suffering from anorexia because of the stress that resulted from the amount of time she spent on homework and not body image issues. The filmmaker includes interviews with experts as well as black-and-white stock footage of scenes from the forties and fifties, all with the intention of showing that schools were better then, students had more time to play, and factory child labor laws had been put into place. The film ends with "Everyone Can"—a call for viewers to take action—before offering specific advice for students, parents, teachers, and administrators.

The DVD comes with a 400-plus–page facilitation guide that is divided into three sections: 1) to be used by parents, guardians, or concerned adults; 2) to be used by educators and administrators; and 3) to be used by students. The company behind the film, Reel Link Films, states their goal as bringing this film and "its message to communities nationwide" (p. 9). In order to do so, they developed this guide as a "starting point" to "help you brainstorm what you can do in your homes, classrooms, schools, and communities tomorrow, next week, and next month" (2011, p. 10). The guide provides each stakeholder group with tools for "build[ing] community, stimulating dialogue, getting the facts, developing tools and strategies, taking action, and staying connected" (p. 13).

Throughout the guide, there are surveys for students to take about their experiences with school and homework, interviews with teachers about homework and testing, and case-study interviews with people who have changed either their own teaching positions or their school's policies regarding homework. There are sample advocacy letters and steps for taking action. There are detailed agendas for advocacy meetings and lesson plans with pedagogical strategies like fishbowl. And there are handouts and discussion questions to use at group viewings. (I should confess that my university sponsored a viewing of this film complete with a panel of experts.) In the final section of the guide, models of successful charter and independent schools are profiled as places that are getting it right. High Tech High, which will soon be featured in its own documentary, is one such charter school. Reel Link Films's next project, *Beyond Measure* (Abeles, 2015), explores public schools that are taking innovative approaches to teaching, such as project-based learning.

This documentary is just one example of how some filmmakers attempt to teach viewers to take action, though I do not know just how often audience members choose to become involved with certain causes that are featured. We see that some filmmakers choose to respond to one documentary (or collective documentaries) by making one of their own, as in the case of *The Inconvenient Truth of* Waiting for Superman. Some documentary filmmakers are very didactic in encouraging audiences to take action; some just plug it in at the credits. But, as social media and technology continue to shape the way films get made, are advertised, and inspire follow-up action, documentaries may move closer to gaining full status as "discourses of sobriety." It is our job as viewers and educators, then, to examine the filmmakers' relationship to the cause as well as the rhetorical and pedagogical strategies they employ with our students. That means combining all three of the approaches mentioned in this chapter into one multi-faceted approach.

Conclusion

As I discussed earlier, this chapter's title comes from a line pertaining to public schools that was delivered by Michelle Rhee in the film *Waiting for Superman*. It's not a nice observation, and she spits it out with confidence and gusto. I also mentioned how I approach the teaching of documentaries in my own courses and the opportunity my students and I had to attend a Skype session with our local public library's book club and Michelle Rhee. The event was sponsored by a book club that we assumed was comprised of teachers in an alternative certification program from New Orleans because they shared the same name as a group we knew about from New Orleans. Our group, we knew, was comprised of teachers from different backgrounds—some from Teach for America, some traditionally certified, some alternatively certified. We were fired up, anticipating that we would meet someone, Rhee or one of the other teachers, who represented an approach to education some of us found offensive. We had questions based on statements Rhee made in her memoir, things she said in the movie, and comments she made during her TED talk.

When we arrived, however, we found out the group was not comprised of overzealous, alternatively certified teachers. They were a group of adults who represented a number of facets of life and read inspiring memoirs. Furthermore, we found Michelle Rhee could relate to our experiences; she answered the questions we asked in a way that we would have answered them. Who was this person? She was not the tyrant know-it-all we had read about and watched. In fact, my students and I nodded our heads during many of her answers. I even discarded my prepared question about policy in favor of a more personal one about being a celebrity.

As in *The First Year* documentary, members of the audience wanted Rhee—who was cast as both expert and celebrity—to suggest solutions to the problems of our own state and school district. One of the final questions the book club facilitator asked her was whether it was too late to fix the problems with education in the United States and how we might affect change in education. Rhee responded that she didn't think it was too late. She suggested showing documentaries about education on airplanes and making everyone watch them. She went on to say that "… every citizen has to demand [that education be improved]. … We must vote because politicians 'go where the wind blows.' It's our job to make sure they understand what we think needs to be upmost in their minds." She added that teachers' and principals' stories are just as compelling, but we don't hear their stories. She summed up with, "Everyone in the room has to be involved. To be an advocate. Much of this is decided in the political realm." Needless to say, there was much applause from the audience.

I took her statements to mean that documentaries are one way to get these stories out there, but people must watch them. Her statements contradict the ones from Ravitch (2013) that I used at the beginning of Chapter 1. In those comments, Ravitch blames films about schools for representing a false narrative of what's wrong and right about education. But, in spite of Ravitch's and Rhee's references to documentaries, there are films based on true stories that encourage viewers to take action—some through foundations, like the Freedom Writers Foundation, some on a more personal level, like those who are inspired to teach after watching a fictional teacher on screen, such as Jaime Escalante in *Stand and Deliver* (Menendez, 1988). The biopic about an outstanding teacher garners the largest audiences, and the most attention from Hollywood is given to narratives that almost always tell a story of the new teacher facing a group of uninterested, unmotivated students in an urban school with insurmountable problems. These films are the subject of the next section.

References

Abeles, V. (Director). (2010). *Race to nowhere: The dark side of America's achievement culture* [Motion picture]. United States: Reel Link Films.

Abeles, V. (Director). (2015). *Beyond measure* [Motion picture]. United States: Reel Link Films.
Bowdon, B. (Director). (2009). *The cartel* [Motion picture]. United States: Bowdon Media.
Freire, P. (2000). *Pedagogy of the oppressed*. New York, NY: Continuum. (Original publication 1970)
Golden, J. (2006). *Reading in the reel world: Teaching documentaries and other nonfiction texts*. Urbana, IL: National Council of Teachers of English.
Guggenheim, D. (Director). (2001). *The first year* [Motion picture made for television]. United States: Public Broadcasting Media.
Guggenheim, D. (Director). (2010). *Waiting for Superman* [Motion picture]. United States: Participant Media.
Lanier, H. K. (2012). *Teaching in the Terrordome: Two years in West Baltimore with Teach for America*. Columbia, MO: University of Missouri Press.
Nichols, B. (1998). *Representing reality: Issues and concepts in documentary*. Bloomington, IN: Indiana University Press.
Phillips, N. C., & Teasley, A. B. (2010). Reading reel nonfiction: Documentary films for young adults. *The ALAN Review*, *37*(3), 51–59.
Ravitch, D. (2010). *The death and life of the great American school system: How testing and choice are undermining education*. New York, NY: Basic Books.
Ravitch, D. (2013). *Reign of error: The hoax of the privatization movement and the danger to America's public schools*. New York, NY: Vintage Books.
Reid, L. A. (2011). *Pop culture and pedagogy: Taking up school documentaries in teacher education* (Dissertation submitted). University of North Carolina at Chapel Hill.
Rhee, M. (2013). *Radical: Fighting to put students first*. New York, NY: Harper.
Rhee, M. (2012). Public education: Are we under, over, or just misspending? Ted[x]Wall Street. Retrieved from https://www.youtube.com/watch?v=RsiLLNzi-cM
Rundle, K., & Rundle, T. (Directors). (2010). *Country school: One room–one nation* [DVD]. United States: Fourth Wall Films.
Sackler, M. (Director). (2010). *The lottery* [Motion picture]. United States: Great Curve Films.
Stoddard, J. D. (2009). The ideological implications of using "educational" film to teach controversial events. *Curriculum Inquiry*, 39, 407–433.
Whiteley, G. (Director). (2007). *Resolved* [Motion picture]. United States: One Potato Productions.
Wurzburg, G. (Director). (1992). *Educating Peter* [Motion picture]. United States: Direct Cinema Limited.

Documentaries, television documentaries, and news series about educational issues

School choice

Nursery University (Simon & Makar, 2009). Follows four families in New York who try to get their students into elite New York preschools.

Waiting for Superman (Guggenheim, 2010). Follows five students, from different cities in the United States, whose families try to get into charter schools. Also considers school reform, educational policy, and teacher unions.

The Lottery (Sackler, 2010). Follows four students in New York who try to get into charter schools and their families.

American Promise (PBS, 2013). Follows two African American boys over several years, both of whom participate in an elite private school's diversity program.

Educational policy and reform

"Stupid in America" (ABC, 2006). This episode is the first of three in a series that examines school culture and the achievement gap. Independent schools and school choice are put forth as possible solutions to the educational problems in the United States.

The Cartel (Bowdon, 2009). Considers the topic of financing public education.

Race to Nowhere (Abeles, 2010). This documentary examines overworked students, those who are trying to get into elite colleges and those affected by overtesting, who are stressed out by homework.

The Inconvenient Truth Behind Waiting for Superman (Bruhn et al., 2011). New York public school teachers challenge the claims made in *Waiting for Superman.*

Portrayal of a school

Dropout Nation (Frontline/PBS, 2012). Promoting itself with the question, "What does it take to save a student?" this program looks at a school in Texas which is trying to help all of its at-risk students to graduate. Considers some of the reasons students drop out of high school.

I Am a Promise: The Children of Stanton Elementary School (Raymond, 1993). Portrayal of an elementary school in Philadelphia.

180 Days: A Year Inside an American High School (Black Public Media, 2013). This film follows a principal and several of her students as they attempt to complete the school year in spite of the difficulties they face.

Last Chance High (Vice, 2014). LCH consists of eight episodes set in and around Moses Montefiore Academy, an alternative high school in Chicago, IL, that serves socially and emotionally disturbed students.

180 Days: Hartsville (Black Public Media, 2015). The second in the series *180 Days*, this two-part program profiles the year of two elementary schools in rural South Carolina and the challenges their administrators, teachers, and students face.

Teachers

The First Year (Guggenheim, 2001). This film follows five new teachers, several of whom are Teach for America teachers, as they struggle with the demands during their first year teaching. The promotional material states that part of its purpose is to inspire people to teach.

American Teacher (Roth, 2011). This documentary follows four teachers over the course of one year as they become parents, try to support a family, and decide to take a more lucrative teaching job.

Morgan Spurlock: Inside Man on Education (Spurlock, 2013). Considers the differences between teachers, schools, and teaching in the United States and Finland. Spurlock teaches a lesson in schools in both countries.

Teacher of the Year (Philips & Korreck, 2016). This film chronicles the year of one social studies teacher in North Carolina. Includes interviews with experts in various fields of education and media studies.

Students

Educating Peter (Wurzburg, 1992). This film follows Peter, a student with Down syndrome, and his inclusion in a third grade classroom.

Chain Camera (Dick, 2001). In this documentary, a crew gives ten students at John Marshall High School in California cameras and asks them to record a week in their lives.

The Pact (Kalin, 2006). This film follows three African American men who are successful doctors as they embark on mentoring young African American males and consider how to get their message out to a wider audience.

American Teen (Burnstein, 2008). This film focuses on the different "categories" of students found in high schools—the jock, the nerd, the princess. The poster even mimics the promotional poster for John Hughes; *The Breakfast Club.* Six students are followed in their everyday lives.

Innovative school programs

Why do these kids love school? (Fadiman, 1999). This film highlights eight schools, but mostly focuses on the Peninsula School in California, whose programs are guided by independent learning, developmentally appropriate approaches, and supportive learning environments.

High School Boot Camp (Braverman, 2000). This film is a look at Eagle Academy, a military-type boarding school in Palm Beach County, Florida.

Boys of Baraka (Ewing & Grady, 2005). A group of African American male students from Baltimore, Maryland, attend a boarding school in Kenya.

Small Steps: Creating the High School for Contemporary Arts (Becker, 2007). A look at a school in Bronx, New York, that is a school within a school that brings together a group of teaching artists to develop a curriculum focused on contemporary arts.

General issues, special programs and extracurricular groups

Spellbound (Blitz, 2002). This film follows eight students in their quest to win the national spelling bee.

Paper Clips (Fab & Berlin, 2004). This film examines the ongoing project of a school who in an effort to try to understand the magnitude of deaths during the Holocaust collects paper-clips to represent each person who died during the Holocaust.

Resolved (Whiteley, 2005). This film examines the field of high school policy debates and follows two teams who challenge the system: one for its elitist qualities, the other to win by finding the right school team.

Ten9Eight: Shoot for the Moon (Mazzio, 2009). This documentary follows students who are at risk of dropping out and take a course in entrepreneurship.

Brooklyn Castle (Dellamaggiore, 2012). This documentary follows the extremely successful school chess club at a school in Brooklyn, New York, that is in danger of losing its program because of lack of funding.

SECTION II

BASED ON ACTUAL EVENTS: BIOPICS

· 4 ·

"I SEE THE SAME F—ING MOVIES YOU DO, MAN"

An Analysis of Three Biopics about Teachers

The title for this chapter comes from a line from the 1995 movie *Dangerous Minds* (*DM*; Smith), a biopic based on the 1992 teacher memoir *My Posse Don't Do Homework* (*MPDDH*; Johnson). In the memoir and film, ex-Marine LouAnne Johnson takes a job at Parkmont High School in Southern California where she faces a challenging group of students. In the particular scene that serves as the basis for this chapter's title, Johnson has just discovered several of her students in a fight—a fight that was a continuation of an earlier one she believed she had diffused. She learns that rather than having prevented a future fight, she had only postponed it.

After bidding goodbye to two of her three students who are taken away in a police car, she visits the other one, Emilio, in order to try to figure out what happened. She finds him in a classroom; a security officer who stands against the wall in the back is guarding him. The following conversation occurs as they both sit in student desks, a directorial decision that negates the stance of the teacher standing over the student, which suggests Ms. Johnson is about to learn a valuable lesson.

Johnson:	You mind telling me what the fight was about in the first place?
Emilio:	Yeah.

Johnson:	I really would like to know what happened. I'm not gonna make any trouble for you. I just want to know. Was it worth it?
Emilio:	Yeah, it was worth it.
Johnson:	Why?
Emilio:	Because it felt good hittin' him in the face. I got him good, man.
Johnson:	Oh, yeah? You like to hit people?
Emilio:	Yeah, I like to hit people.
Johnson:	Why? You feel angry a lot of the time?
Emilio:	So now you're gonna try and "psychologize" me? You're gonna try and figure me out? I'll help you. I come from a broken home, and we're poor, okay? I see the same fuckin' movies you do, man. ... How the fuck you gonna save me from my life, huh?

While Emilio doesn't specify which movies they both have seen, his candid comeback can be read as a summary of the plot found in many school films. In fact, his response is a commentary on just about every film in which a teacher comes into a school with good intentions, high expectations, and naïve pedagogical approaches, only to find a group of disinterested and often unruly students with insurmountable problems in their lives inside and outside of school. Then, it is up to the teacher to "figure out" how to reach these students—hence, Emilio's use of the phrase "psychologize me." Scholars have shown how these films share a similar template—the reluctant student, the teacher as outsider, the coming together of students and teachers to resist/fight some cause, and the cheerful ending where the teacher stays (Ayers, 2001; Bulman, 2004; Chennault, 2006; Dalton, 2010). Emilio and Johnson are just filling their slots as the resistant student and the teacher-as-hero. While this scene does take place in Johnson's book, it does not include the reference to other teacher movies; therefore, Emilio's line in the film threatens to unravel the potential for the film's message to claim any connection to the success Johnson may have had with her students.

If Emilio is referring to school films, then what is the audience, knowing this film is based, in part, on real events and persons, to think of his statement? If this teacher movie resembles other teacher movies, then should we as an audience discredit its representation of Ms. Johnson's teaching? Is she just another teacher whose concern for her students is constructed for the purposes of the film or is she the "real thing"? Or do all biopics hold some truth about schools, leaving it up to the audience to recognize what comes from actual events on which the film was based and what has been dramatized? As viewers, we understand that the images from teacher films that have been repeatedly recreated, revisited, and remade tend to be based on actual teachers, and these dramatic moments, these unforgettable moments, are purportedly based on true stories. Emilio's declaration, then, is a line that threatens to undo the very purpose of teacher biopics by calling attention to how Johnson's narrative has been manipulated by Hollywood as well.

The purpose of this chapter is not to debate the value of the film versus the book (although in my opinion, the book is always better). Both contain elements that may be truthful or not truthful given the characteristics of their genres. Instead, my purpose is to trace what gets added, left out, or manipulated for a film from a "true story" and how that representation interacts with the original source text(s). I hope to identify what the Hollywood narrative might have been if the cinematic adaptations of these works had more faithfully followed their original stories. In my analysis, I argue that these teacher biopics shift the reason most responsible for the students' success onto the teacher–student relationship, change the curriculum for purposes of supporting the films' messages, and sometimes soften a teacher's character to make him or her more sympathetic and admirable. In doing so, they attempt, but ultimately fail, to capture the multiple levels of power that exist in schools. This examination explores the aspects of teachers' narratives that have been silenced to fit the Hollywood model for biopics as well as how those stories represent particular narratives to the public about schools.

In an attempt to understand the complicated piecing together of source texts and films that unfolds when a story based on actual events is adapted for film, this chapter examines three biopics—*Freedom Writers* (LaGravenese, 2007), *Dangerous Minds* (Smith, 1995), and *Stand and Deliver* (Menendez, 1988)—that not only received some degree of box office success, but also comprise much of the conversation surrounding representations of good and bad teachers, and good and bad teaching, in school films. They are also all set in Southern California. While there are other films that could make this list because they were either based on actual teachers, such as *Dead Poets Society* (Weir, 1989), or true stories found in the media, as in *Won't Back Down*, (Barnz, 2012) I am going to focus on movies with memoirs, and in one case, a biography, because of this genre's interaction with and attempt to capture actual events and situations. This chapter weaves together the reception of these biopics by film critics and scholars and the reactions from subjects of the biopics themselves in response to seeing their stories adapted for the screen.

The Biopic

According to Custen (1992), a "biographical film [biopic] is one that depicts the life of a historical person, past or present" (or a portion of that life) and uses the person's real name (pp. 5–7). Custen notes the influence of the biopic that comes from the shifts that occur in the genre with each generation. They are

> ... an enormous, engaging distortion, which after a time convinces us of its own kind of authenticity. Hollywood biographies are real not because they are believable. Rather one must treat them as real because despite the obvious distortions ranging from the minor to the outright camp, Hollywood films are believed to be real by many viewers. (p. 7)

Many scholars of school films agree that audiences treat these films as real. While the Hollywood narrative of school films has been well documented by scholars, the distinction between the biopic and the fictional film is nearly nonexistent. Biopics about schools are expected to be based on an actual teacher, to retain the majority of that teacher's experience, and to be based on a real story. What, if any, obligation does a biopic have to the original story on which it is based?

There have been few studies of K–12 teacher biopics, in part because of the genre's tendency to focus on a figure of historical importance. In her book, *Bio-pics: A Life in Pictures*, Cheshire (2014) devotes an entire chapter to academics in biopics, but never mentions one biopic featuring a K–12 teacher. She claims that the one characteristic that links biopics "is quite simply [that] the films depict the life of an important real person" (p. 4). Can teachers reach the level of other subjects of biopics, including Ali, Curie, and Lincoln? Many of the teachers featured in biopics did receive attention from the press or sell many copies of a book before their biopics were made.

In his chapter, "A Teacher Ain't Nothin' but a Hero," Ayers (2001) discusses five teacher films, and he concludes that these films—indeed, the majority of teacher films—contain teacher heroes who have to first gain control of their students before they are able to teach. Three of the films he examines are based on real stories: *Conrack* (Ritt, 1974), *Lean on Me* (Avildsen, 1989), and *Stand and Deliver* (Menendez, 1988). While he does note which films are based on true stories, he dismisses the importance of that fact, claiming that they are only loosely based on the truth in order to perpetuate the myth that teachers can accomplish great things: "It [*Conrack*] is, of course, true in the sense that the later *Lean on Me* or *Stand and Deliver* are true—a few readymade verities, a handful of simple formulas, a couple of slogans thrown out and passed along. It is a comfortable kind of truth, a painless and uncomplicated romance, and an easy belief" (p. 204).

For Dalton (2010), these films, whether they are based on true stories or not, follow a similar pattern: the "teacher as outsider," "personally involved with students," "teachers learning from students," and "tension between teacher and administrator." This formula includes uncomplicated notions of teaching a lesson, which are determined by the context in which teachers find themselves, which hold that good teaching is accomplished through individual work, and which espouse showmanship. But these arguments are also applied to their counterpart fictional teacher films, like *Bad Teacher* (Kasdan, 2011) and *Blackboard Jungle* (Brooks, 1955). What if it's true? What if teaching really is this hard and one can only be truly successful through extreme attempts to reach students and fight the evil educational system?

A notable and frequent effect of adapting a book into a biopic is the distortion of time, as the film adaptations attempt to condense events that may happen over several years into one. Johnson's (*DM*), Gruwell's (*Freedom Writers*), and Escalante's (*Stand and Deliver*) stories cover several years of their teaching experiences, some even teaching the same students for more than one year. On the other hand, the biopics tend to focus on one year, combining the many ups and downs of several years' experiences. As a consequence, this adaptation for the screen makes it appear as if they achieved their success in a much shorter time than they actually did. The lesson that is lost on the audience is the ongoing reflective process that teachers often endure their first couple of years.

Another omission from the memoirs' adaptation into biopics is the tremendous amount of work that teachers face—the time spent lesson planning, grading, doing administrative tasks. According to these films, the secret to great teaching is in the delivery of a lesson, not in the preparation. Admittedly, even a montage of teachers reading classroom management books and child psychology texts (as in *DM* and *To Sir With Love*) would only scrape the surface of the complex thought that goes into teacher planning. And audiences do get glimpses of this work, as there are several scenes in which the protagonists are shown reading books on child psychology. However, prolonged scenes of teachers reading or attending workshops would probably not transfer to the screen in an entertaining way.

Some acknowledgment of teaching evolution does exist. There are several montages of early failed lessons until the teachers "get it right." That might be the changing of what one wears to teach, the throwing out of books, or the chopping of apples, but the message is clear: no new teacher can go right in and start teaching. Given these decisions, teaching in these films appears to come from great performances and building relationships; teachers require very little training other than the on-the-job training.

Another notable area of critique around these films is their consideration of race and ethnicity. Whether it's a white teacher facing a class of students of color, or a teacher of color up against the larger system, it's hard to say if these moments are part of the director's larger agenda and/or a part of these teachers' lived experiences. What is important to note is the degree to which these racial tensions are highlighted or downplayed. For example, the racial make-up of both Gruwell's and Johnson's students is changed for the screen (albeit not as drastically in *DM*) to make it appear that they worked mostly with minority students. *Stand and Deliver* addresses notions of racism directly, but not nearly as nuanced as in the biography. Race becomes even more prominent in *Up the Down Staircase* (Mulligan, 1967). In a 1993 conference presentation, Thomsen examines the public's attitudes toward schools as evidenced in the Phi Delta Kappa Gallup poll. He credits *Blackboard Jungle* with establishing the template for the great teacher myth and writes, "In the movie, *To Sir, With Love*, produced only a few years later, Sydney Poitier takes on the same role—a teacher forced to stand up against apathetic teachers and students." Likewise, in an essay on *Freedom Writers*, Delgado (2001) wonders:

> I find it hard to put a finger on what bothers me about Hollywood's teacher movies. Is it the young white teacher saving kids of color? Is it the guilt I feel as a teacher who may not have succeeded as well as these superheroes? Is it the notion that teachers should be mother, father, college counselor, and best friend to our students, despite the incredible personal toll that takes? Or is it the movies' individualized solutions to structural problems? (p. 226)

The films all end the same way—by answering the questions posed by the (arguably) first teacher-as-savior film, *Blackboard Jungle:* does the teacher stay and/or do the students succeed? Perhaps most notable is the change of the ending between *MPDDH* and *DM*. *MPDDH* ends with Raul promising to graduate and repay the money he owes Johnson. *DM*, on the other hand, ends with Johnson and her colleague, Parker, walking together on the last day of school after Johnson's students convince her to stay. Parker asks, "How did they get you to come back?" Johnson responds with, "They gave me candy and called me 'the light,'" referring to her method of getting students to answer questions and the Dylan Thomas poem they read in class. While all of the teachers stay at the end of the film, all three leave the profession within several years of the film's production, citing, among other factors, the tension between them and their colleagues as a result of their post-film notoriety.

Finally, none of these teachers, according to the books, accomplished these feats on their own. In the memoirs (and biography), they specifically set out to acquire support from anyone who was willing. When they couldn't get it from their colleagues or administrators, they went to the public and private sector to find people who would support them—professionally and even financially when classroom needs couldn't be met with their salaries and extra jobs. At least two of these authors acknowledged the near impossibility of sustaining these approaches to teaching. They admittedly took approaches that bordered on the unethical: they threatened, they cajoled, they made promises, and when they couldn't get their way, they circumvented the system. In these ways, they echo many of those who purport to understand how to improve the educational system: we need to expect more from our students, adhere to higher standards, implement more teacher accountability, and fund programs that work. But as scholars point out over and over, these approaches are not sustainable, so when these accounts transfer to the screen, audiences are left with only part of the story.

Dangerous Minds: Taking the Unsightly out of the Character

The biopic *Dangerous Minds* (Smith, 1995) is based on LouAnne Johnson's *My Posse Don't Do Homework* (1992). Her memoir begins and ends with a promise that one of Johnson's students, Raul, makes to her—that on the day he graduates, he will repay her the money she lent him for a jacket. Johnson reveals that the reason Raul had bought the jacket was to wear to a dinner at a fancy restaurant, a dinner he earned for his good grades. In between the introduction of this loan and its status at the end of the book is a series of stories about Johnson's experiences teaching at Parkmont High, where her student teaching placement turned quickly into a full-time job left by a retiring teacher. The book is comprised of vignettes, told in no particular order, of her interactions with students, her struggle to connect her students with the curriculum, her experiments to determine why some students are labeled as advanced, and her interactions with her colleagues. Johnson would eventually write a sequel, *The Girls in the Back of the Class* (1995), along with a novel and several books on effective teaching strategies for educators.

In the film version, *Dangerous Minds*, ex-Marine LouAnne Johnson (played by Michelle Pfeiffer) finds herself teaching at a Los Angeles high school. The film focuses more on Johnson's relationship with troublemaker Emilio and her attempts to follow her student Callie's advice, "Ms. Johnson, if you want to get the class to listen, get Emilio." With the support of her colleague, Johnson challenges herself to change radically her pedagogical approaches in the classroom with a makeover (literally) that begins to help break down the barriers between her students and her. She soon finds herself able to help students relate to the "college level" poetry of Dylan Thomas by first getting them interested in Bob Dylan's songs. In spite of the traumatic episodes with some of her students—two being pulled from her classroom by their grandmother, one being murdered—Johnson ultimately stays with her students after they convince her through Dylan Thomas's words "not to go gently into that good night."

As Bulman (2004) notes, if a film is set in a lower socioeconomic school, the focus of the film is on the teacher. For *DM*, the decision to cast Michelle Pfeiffer in the role of LouAnne Johnson and the decisions about how to represent the ex-Marine on the screen became distracting for film critics. In Maslin's review in the *New York Times*, titled "If the Teacher Is Pfeiffer, Can All Youths Be Bad?" (1995), she concentrates on how the film takes the teacher–author from the book and transforms her into a beauty queen for the screen, a one-dimensional character who comes to resemble the cinematic teacher who "tames the rebellious teen." Maslin writes, "It doesn't matter whether these were Ms. Johnson's real educational tactics. In a movie, as performed so prettily by Ms. Pfeiffer, such tricks aren't believable for a minute." In his review for the *LA Times*, "Two Stars in a Dim Galaxy: Michelle Pfeiffer gives a realistic performance in an otherwise simplistic and predictable *Dangerous Minds*" (1995), Turan concurs that the focus on Johnson's character distracts the essential message of the memoir:

> Unfortunately for the movie-makers, her book was a series of loosely connected vignettes, not a conventional narrative with a plotted arc and a dramatic ending. To make it into a film, a story would have to be constructed around Johnson's character. (¶5)

Finally, McManus, reviewing for *The Washington Post*, stated simply, "As a divorced ex-Marine who throws herself into teaching 'at-risk' teens in East Palo Alto, [Michelle] Pfeiffer is a kick to watch" (1995, ¶3). He continues, "With her leather-flannel-and-denim ensembles, she looks like a gal who really could charm a rainbow coalition of adolescent gangstas and burnouts"

(¶3). But for the movie's producers, the formula of assembling the well-known production team of Simpson/Bruckheimer (*Flashdance*, 1983; *Top Gun*, 1986) with a talented star, an impressive soundtrack, and a well-trod narrative structure paid off. *DM* grossed $84,919,401 in the United States and $179,519,401 worldwide.

Educational scholars also noticed the manipulation of LouAnne Johnson's character for the film, especially in regards to how she inhabits the "good" teacher, the "colonial teacher," the "charismatic teacher," and the last teacher in a long line of films that feature the white, female, do-gooder who is intent on making a difference (Henke, 2008). According to Henke (2008), "it eulogizes the last hope of public education" (p. 99). But educational scholars, like the film critics, point out that she is cast as an attractive teacher (which is not to say Johnson is not attractive). Bauer (1998) notes how teachers in films now represent a "sexual proposition" and subjects of desire (p. 307). Those like Pfeiffer/Johnson represent "the rather asexual newly divorced teacher [who] finds herself in an eroticized zone, supercharged with violence, disrespect for authority, and moral chaos" (p. 307). The storyline also becomes part of these (re)visions as Henke (2008) argues, "Johnson tells the tale, but it is not her tale after the telling … as the film simultaneously eclipsed and reinvented its own originary text" (p. 99). Henke notes that *DM* "escapes the baggage of 'realism' of a documentary, while managing to profit from the feeling that is evoking something real" (p. 102). It is almost as if these (re)presentations will make the real *more* real to viewers, counting on their assumptions of schools, students, and teachers.

The students also go under a makeover, as Johnson's original students were a third Hispanic, a third African American, and a third white. In the introduction to the revised version of the book that came out after the production of the film, Johnson explains a significant difference between the way she tells her story and the way it is told in the film. The film is told as a narrative, beginning with Johnson's first day and ending with the last day of school. *MPDDH*, on the other hand, is told through a series of "snapshots" that span four years. Johnson tells her stories out of order: "Since my students are my primary focus, I chose to emphasize them instead of the clock and the calendar" (p. 1). Furthermore, she teaches several of these students for multiple years, whereas the film only covers one academic year. While both tales capture Johnson's struggle for power, the film also captures her students' struggle for power within the institution. Both perspectives on struggle fit comfortably within the tradition of school films.

The scene that opens this chapter is quite similar to the way Johnson records it in her memoir, but there are two notable exceptions. First, the dialogue in the memoir changes after she asks Emilio if he feels angry all of the time. In the memoir, Emilio admits that he does and responds to her questions "Do you feel mad?" and "Why do you feel mad?" with the response: "I don't know," he said. "Things" (p. 226). Emilio then goes on to explain that he is from El Salvador, that the fight was over a pair of shorts believed to have been stolen, and that he doesn't like school because the teachers exert too much control.

The second important difference between this scene in the memoir and the film is that at this point, Emilio is not Johnson's student. During the conversation in the memoir, she asks Emilio why he is not in the Academy Program and invites him to stop by her classroom after school. When he does, she's surprised. She gives him a journal and asks him to write down his life story, which he does, and their relationship grows as she takes the time to learn about him. Johnson reflects how she experiences the most success when she's honest with her students—why she's there, how they made her feel, how she reacted, why that was wrong, and can they start again. Henke (2008) points out how this scene in the memoir is an example of the "colonial agent exemplar," and one might wonder which is the better scene for Emilio and Johnson. In the film, the point of view is not first person, and the stakes for the onscreen Emilio are temporary; for the Emilio in the memoir, those stakes may be longer lasting, in that he may view the Academy Program as a way to succeed in school and/or join his friends. It's even possible he recognizes this encounter with Johnson as a rare moment where a teacher has taken an interest in him. Teachers like Johnson are repeatedly, and often fairly, examined in a way that uncovers white privilege and colonial tendencies, but Emilio's motives are overshadowed in the book and the film by Johnson's efforts.

Another scene not originally from the book is included briefly at the beginning of the film. On the second day of class, there is the infamous scene in which Johnson, now clad in a leather jacket and jeans, lets the students assume she can kill a man with her hands. She then has two students demonstrate a karate move. While this scene is not from the memoir, Johnson did not hesitate to threaten her students with bodily harm. At one moment in her memoir, she even goes so far as to say to one student:

> "Go ahead and hit me," I snarled, "but make it good, because you're only going to get one hit. Then I'm going to kill you." … It was my father's voice and my father's words. (p. 88)

Perhaps this moment reveals why Johnson is able to ask the questions she does of Emilio, beginning with the "What makes you angry?" that allows him to open up to her.

Another important distinction between the film and the book is Johnson's relationship with the other teachers and administrators. In her memoir, she teaches as part of the Academy Program, a school-within-a-school program that assists students through team-teaching with smaller class sizes. She speaks of working with the Academy team faculty and frequently uses the pronoun "we" when discussing curriculum issues and student engagement. Her colleague, Parker, plays a large role in mentoring her, just as he does in the movie. She often discusses with senior faculty ways to reach her students that some teachers have given up on; for example, they doubt she should bother teaching Shakespeare. In the film, however, the Academy Program appears to be just a program, and audiences don't see the teacher meetings, the community support (for example, a local restaurant donated the dinners to students, like Raul, who were making good grades; Johnson didn't pay for them out of her own pocket as the film suggests), or the collaborative efforts to work with students. In addition, the power struggle between the advanced program and the academic program is diminished, as those students remain in the margins of the film.

In short, the decision to focus on Johnson rather than on her relationships changes much of the focus and purpose of her memoir, which was to highlight the collaborative, relationship-building aspects of teaching. Instead, it emphasizes *one* of the tenets of Johnson's teaching philosophy—that her students have choices, and their choice to be in school sets them apart from their peers who have chosen not to attend school. The close relationships Johnson builds in the films with the teen gangster, the pregnant teen, and the underachieving student were manipulated for the screen as a way of threading narratives of the consequences of their choices into the film.

The ongoing stories of the authors of biopics reveal mixed feelings about their experiences with adaptations into films. While Johnson agrees with much of how she and her philosophy of choice were transferred to the screen, she was frustrated with the liberties the publisher and production company took with her book and with her. *DM* eventually became a television show with the same name that ran on ABC for one season (1996–1997) and starred Annie Potts. In an interview with Ira Glass (1996) on NPR's show *This American Life*, Johnson describes her feelings about what happened to her book, including her disappointed reaction when she discovered that on the post-film reprinting of the book, the publishers had changed the title to *Dangerous Minds* and put the stars of the film on the cover.

In that same interview, Johnson also describes how the television show turned the school into a war zone, emphasized racial and ethnic conflicts, and that ABC, owned by Disney, was turning her and her character into a character that they owned, like Mickey Mouse or Dumbo. She was also concerned with the fabricated storylines that she believed did not reflect her experiences in an inner-city school. Glass interviewed the show's producers, Andrew Schneider and Diane Frolov, about the liberties Johnson believed they were taking with her story. Schneider responded:

> The war zone aspect of life in school is something that we will concentrate on more, only because you need conflict, you need dramatic situations, you need stakes to be high. Otherwise, I'm not sure how you make a show. I mean, you have to deal with issues that have impact.

In the closing remarks to the segment, Glass attempted to attribute the producers' choices to the form of television. He concludes:

> In a sense, this is the Faustian bargain the producers of *Dangerous Minds* have made. The high school in their show has more war zone moments, more heroic attempts by teachers to save kids, more crises and near crises than any real inner-city high school, because they need three stories per episode, and they have to be dramatic.

Johnson's story shows the complications that occur as a real character becomes fictionalized and the original author loses control over that representation. While a memoir can become just as dramatized as a biopic, it is the author who has control over that story; once writers, directors, and producers become involved, the narrative is bound to evolve. The point is, each form—memoir, film, and television show—has a traditional structure, and perhaps the memoir has the fewest restrictions. When *Freedom Writers*, the next film based on a memoir featuring mainly student voices, was produced, a similar decision was made to cast a high-profile actress in the leading role, but that film would attempt to retain more of the students' stories and balance those with the personal narrative of the teacher.

Freedom Writers: First a Book, Then a Movie, Then a Memoir, and Then a Documentary

Erin Gruwell's story is one that has been told through her and her students' written narratives that were collected and published as *The Freedom Writers*

Diary: How a Teacher and 150 Teens Used Writing to Change Themselves and the World around Them (*FWD*, 1999), then in the film, *Freedom Writers* (*FW*, LaGravenese, 2007), then in her memoir, *Teach with Your Heart* (*TWYH*, 2007). Together these texts reveal the four years Gruwell spent as a teacher of a group of students, their journey to publish and then film their stories, and their ongoing efforts to improve education today through their foundation.

FWD is a collection of 142 diary entries written by Gruwell and her students and organized by the semester of each of the four years she spent with them as their English language arts teacher. The diary entries read like a series of vignettes in which students discuss "events that changed their lives." Woven into these stories are references to lessons, literature, and assignments students experienced in Gruwell's class, as well as their thoughts about her and her approach to teaching. In her entries that begin each section, Gruwell explains how this collection of diaries came out of their classroom lessons, through which they became driven by the desire to change themselves, the system, and the world.

Like Johnson's memoir, *FWD* takes place over the course of multiple years, in this case, four years. However, unlike *MPDDH*, students in *FWD* tell their own stories alongside their teacher's, rather than the teacher telling their stories. Gruwell lived in Newport Beach, California, and was destined for law school until the night she watched the Rodney King riots. Convinced that she could contribute to making a change, she decided to become a teacher and applied at Woodrow Wilson High School, an integrated school in nearby Long Beach. Her first year teaching freshmen mirrored many other teacher narratives—she was appalled by the conditions of her classroom and the lack of interest in the content from her students. She soon recognized that she wasn't connecting with her students, so she worked to build quality relationships.

One of the incidents that determined Gruwell's future direction as a teacher occurred when a racist picture of Sharaud, one of her more disruptive students, was being passed around her classroom. (Note that these are not the students she goes on to spend four years with.) The way she recorded that scene in her diary transferred nearly word for word to the screen:

> Sharaud became the butt of a bad joke. A classmate got tired of Sharaud's antics and drew a racial caricature of him with huge, exaggerated lips. As the drawing made its way around the room, the other students laughed hysterically. When Sharaud saw it, he looked as if he was going to cry. For the first time, his tough façade began to crack.
>
> When I got a hold of the picture, I went ballistic. "This is the type of propaganda that the Nazis used during the Holocaust," I yelled. When a student timidly asked me, "What's the Holocaust?" I was shocked.

> I asked, "How many of you have heard of the Holocaust?" Not a single person raised his hand. Then I asked, "How many of you have been shot at?" Nearly every hand went up.
>
> I immediately decided to throw out my meticulously planned lessons and make tolerance the core of my curriculum. (pp. 2–3)

Her curriculum became guided by this theme—not only through the texts she chose for them to read, but also through how she approached each text. For example, in her diary, she considers excitedly how she will introduce Shakespeare to her students:

> So, to whip them into shape, I'm going to have to get down and dirty. I'll have to burst their "Beverly Hills 90210" stereotype of me by getting into the trenches with them. Since I'm tackling Shakespeare soon, I need to convince them that this guy in tights who talks funny "has it going on." I need to show them Shakespeare's got a little "something something" for everyone. So what I'm going to do is make the Montagues and Capulets into a modern-day posse. (p. 32)

Gruwell and Johnson share several similar approaches to teaching—they think about how to relate the curriculum to their students' lives, they both employ journals as a way to learn about their students' lives and build relationships, and they both sustain ongoing relationships with many of their students. But Gruwell's project becomes a joint endeavor as she shares the responsibilities with her students.

The film *FW* attempts to create a balance of Gruwell's journey with her students' journeys by interspersing the narrative of Gruwell's experiences with scenes from her students' diaries. The scenes go back and forth from Gruwell's classroom to her home to her students' neighborhoods. A notable difference between *FWD* and *FW* is the latter's increased attention on Gruwell and her life outside of the classroom. Unlike *FWD*, Gruwell's personal life is explored in much the same way as her students', that is, by sharing personal experiences. Many of those experiences revolve around adults who criticize her approaches. In fact, her husband, her father, a colleague, and her department chair question her overwhelming devotion again and again. Her portrayal of a superstar teacher is best captured by her cinematic department chair who exclaims in a meeting with the principal, "Her methods are impractical, impossible to implement with regularity" (*FW*, 2007).

In addition to Gruwell's storyline, the film attempts to create a narrative that connects and (re)constructs three storylines from the memoir: a homeless student's longing to return home, a student who must decide whether to perjure herself at a murder trial, and a student who deals drugs. Many snapshots of other students' stories are included using a voiceover reading of excerpts from their entries. At the end of the first year of teaching this group of students, Gruwell feels as if there's more to be done with them, so she fights to keep them another year. At the end of the movie and the book, her notoriety as a public figure has grown as she has garnered national support for her students and turned her career into a movement.

It's a thrilling story that's been both harshly critiqued and generously praised by film critics. As with *Dangeous Minds*, film critics focused on the leading actor in *Freedom Writers*, Hilary Swank, best known for her award-winning roles in *Boys Don't Cry* (Peirce, 1999) and *Million-Dollar Baby* (Eastwood, 2004). In the *New York Times Review*, "To Ms. With Love: A Teacher's Heart Fords a Social Divide," Dargis (2007) writes, "*Freedom Writers*, a true story about a white teacher trying to make a difference in a room crammed with black, Latino and Asian high school freshmen, has the makings of another groaner" (¶2), but she goes on to praise the balance of the teacher's story with her students. In a letter to the *New York Times*, a teacher who taught writing courses in inner-city schools disagreed with a review written by film reviewer Moore (2007), "I would argue that *Freedom Writers* is a break-out film, by placing the stories of the students front and center, and demonstrating realistically that disadvantaged kids need more time, attention, and creative lesson-planning than our static public schools allow" (Ross, 2007, ¶3). Thomson (2007) from the *Washington Post* asks, "So is it a good thing or bad that *Freedom Writers*, which stars Hilary Swank, adheres so closely to the clichéd syllabus?" (¶3). While ultimately for Thomson, it's a bad thing because this addition to the genre of school films still leaves audiences searching for an authentic look inside our schools, *FW* earned $36,605,602 in the United States and earned $43,090,741 worldwide.

Educational scholars, for the most part, associate *FW* with a long tradition of teacher films that portray the good, white, female teacher intent on saving her students. One form of that criticism is directed at the text choices Gruwell makes on screen. The curriculum for the film consists mainly of *The Diary of Anne Frank*, since the department chair refuses to let her use a class set of *Romeo and Juliet* and offers her a condensed magazine version instead. Delgado points out that her decision to use the texts she does "raises several questions."

> Rather than studying their own histories—U.S. slavery, the violence of colonization and border creation, the Khmer Rouge regime in Cambodia—the students study the Holocaust. Even where the Holocaust is a vehicle for the students to tell their own stories, that connection to a white experience is key. The Holocaust should be

> studied in its own right—but so should the current lived experiences of youth of color in the United States. (pp. 227–228)

In my article on the teaching of Shakespeare via school films (Bach, 2009), I read this scene differently—Gruwell picks Shakespeare off the shelf to teach it as a gang story, thereby making assumptions about her students and what will get them excited about reading. From this perspective, these comments speak to the limitations of film adaptations and their tendency to present incomplete pictures.

Whether or not you applaud Gruwell and believe her approach can be implemented with regularity, she, out of all the other teachers, has left a most notable legacy and continues to do so. Henke (2008) states that *FW* is the last in a long line that began with *Blackboard Jungle*; the production of *High School High*, a parody of these films, signals the audience's awareness of the common elements found in movies in this tradition. While those films have been replaced by teachers who are goofy characters whose behaviors are often unethical (*School of Rock*, *Bad Teacher*, *Here Comes the Boom*), films like *Dangerous Minds* still exist, and audiences still seek the feel-good messages that are so often criticized by scholars and critics.

Like Johnson's and Gruwell's movies, *Stand and Deliver*, the final biopic and accompanying biography I discuss in this chapter, is an attempt to honor and reveal the secrets of good teaching and to capture the true story for the public. While the first two authors wrote their own stories, Jamie Escalante's story was captured first by the news media, then in cinematic form, and finally in a biography.

Where Have All of the Other Teachers Gone?

The 1988 film *Stand and Deliver* (Menendez, 1988) is the story of Jaime Escalante's determination to meet the challenge of having his students, mainly Hispanic, pass the notoriously difficult AP Calculus test. Their success on such a test could help his school improve its ranking and help with accreditation issues. The film covers two years of Escalante's teaching, the first of which is characterized by his stumbling efforts that soon morph into gimmicks designed to garner interest and group success, like chopping apples and reciting math rules as a group. Escalante identifies his most promising students and accelerates their instruction, leading to a group that prepares relentlessly for the AP Calculus test. But this extra effort doesn't come easily, as we see Escalante argue with both the students and their parents to put Calculus prep above all else.

Escalante's health suffers as does the financial situation for many of his students, due to the number of hours—outside of school and in the summer—spent preparing for the test. Several months after they take the test, the results show that all of his students pass. However, the results are accompanied by the news that the Educational Testing Service is challenging the test scores of the majority of those students, citing examples in the written responses that appear to be evidence of cheating. Escalante, extremely angry, accuses the ETS of discrimination, but they offer an ultimatum to the students: retake the test or forfeit their scores. The students decide to retake, spend two days studying, and all pass again. The film ends with Escalante triumphantly walking down a school hallway while across the bottom of the screen roll statistics showing the increasing number of students at Garfield who take and pass the AP Calculus test.

The Best Teacher in America (Mathews, 1988) is a biography tracing the story of Escalante, a teacher who helped build a successful AP Calculus program at a Los Angeles High School. Escalante, who immigrated to the United States from Bolivia after having taught there successfully for several years, moved to California in the 1960s to provide more opportunities for his family. However, once there, Escalante discovers he is unable to teach because of his lack of credentials and has to retake four years of college. He finishes the program, leaves a profitable job in engineering, and takes a job at the troubled Garfield Senior High School in Los Angeles. There, as depicted in the film, he starts up a small but successful Advanced Placement Calculus course; students who score a 3 or higher (on a scale of 5) on the national test can receive college credit from most universities for that course. In 1982, the first year his students took the test, 12 of them were accused of cheating on the exam by the company who created and scored the test, ETS. Ten of them retook another exam three months after they had graduated and managed to earn passing scores again, though most of them scored lower on that second test. At the end of the book, Escalante and his colleagues continue expanding their program and their number of passing scores.

Mathews, who was asked to write this biography (in part as a response to the alleged cheating scandal), traces not only Escalante's path to Garfield High School from Bolivia, but also the career paths of several of his colleagues and administrators. Several of Garfield's teachers also sought to increase the number and passing rates of students who took AP tests in other areas, and Mathews highlights the tension that occurred when various faculty members recruited the same students for these demanding courses. Mathews's account highlights not only their role in Escalante's mission, but also many of the students who enrolled in the Calculus course. Through his depiction of several of the students, Mathews reveals the decisions students had to make about how to spend their time—such as whether to keep jobs that helped support their family; whether to spend time in activities they loved, such as marching band; or whether to devote their attention to their other courses. It's a narrative that shows that great teachers need to be left alone, as Mathews concludes, but they also undoubtedly benefit from the support of colleagues who prepare and endorse a vision. Finally, Mathews recognizes the sacrifices Garfield's students made and highlights (and this is captured by the quotations on the back of the book) concrete ways to increase student engagement and achievement.

Stand and Deliver became a story about Escalante and his students—a distortion that downplays the role other teachers played, aside from those who were disbelievers and antagonists. One of the film's directors read about Escalante and his students in the newspaper and began the process of transferring the story to film. While the two directors, Musca and Menendez, spent two months observing Escalante's classroom and interviewing his students, there are "distortions" (¶12), as one reviewer for the *New York Times* points out; however, "to sit at the back of Mr. Escalante's classroom for an hour is to realize that the emotional truth has not been distorted at all. Teaching as brilliant improvisational theater is at the heart of the movie and at the heart of the real classroom" (¶31). But one director also wonders about how the film will affect Escalante: "Mr. Musca muses: 'I wonder what effect we will have on Jaime's life. After all, all I am is a parasite. I take someone else's life and deliver it to the public'" (p. 3). Many reviewers marveled at how the film was able to make a subject like mathematics interesting.

Likewise, those who study teacher films are mixed about *Stand and Deliver*. The film is associated with the teacher-hero narrative; the film is praised for its positive representation of Hispanic teachers and students. Dalton (2010), for example, notes that while Escalante points out the prejudicial treatment his students will face, he is preparing them to succeed in the dominant culture, rather than finding ways to dismantle it. Berg (1990) captures the tradition of contradictory representations of Hispanic characters on screen and theorizes:

> One way to apply object-relations theory critically is by noting that historically Hollywood films have demonstrated the oscillation between two such positions. They alternate from the first position, creating Hispanic stereotypes that project degradation and idealization, to the second position, showing their guilt for having constructed the Other so negatively. (p. 290)

Films like *Stand and Deliver*, which was helmed by Hispanic film makers, are challenging the stereotypes found in earlier films.

The film juxtaposes the jumps Escalante makes in teaching content with the increased close relationships he is able to cultivate with his students. In an early scene in the film, Escalante is teaching his basic math students about fractions by cutting up an apple and asking them what percentage of the apple they have. He deals with students who resist his attempts to reach them—such as the student who flips his middle finger at Escalante and is dubbed "Fingerman"—by subtly teaching them using their misbehaviors. The end of the film attempts to capture the lasting and growing influence of Escalante's AP program as captions at the bottom of the screen just before the final credits show the numbers of students, year by year, who go on to pass the test. Still, Escalante is heralded as the lone teacher responsible for this success, and the film fails to capture the collaboration that resulted in Garfield's success.

According to Mathews, "Even before the 1982 triumph, rumors and dissent had haunted [Escalante's] program. When filmmakers Ramon Menendez and Tom Musca in 1987 began shooting their riveting feature film, *Stand and Deliver*, starring Edward James Olmos as Escalante and based on the ETS controversy, more than the usual hate mail landed in Escalante's mailbox. … Some of the anonymous letters suggested he was getting too much credit, or that the true story had never been told" (p. 174). What both the film and the book attempt to keep is the role of connection with Escalante through their shared status of being immigrants or coming from families from Mexico or Central America. After describing what the process must have looked like during the grading of the free-response section on the AP text, Mathews writes:

> She [the ETS grader Pat Henry] reached for a suspected violation report blank, something she rarely had to do. It was not just the idea of cheating that bothered her. She had read the names. They were all Hispanic. Pat Henry had been born in Minnesota but moved to Utah as a girl and later married a man named Fernández. Her five children all bore the name Fernández. She did not like this at all. (p. 148)

This connection takes a more prominent role on screen. In Mathews's biography, he explains how Toni Rosenbaum became the ETS employee who bore the brunt of the Garfield controversy (p. 156). Escalante eventually confronts Frank Romeo, who was the head of the western division of ETS. Let's examine the interrogation scene in Mathews' biography and then with the scene in the film with Andy Garcia, cast as Tony Ramirez, an ETS official.

"I don't believe that," Escalante snapped. "That's bullshit. I don't buy that. I want to see the mistakes they made."

"I'm sorry you feel that way. Let me explain to you the whole process and let's see if we can resolve this."

Escalante stared at the tall, slender, youthful administrator. "You know, when I came over here, I expect to see a *gringo*. And then I see you, but you know, you're not one of us."

Romero fought to control his anger. "You're wrong, I'm only doing my job."

"Doing your job." Escalante said snorting in disbelief. He was getting nowhere, but he wanted the last word. "You're a blind man. You're chasing a black cat in a dark room. You know, I know a lot about computers. Maybe you had a code or something that identified the kids like ours taking the test. You know, the ones that have a last name like yours."

"I know well how to spell discrimination. You're not going to *give me any of this shit*." (p. 165)

In *Stand and Deliver*, Escalante takes the accusation of the cheating personally. Andy Garcia's Tony Ramirez argues against that in the following scene:

Escalante:	By making a blanket accusation, you're saying there was a conspiracy. Every conspiracy has a leader. Who better qualified to be the leader than the teacher?
Ramirez:	Mr. Escalante, no one here is accusing you of anything.
Escalante:	Not only me. The school, the parents, the entire community.
Ramirez:	Scores this high, I guarantee you, would be questioned regardless of the school.
Escalante:	Yes, but if this were Beverly Hills High School, they wouldn't have sent you two to investigate.
Ramirez:	Mr. Escalante, I hope you are not insinuating that we haven't earned our position here. Because no one's given me a damn thing. I suggest you're letting your emotions get the best of you.
Escalante:	If no one has given you a damn thing, you should not be taking anything from my kids.
Ramirez:	The identity of the students was concealed until it was determined that irregularities existed.
Escalante:	Those scores would have never been questioned if my kids did not have Spanish surnames and come from Barrio schools. You know that!
Ramirez:	We've been patient explaining our position to you and listening to your complaints. Now, our conversation is over.
Escalante:	There's something going on here that nobody is talking about. And you know what it is.
Ramirez:	No one has the right to accuse me of racism. No one [shouts] has the right to accuse me of racism.

Escalante:	I know well [shouts] how to spell discrimination. I thought this was over a long time ago. Are you doing this to my kids?
3rd agent:	There are two kinds of racism, Mr. Escalante. Singling out a group because they are members of a minority or not singling them out because they are members of a minority.
Escalante:	My kids could teach you a thing or two, Charlie.
Ramirez:	I'm going to call security if you can't control yourself, Mr. Escalante.
Escalante:	Go for it. My kids didn't do anything. I'm going to prove you guys wrong.
Ramirez:	I hope you do. Because this is not between you and me.
Escalante:	Maybe not. But if I catch you on the street, I'll kick the shit out of you.

Stand and Deliver does send a message that should concern many. While it provides a commentary on racism (assumptions about students based on their cultural heritage and perceived lack of ability; for Garcia's character, a minority investigating a controversy for other minorities, the notion that Escalante is "the best teacher in America" is potentially misleading. Escalante is a great teacher and has many of the natural abilities that make him a great teacher, but he also worked hard to learn his craft. And, while he may be responsible for his students' success at Garfield, that success became greater because of the collaborations and vision he had for growing his program. As Mathews points out, there were other successful programs at Garfield, other teachers committed to their students' success, and the cultural change that the school underwent played a large role, no doubt, in this story of academic success.

Conclusion

> "Movies like this are inevitably 'based on a real story.' Maybe they tell you that because otherwise you'd think they were pure fantasy."
>
> —Ebert (1995)

At the end of *The Best Teacher in America*, Mathews presents a list of what makes a great teacher based on what he saw at Garfield:

- "Teachers who bring students up to high standards are precious commodities" (p. 288).
- "If left alone, teachers who work hard and care for their students will produce better results than ten times their number dutifully following the ten best recommendations of the ten latest presidential commissions on education" (p. 288).

- "A third lesson seems to apply just to minorities, but it ought to work with nearly all human children: Demand more than they think they have to give" (p. 288).
- "Pick some unusually difficult goal, such as an Advanced Placement examination, and organize students as a group to reach it" (p. 290).

Mathews ends Escalante's biography with this observation for improving schools: "But you have to start with good teachers, and leave them alone" (p. 293).

Examining these three teachers, their stories reveal that from the page to the screen or from the screen to the page, the films magnify the notion that a great teacher can make all the difference; that focusing on racial, cultural, and personal differences makes education interesting; and there are consequences of being a teacher-celebrity when one's story becomes part of the larger narrative of great teachers. However, the tension that exists in the biopic genre is interesting. On the one hand, the narratives are often written not for the screen, but rather to highlight the work of teachers, to showcase the success of one's students, or to "set the record straight." On the other hand, when these stories go through the machine that is Hollywood, they come out remarkably similar. Why? Probably because they were similar to begin with. Perhaps, when all is said and done, there is really no other way; school is chronological, and tangible success can be seen in a test score. But we also hope that through our efforts, our students also become better citizens.

References

Avildsen, J. G. (Director). (1989). *Lean on me* [Motion picture]. United Kingdom: Warner Brothers.

Ayers, W. (2001). A teacher ain't nothin' but a hero: Teachers and teaching in film. In P. B. Joseph & G. E. Burnaford (Eds.), *Images of schoolteachers in twentieth-century America* (2nd ed., pp. 147–156). New York, NY: St. Martin's Press.

Bach, J. (2009). One size does not fit all: Cinematic representations of the teaching of Shakespeare. *Changing English, 16*, 323–331.

Barnz, D. (Director). (2012). *Won't back down* [Motion picture]. United States: Walden Media.

Bauer, D. M. (1998). Indecent proposals: Teachers in the movies. *College English*, 60(3), 301–317.

Berg, C. R. (1990). Stereotyping in films in general and of the Hispanic in particular. *The Howard Journal of Communications*, 2, 286–300.

Brooks, R. (Director). (1955). *Blackboard jungle* [Motion picture]. United States: Metro-Goldwyn-Mayer.

Bulman, R. (2004). *Hollywood goes to high school: Cinema, schools, and American culture*. New York, NY: Worth Publishers.

Chennault, R. (2006). *Hollywood films about schools: Where race, politics, and education intersect*. New York, NY: Palgrave.

Cheshire, E. (2014). *Bio-pics: A life in pictures*. London: Wallflower.

Coraci, F. (Director). (2012). *Here comes the boom* [Motion picture]. United States: Columbia Pictures.

Custen, G. F. (1992). *Bio/Pics: How Hollywood constructed public history*. New Brunswick, NJ: Rutgers University Press.

Dalton, M. (2010). *The Hollywood curriculum: Teachers in the movies* (2nd ed.). New York, NY: Peter Lang.

Dargis, M. (2007, January 5). To Ms. with love: A teacher's heart fords a social divide. *New York Times*. Retrieved from http://www.nytimes.com/2007/01/05/movies/05free.html?_r=2&

Delgado, C. (2001). *Freedom writers*: White teacher to the rescue. In E. Marshall & Ö. Sensoy (Eds.), *Rethinking popular culture and media* (pp. 227–233). Milwaukee, WI: Rethinking Schools.

Eastwood, C. (Director). (2004). *Million dollar baby* [Motion picture]. United States: Warner Bros. Pictures.

Ebert, R. (1995). Review of *dangerous minds*. Retrieved from http://www.rogerebert.com/reviews/dangerous-minds-1995

Glass, I., & Johnson, L. (1996). Faustian bargains. *This American Life* Podcast. National Public Radio. Retrieved from http://www.thisamericanlife.org/radio-archives/episode/43/transcript

Gruwell, E. (1999). *The freedom writers diary: How a teacher and 150 teens used writing to change themselves and the world around them*. New York, NY: Broadway Books.

Gruwell, E. (2007). *Teach with your heart: Lessons I learned from the freedom writers*. New York, NY: Broadway Books.

Harmetz, A. (1988). Math stars in a movie. *New York Times*. Retrieved from http://www.nytimes.com/1988/03/20/movies/film-math-stars-in-a-movie.html

Henke, S. (2008). Dangerous minds: Constructing urban education between hope and despair. In S. Schramm-Pate & R. B. Jeffries (Eds.), *Grappling with diversity: Readings on civil rights pedagogy and critical multiculturalism* (pp. 97–115). Albany, NY: State University of New York Press.

Johnson, L. (1992). *Dangerous minds* (previously published as *My posse don't do homework*). New York, NY: St. Martin's Press.

Johnson, L. (1995). *The girls in the back of the class*. New York, NY: St. Martin's Press.

Kasdan, J. (Director). (2011). *Bad teacher* [Motion picture]. United States: Columbia.

LaGravenese, R. (Director). (2007). *Freedom writers* [Motion picture]. United States: Paramount.

Linklater, R. (Director). (2003). *School of rock* [Motion picture]. United States: Paramount Pictures.

Lyne, A. (Director). (1983). *Flashdance* [Motion picture]. United States: Paramount Pictures.

Maslin, J. (1995, August 11). If teacher is Pfeiffer, can youths be all bad? *New York Times*. Retrieved from http://www.nytimes.com/1995/08/11/movies/film-review-if-teacher-is-pfeiffer-can-youths-be-all-bad.html

Mathews, J. (1988). *Escalante: The best teacher in America*. New York, NY: Henry Holt.

McManus, K. (1995, August 11). Dangerous minds. *Washington Post*. Retrieved from http://www.washingtonpost.com/wp-srv/style/longterm/movies/videos/dangerousmindsrmcmanus_c027c4.htm

Menendez, R. (Director). (1988). *Stand and deliver* [Motion picture]. United States: Warner Brothers.

Moore, T. (2007, January 19). Classroom distinctions. *New York Times*. Retrieved from http://www.nytimes.com/2007/01/19/opinion/19moore.html

Mulligan, R. (Director). (1967). *Up the down staircase* [Motion picture]. United States: Warner Bros.

Peirce, K. (Director). (1999). [Motion picture]. United States: Fox Searchlight Pictures.

Ritt, M. (Director). (1974). *Conrack* [Motion picture]. United States: Twentieth Century Fox.

Ross, N. (2007, January 22). Heroic teachers, on screen and off (4 letters). *New York Times*. Retrieved from http://www.nytimes.com/2007/01/22/opinion/l22teach.html?_r=0

Scott, T. (Director). (1986). *Top gun* [Motion picture]. United States: Paramount Pictures.

Smith, J. N. (Director). (1995). *Dangerous minds* [Motion picture]. United States: Don Simpson/Jerry Bruckheimer Films/Hollywood Pictures.

Thomsen, S. R. (1993, April). *A worm in the apple: Hollywood's influence on the public's perception of teachers*. Paper presented at the Joint Meeting of the Southern States Communication Association and the Central States Communication Association, Lexington, KY.

Thomson, D. (2007, January 5). School story repeats lessons often learned. *Washington Post*. Retrieved from http://www.washingtonpost.com/wp-dyn/content/article/2007/01/04/AR2007010401928.html

Turan, K. (1995, August 11). Two stars in a dim galaxy: Michelle Pfeiffer gives a realistic performance in an otherwise simplistic and predictable *Dangerous Minds*. *Los Angeles Times*. Retrieved from http://articles.latimes.com/1995-08-11/entertainment/ca 33858_1_dangerous-minds

Weir, P. (Director). (1989). *Dead poets society* [Motion picture]. United States: Touchstone Pictures.

· 5 ·

TRAPPED BY FUTILITY

The Problems with Claiming Connections to Real Classrooms in *The Class*

As with *Chalk* (Akel & Mass, 2006), my introduction to *The Class* (Cantet, 2008) started at a colleague's home where a group of us met to watch the film together. We had heard the buzz surrounding this French film, including its winning the Palme d'Or at Cannes, and we were eager to see what the fuss was about. I have spent many years trying to find a film that captures what I believe to be a representation of real teaching to use in my education courses. While there are plenty of videos of teachers demonstrating "best practices" in the classroom, I don't always want to show my students what's good; sometimes, I'd rather discuss what happens when things go wrong, which is why I used the mockumentary *Chalk* in my courses for several years before discovering *The Class*.

Based on François Bégaudeau's book *Entre Les Murs* (2006) (which translates into *Between these Walls*), which many scholars consider an autobiographical or semi-autobiographical novel, the film is about the relationship between a French teacher and his students—an ethnically diverse group, many of whom are from immigrant families from Africa, Asia, and the Caribbean. *The Class* is technically neither a fictional nor nonfictional film, since it employs the codes and conventions of both, such as creating fictional characters and employing documentary styles of filming. It's painful for me to read the book or watch the film, and I can honestly say that the teachers in both the film and the memoir are my least favorite of all those I have mentioned in this book. In the end, *The Class* attempts to, as stated in its title, explore what goes on between these walls, but the real learning for both students and their teacher occurs outside of the classroom.

The film was praised for many reasons, but perhaps the most frequent compliment was how it represented the realities of the urban classroom. Noted film critic, Roger Ebert (2009), praised the film for its authenticity:

> *The Class* might have been set in any classroom in the Western world, and I believe most teachers would recognize it. It is about the power struggle between a teacher who wants to do good and students who disagree about what "good" is. The film is so fair that neither side is seen as right, and both seem trapped by futility. (¶1)

While I agree with Ebert that the film captures the power struggles inherent in a classroom, I have a problem with those critics and scholars who praise it for its reality and use it as a way to talk about contemporary education problems. They are trapped in a conversation in which they must acknowledge that while they believe it reflects the contemporary real classroom, it is also a movie with fictional elements. Some of those elements, which I will discuss in this chapter, may in fact reinforce stereotypes and assumptions about schools, teachers, and students. In other words, while Bégaudeau's story may contain elements of truth, it is a story told through a genre (memoir) that is often criticized for its representation of past events based on the author's memory and interpretation of them.

But it is what critics and scholars sensed as the truth that attracted them to the film, and those truths are based in reality as well as the body of school films as a whole. According to film scholar Gueye (2009), "[I]t is the film's realism which explains why social scientists are drawn to *The Class*" (p. 161). In spite of these realistic depictions of the challenges faced in many classrooms, the film still reinforces many of the stereotypes associated with schools serving large populations of students from ethnically diverse backgrounds who live in lower socioeconomic urban neighborhoods. And, while *The Class* problematizes those experiences through a compelling narrative that seems real to many, this film still echoes some of the representations found in *Blackboard Jungle* (Brooks, 1955). I don't subscribe to the "realism" that it presents because that means we are still dealing with the same educational problems, both between and outside the classroom walls, that we educators keep hoping to fix.

The film from the start sets out to blur the lines between fiction and reality. Like *Chalk*, which I discussed in Chapter 2, *The Class* starred the actual teacher, François Bégaudeau, on whose story the film was based. Furthermore, as in *Chalk*, the director used real students instead of actors to portray the class. Both teacher and students engaged in a yearlong series of workshops that led Ebert (2009) to observe: "So convincing is the film that it seems documentary, but all of the students, I learn, are playing roles and not themselves" (¶4). Furthermore, critics praised the story for diverting from the usual teacher-hero narrative. In his review for the *New York Times*, Dargis (2008) writes, "For audiences accustomed to big-screen pedagogical imperatives soaked in guilt and deep-fried in piety, this makes for an exotic change (though the HBO show *The Wire* [Simon, 2008] covered similar ground) and might sound perilously dry" (¶3). In this sense, this is a film that does not seek to honor a transformation in a teacher, student, or school, and the ending is not a triumphant victory over the inequalities of education.

Reviewers also praised the film for the director's use of documentary-style camera techniques and for Marin's unique (for school films) portrayal of a teacher; Marin is unlike the idealistic teachers from previous school films, and he persists in spite of what Anderson's (2009) *Washington Post* review describes as a difficult group of students to teach. Much of the contention in the classroom occurs because of the cultural differences between Marin, who represents a French identity, and the students, who represent a number of ethnicities and cultural backgrounds. Anderson reflects:

> The students, in total, are an immigration metaphor; individually, they're victims of a broken system and the offspring of the cult of victimhood. Their behavior is often vile, self-defeating and vulgar, and yet they search endlessly for symptoms of cultural bias, racism and sexism in everything Marin says. In the face of their insults and insolence, his behavior must remain impeccable. And the system backs up the class, rather than the teacher. To them, he represents the enemy, even if he's the best friend they'll ever have. (¶6)

Yet, what troubles me with *The Class* is that Marin is not what I consider a good teacher, no matter how much he seems to care about his students' futures, and many of his actions and comments are not professional. For instance, I see that his antagonistic approach to motivate his students to produce better work brings out the worst in them. In fact, in thinking about Ebert's discussion of good versus "good," I would argue that Marin's students' idea of good is the better one.

Critics also tried to make connections between the film and the state of education in other Western countries. For example, in his review for *The New Yorker*, Denby (2008) writes:

> In all, *The Class* is a prime document of French post-colonial blues, though its relevance to American urban education could not be any greater if it had been made in the Bronx or Trenton or South Los Angeles. I would be surprised if this brilliant and touching film didn't become required viewing for teachers all over the United States. Everyone else should see it as well—it's a wonderful movie.

Likewise, Dargis (2008) writes about the behavior of the onscreen students and how that behavior reflects the majority of adolescents stuck in classrooms: "With their cellphones and pouts, these bored, restless junior high students look pretty much like the fidgety progeny of Anytown, U.S.A" (¶1). He goes on to note the role identity plays in many of the onscreen struggles: "One difference being that these African, Arab and Asian Parisians live in a country that insists its citizens have only one cultural identity, even if it is an identity—as France's smoldering suburbs vividly suggest—many of these same young people don't feel welcome to share" (¶1). These exchanges, a result of this tension, led some scholars to compare the film with urban education (Gueye, 2008; Yang, 2009), and Yang wonders about the fairness of the comparisons to what she ultimately claims is a fictional film.

Another aspect of *The Class* that critics praised was its focus on the way the onscreen conversations connected with life outside of the school walls to create real learning experiences. Bradshaw (2009) of *The Guardian* reflected in his review:

> I could watch it [the movie] all afternoon. The teacher simply dealing with all the backchat is endlessly fascinating: it is a particularly gripping kind of reality television, but a reality TV that isn't concerned with humiliation or embarrassment but with idealism, and trying to learn something. (¶7)

In his review for *Entertainment Weekly*, Milon (2009) points out how the classroom interactions are real reflections of students connecting school with real life. He writes "*The Class* is one of the most alive and engrossing movies ever to take on the rich, infinitely renewable topic of school-as-life, and make it feel real. Unscripted. And above all, honest" (¶2). For Milon, that honesty appears in the differences between this film and previous films about school-as-life, such as *Dead Poets Society* (Weir, 1989), most specifically the differences between Keating's and Marin's approaches to teaching.

The first notable difference between *The Class* and other films about schools is that it opens in a coffee shop—not a typical setting associated with a school that we find in other documentaries and biopics. (In the book, Bégaudeau admits to stopping at the coffee shop to prolong his summer just a bit more.) Marin walks to school and greets colleagues on the way. He's clearly at ease and isn't approaching a graffiti-ridden school, unlike the teachers I see in American films who are nervous or excited about their first days. Another oddity is that there are custodians cleaning his classroom for him. As Gueye (2008) points out, this scene reinforces the roles of custodians and blue collar workers as held by people of color, but for me, it contradicts the many scenes in which onscreen teachers clean their own wrecked classrooms with gusto and hope. Even in *The Wire*, a television show whose fourth season was celebrated for its real depictions of education, the teacher must clean his own classroom.

The film continues with its chronological approach to the beginning of Marin's school year, which helps establish the realism it hopes to construct. It does so by presenting the unexciting tasks that mark the beginning of the school year before the students appear. The audience is allowed to see some of the mundane occurrences that go along with the beginning of the year, such as the first faculty meeting. There, the teachers introduce themselves to each other and offer tidbits of advice, comments (not necessarily helpful), and encouragement; one says he is "as ready as ever"; another warns a new teacher that "the students can be rough—consider yourself warned." When asked how long he has been at the school, the mathematics teacher's response is "too long." Marin introduces himself as a fourth-year French teacher. Then there is the passing out of class lists. Two teachers sit next to one another as one of them goes down the list of names and says, "Good, good, good boy here. This guy's bad" and so on. "Infinite courage" offers the teacher who plans to retire at the end of the year. The next shot is of the first day of school. Marin is now dressed in a button-down shirt and blazer. He greets his students at the door with a "Morning." Inside the classroom, his students fight for seats. And then class begins.

After my first viewing, Marin's interactions with his students do not seem very different from the other scenes of classroom interactions in school films. The teacher tries to get his or her students' attention and they resist. However, for Wilson (2009), who is a teacher, the difference lies in the fact that Marin "doesn't have all the answers and Marin like most teachers is neither a martyr nor a saint. He's a person trying to make some difference in a vast system" (¶9). What bothers me is the way Marin goes about trying to make a difference. In truth, he does want to get to know his students, but he wants to accomplish that through the calm, controlled manner of classroom discussions and writing assignments, not through the transformation of his approach to teaching the curriculum.

While Marin's approach to teaching French appears to be benign, if not a bit dull, his classroom discussions are extremely antagonistic. In both his memoir and his film, he begins that first class by chiding his students about the length of time they take to get started. He calculates that they waste about 15 minutes of each class hour before they begin the lesson. Esmerelda, one of his most outspoken students, challenges his claim—a claim she says other teachers make as well—saying that they never meet for an hour because class is only 55 minutes. She continues, "You're [Marin] always saying that. Eight thirty to 9:25 doesn't make an hour." Marin dismisses her comments with a "you know what I mean" reproach and they move on to the tasks of the first day.

Marin then asks them to make nametags for their desks. Now, any teacher with any experience teaching adolescents could have told you what would happen next—his students would turn this simple task of identifying themselves into designing elaborate representations of their names on paper. Since they take much longer than he thinks they should, he chastises his students again for wasting class time: "Taking five minutes to write your name is ridiculous." Again, some of his students challenge his decision. Esmerelda again interrupts the silence and questions why he needs nametags: "Seriously, we had you last year." Marin responds, "Look around Esmerelda, half the kids are new." She, in turn, asks why *his* name is not on the board. He turns and writes it on the board. This is a great scene to use with preservice teachers during a discussion of routines and procedures, but it also demonstrates how, by engaging in back-and-forth conversations with his students, Marin wastes time as well.

Another issue that I share with my students is how Marin's approach to teaching favors those students who can deliver the right answer to his questions quickly. Because his assessment of student learning takes place within classroom discussions that resemble free-for-alls, some of his students find themselves overlooked or passed over. During one lesson in which he asks several students to share words that they don't understand from the reading, he calls on quiet Henriette, who pauses and tries to find a word. The girl next to her, Louise, sensing her confusion, feeds the word "henceforth" to her. Asking Louise to let Henriette speak for herself, Marin quickly turns to banter with Esmerelda rather than waiting for Henriette to find her own word. He then turns his attention to Souleymane, who sits at the back of the room and is not writing anything down. Souleymane, who becomes a defender for his classmates against Marin's criticisms, challenges Marin's quick-fire approach to classroom discussions: "Really? You don't call out kids like this." Souleymane soon joins Esmerelda in critiquing Marin's pedagogical approaches, which do, in fact, create an "us-versus-them" atmosphere. By winding his students up with insults, prodding, and teasing, he can't really be sure of who is learning and who is not.

At the heart of *The Class* is the relationship (or lack thereof) between Marin and his students. That relationship is complicated by several elements; tensions result from differences in class and age, but many of the altercations in his classroom are a result of cultural differences. That he may need to acknowledge these differences in his approach to teaching doesn't seem to register for Marin until his students point it out to him, beginning with the scene about the names he uses on the chalkboard. In this scene, which also appears in the memoir, Esmerelda and Khoumba point out that all the names on the board in his example sentences are Aryan and "bizarre," like (in the English version) Bill and Daniel. Khoumba and Esmerelda suggest he use names like Rashid or Aissata. Marin looks startled and, rather than simply accepting or rejecting their suggestion, responds, "If I start using of all your names from your ethnic backgrounds, it'll never end." The two girls then encourage him to just "change it a little bit" and decide he should use the name Aissata.

This scene is followed by a discussion Marin has with the history teacher about the texts for their courses. The Western civics teacher is trying to overlap with Marin's curriculum since they teach the same students. Marin rejects the teacher's suggestions by calling them too tough for the students. The film then cuts back to Marin's classroom where a student interrupts a lesson by declaring that his pen is leaking, suggesting the juvenile nature of his students. But Esmerelda, who is frustrated by the imperfect subjunctive, soon starts a sophisticated conversation. She claims that no one uses the imperfect subjunctive and asks why they have to learn it. The rest of the students soon join in on her argument with comments such as: "Sir, why are you criticizing us?" "It's from the Middle Ages." "It's bourgeois." Marin tries to agree with them by saying that snobs use it. Boubacar thinks that he means a gay person after Marin describes a snob as someone a bit affected. At this point, Souleymane seems to want to make a comment but is reluctant. Marin pushes him until Souleymane says that he has heard people say that Marin is gay. Marin wants to know if it matters to Souleymane, if he finds men liking other men odd. As they go back and forth, Souleymane insists it doesn't, but that it might. Marin finally ends the conversation by saying, "No, it's not true. Sorry to disappoint you."

The next scene shows Marin looking down at his students from his classroom window during recess. They are playing on their electronics, talking, and Souleymane is taking pictures of his classmates with his cell phone. The distance between Marin and his students is emphasized through this shot of him looking down (some critics pointed out that the courtyard looks like something one might find in a prison), and the scene with the cell phone camera serves as foreshadowing for a scene to come. The film soon returns to the classroom where Marin's students are attempting to help a classmate conjugate the verb "swim" on the board. Frustrated at their slow progress, Marin says they have the attention span of young children. Khoumba tells him that his kidding goes too far and that everyone says so. Marin's response is that he does it so they can get somewhere in life. It's as if he's embraced the idea that teachers need to hold their students to high expectations, but the only way he knows to motivate them to do better is by insulting them.

While we never see other teachers interact with these students, we can surmise that these students behave in a similar manner in other teachers' classrooms. In the scene following this one, the computer teacher, Vincent, storms into the faculty room and claims that he is "sick of these clowns. I'm not going to help them. [They can s]tay in their crappy neighborhood, they probably will stay there forever anyway." He finishes with the declaration, "I'm done," as another teacher says, "Come on, let's get some air." Vincent's and Marin's frustrations seem to jibe with the familiar fictional and nonfictional teacher narratives that support the notion that teachers enter the profession because they want to help their students leave their "crappy neighborhoods." But it's quite possible that these students sense that although their teachers know them "between the walls," they do not know them in their homes, in their neighborhoods, or in the countries from which their families came. From this perspective, earlier films set in urban classrooms and *The Class* share an idealistic view of teacher motivation, but they differ in their depiction of approach and outcome—the teachers in the earlier films are shown to make a difference through their connections with their students *outside* of the classroom. Which is the "real" teacher? Which is the good teacher?

A series of scenes that I use with my students, and perhaps the most real to me, involves Marin's self-portrait assignment in which he asks students to write about their lives. His assignment coincides with their reading of *The Diary of Anne Frank* (1947/1993). This seems to be a favorite of both actual and onscreen English language arts teachers, as I have found the assignment in many of the memoirs and films featuring such teachers as well as in my own students' lesson plans. We watch these scenes with the purpose of critiquing Marin's approach to this assignment. (Interestingly, in his memoir, he gives this assignment to stall the teaching of his content at the beginning of the year.) In one scene, he is again chastising students for "not making good use of time. I want you to work." He then tries to get Khoumba to read aloud from the diary and she refuses. He argues with her for several minutes (again, he seems oblivious to the amount of time he wastes) and eventually gives up. He turns to Esmerelda and asks, "Are you on strike, too?" She says no and reads.

He then tells the students that they will write their own self-portraits, and he expects to learn about each of them through the facts and feelings they include in their portraits. His students resist this assignment, as they believe that that have nothing passionate to reveal at their ages. Marin responds, "It's odd to me that you don't think your lives are interesting," to which they point out the boring routines in their lives: school, eat, sleep, and school again. Marin tells them, "What you feel is what I'm interested in." His students respond that their feelings are private and that he's only interested in their feelings because he's the teacher. Of course, Marin can't let his point go; he pushes them to share examples of when they have felt ashamed as an example of what they may write about.

Once again, veteran teachers most likely cringe at Marin's pushing students to reveal personal information in front of the class, but some of his students try. What results is a conversation in which Marin is unable to cross some of the class, cultural, and generational gaps between himself and his students. For example, Boubacar tries to explain why he felt ashamed when a friend offered him a sandwich to eat, but he didn't want to take it because it would mean he would have to eat it in front of his friend's mother. He tries to explain, "I don't eat with her out of respect. I'm ashamed to talk about it." Marin, confused, says to the class, "So if Boubacar eats in front of us, that means he doesn't respect us." Boubacar finally gives up trying to answer Marin's questions: "You can't understand." There are gaps among the students as well. Wei, for example, claims that "Kids today have no shame. They yell, they hit each other. … No shame." Marin turns to Louise: "Tell me, Louise, are you ashamed of something physical?" She responds, "My ears." Marin asks, "Can we see them?" Finally, the bell stops him from asking more questions.

That his students might be experiencing issues of identity and adolescent anxiety never seems to occur to Marin, but it probably should to a teacher who has been in the classroom for four years. As the students walk out, Marin remembers to call Khoumba back after the bell to discuss her refusal to read.

"What happened this summer? We got along last year." Khoumba responds, "Sir, can you hurry, I want to go to lunch." It's clear she's very aware of the two girls standing in the hallway watching Marin try to make her apologize using a sincere tone, whereas Marin overlooks how their presence might be affecting his talk with Khoumba. She tries to explain, "I can't be a little girl forever." For me, Marin's problem from this point on in the film is his lack of self-reflection and effort to change his ways, even if it means admitting he might be wrong or have done the wrong thing. When his students tease him for his love of the subject and his bourgeois ways, he dwells on their comments, denies them, or tries to rationalize why he is right. Cultural differences aside, the point is that Marin never laughs at himself, and he never laughs with his students. In the conversation with Khoumba, he asks her what happened in the summer, but he never considers that *he* might need to change, too. These are bright kids who want to know why they are learning verb tenses that they will probably not use in everyday conversations (and it's possible they already understand why). But Marin's rigid attempts to be right and to defend his subject, his pedagogical approach, and his teaching philosophy contribute to a rift between his students and him.

Marin's colleagues play an interesting role in the film as well. Marin interacts with them during faculty meetings, in the faculty room, in the hallways, and in the principal's office, but never in the classroom. For the most part, they are all baffled as to how to reach their students, and consistency among faculty members seems to be at the root of many of their issues. At one faculty meeting, they discuss implementing a penalty point system for breaking rules because "punishments seem to have no effect." One teacher explains how such a system might work: "When they [the students] get down to zero, they go before the disciplinary committee." A parent representative says this idea is just another one of the school's bad habits, "[The school] never praise[s] the students." A teacher responds, "Good grades should be enough. Honor is all that counts." Marin makes a point that I imagine would resonate with many teachers: "When you're dealing with punishments that are cut and dried, you can't adapt them to each case." After a lengthy conversation about implementing such a system and the inability of teachers to all adhere to the same rules, they give up. In a quarter of the time it took to discuss the point system, they manage to tackle "a vital issue," according to the principal, and decide not to replace the coffee vending machine with a coffee pot.

Another realistic aspect of the film that focuses on the diverse group of students within any class is the parent–student conferences. Here the meetings revolve around what might be considered stereotypical representations of this type of conversation. Marin meets with Wei's parents who are from Asia. They are worried that the amount of time their son spends on computer games will result in his school work suffering. Marin assures them that Wei is performing well. One mom is defending her Goth son's behavior. Another mom wants her son to go to the best high school and asks Marin, "Why don't you try to push the better students a little harder? They get bogged down by those students who are not as smart as they are." Souleymane's mother meets with Marin, using Souleymane's brother as a translator. Marin tells her that Souleyman is absent, unprepared, and unruly. The mother doesn't believe it, and Souleyman's brother says that he's just the brother and he can't do much about Souleymane's behavior. These conversations demonstrate that the disparity among the parents is reflected in their children, and suggest the apparent impossibility of Marin meeting all of their needs.

The film then captures perhaps the one moment of authentic learning in the classroom, in which Marin creates an assignment which none of his students contest, and of course it is not in Marin's classroom, but rather in the computer lab. The lesson? Marin asks his students to type up their self-portraits. Marin, who has been filmed so far only at the front of the classroom, walks among the students, bending down and nearly getting on their level to read what they've typed into the computer. Here, the students are using computers in innovative and orderly ways, and one wonders what lessons the computer teacher, who was fed up with them earlier, is teaching. Marin learns much about his students. He's surprised to learn that Esmerelda and Khoumba go to different parts of Paris to shop and visit friends. Souleymane has brought photos for his self-portrait, and Marin sees Souleymane's life outside of the classroom walls. Impressed by Souleymane's pictures, or perhaps just trying some positive praise, Marin puts Souleymane's pictures on display. Souleymane seems pleased but skeptical. He says to Marin, "You're just doing this to mess with me." The effects of this praise don't last long; when they return to the classroom, there are arguments over what teams should play and/or be supported in the African Cup of Nations. Carl, a new student, and Souleymane get into an extremely heated argument, and Marin takes Souleyman to the principal.

Perhaps the most problematic scene for me is what goes on in the grade-level meeting because it seems so unreal. At first, grade-level meetings in which the faculty discuss individual student progress seem like a great idea; it's certainly one we share with our students who are in teacher certification programs—imagine if we taught students in cohorts, conferenced about them together, and then evaluated them holistically as a team? The scene in which this occurs begins in a very constructive manner. The team of teachers is sitting in a room facing one another. The camera stops on Louise and Esmeralda, who are the class representatives at this meeting and who are listening to their teachers evaluate each individual student. Louise and Esmerelda giggle, whisper, and make other noises during the meeting, but it's clear that they are paying attention. When the group begins discussing Souleyman and the problems they are having with him, Esmeralda points out that his grades have gone up. The teachers respond that they are not discussing grades, but behavior, and that has not improved. Marin, in an attempt to soften the comments recorded on Souleymane's record, suggests that they write, "Souleymane is limited because he's reached his limit scholastically." Esmeralda can be heard saying, "It's not right saying that."

The film then cuts to the next day and a shot of Henriette looking at the chalkboard but not raising her hand as others attempt to answer Marin's questions. Esmeralda and Louise have been telling students what happened in the grade meeting the previous day. Marin sarcastically looks surprised, claiming he didn't realize they were paying attention because they were talking and making sounds. Louise shows him the pages of notes she took. Souleymane then says to Marin, "I hear you sold me out at the meeting," and goes on to say that he doesn't understand why teachers take revenge. Marin tries to explain that there's no revenge: "It's discipline. This isn't the streets." Esmeralda says, "He really laid into you." Marin, frustrated, embarrassed, and perhaps realizing the consequences of his remark on Souleymane, tells Louise and Esmerelda that they looked like skanks during the meeting because of their behavior. Souleymane tries to defend the girls and confronts Marin—the only time in the classroom that Marin and a student stand face to face in the classroom. Souleymane decides to leave, and on his way out of the classroom, his backpack smacks Khoumba in the face and cuts her eyelid, requiring stitches.

Marin writes up an accident report. The principal meets with Marin and asks him what they should do about Souleymane. Marin is hesitant, undecided about how to proceed; he lets the principal convince him to put Souleymane in front of the disciplinary committee. While Souleymane is suspended for 48 hours, Julie, the lead teacher for the grade, asks if Marin called some of his female students skanks, and if so, why he didn't mention it in his incident report. He responds that he didn't mention it because he didn't mention it. Then, he confronts Esmerelda in the courtyard about their sharing this information, and she says they have the right to report him just as they report other incidents *to* him. He claims that he didn't realize *skanks* to them means *prostitutes*. They are face to face in this space, as outside of the classroom walls, the power has shifted. Khoumba also approaches to tell Marin that if Souleymane gets expelled, he'll get sent back home to Mali.

Souleymane's hearing is another painful part of the film because the audience knows Marin's role in Souleymane's final outburst. Marin also made the decision to hold the hearing. Still, it's hard for me not to root for both Souleyman and Marin, whose confession about the role his comments about his students played in this situation could show his growing understanding of his students. At the meeting before the disciplinary committee, Souleymane must translate for his mother. Marin's report is read, the sole record of the facts that led to the hearing. The history teacher admits that he and Souleymane's other teachers could have reacted sooner, but that Souleymane doesn't control what he says or what he does. They give him a chance to speak. He's says, "I have nothing to say." His mother chastises him and makes Souleymane translate her words, which he does: "She says my son I'm a good boy. I do my homework. I help my brothers and sister with their work when I can. I always wash the dishes and help her around the house." Souleymane becomes a bit choked up by her comments, and she urges him to say them again. The principal responds by saying, "I'd like to get back to his school record." One of the members who is not on staff at the school or a parent of a student tries to note that it's odd for Marin to be both the judge and litigator on this committee. At the end of the meeting, Souleymane's mom apologizes on his behalf, and he and his mom wait outside the room. The paper votes are put in the box. He is expelled. The message in this meeting is clear; it is only what happens between the walls that counts.

Cut to the end of the year. Marin is conducting a class discussion in which each student must answer the question, "What did you learn this year?" Ever focused on the precise use of language, Marin corrects one student who says he likes science: "What did you learn, not what did you like?" Another student replies, "Why teach it to us if there's no interest in knowing it?" When Esmerelda is called upon, she responds, "I didn't learn anything." When Marin doubts her, Esmerelda responds that she read Plato's *The Republic* (380 B.C./2004) after her sister, who is studying law, suggested it. When Marin expresses surprised admiration, she smiles and responds, "It's not a skank book," thereby getting the last word. Marin then passes out copies of their self-portraits, which he has bound together for them. He claims that they are a way for them always to remember this class.

The Class ends with Henriette confessing to Marin that she hasn't learned anything all year, and Marin is dumbfounded. This is the only scene in the film in which a student stands over him as he sits at his desk. She tries to clarify what she means, "Compared to them, I learned nothing. I don't understand what we're doing … in everything. I don't want to go to vocational school." Like the ending of *Chalk*, the year ends, our students leave, and we can never be sure if they've learned anything. Has his year been successful or not? It's highly unrealistic that a student would take the time to share this with Marin; such a thought indicates a high level of thinking. Or is it another indication of no learning occurring in the classroom? The last few moments of *The Class* are of the students and teachers playing soccer. Even the principal takes part, still wearing his tie. The students and teachers who are not playing stand on the sidelines and cheer. The camera then shows Marin's empty classroom. The audience can hear sounds from outside. The classroom looks exhausted to me.

While *The Class* still suffers from many of the same tired approaches to teacher movies—they only focus on one class, the students are rowdy, the teacher tries to reach them through assignments and readings (although the curriculum choices Marin makes do seem to be ones he has used successfully in the past)—the questions the film deals with mirror those in many fictional and nonfictional school films: Who gets controlled, who is in control? Who is the teacher, who are the students? Who gets to punish, who is punished? There are no firm answers to these questions in this film.

Needless to say, I don't show *The Class* to my students anymore. While the scenes are great ways to critique how *not* to give an assignment, how *not* to speak to your students, and how we won't be able to assess fully all of our students' learning, I'm just not sure Marin is a good teacher.

References

Akel, M., & Mass, C. (Writers & Directors). (2006). *Chalk* [Motion picture]. San Francisco, CA: Someday Soon Productions.

Anderson, J. (2009, February 20). Movie review: *The class*. *The Washington Post*. Retrieved from http://www.washingtonpost.com/wp-dyn/content/article/2009/02/19/AR2009021902983.html

Bégaudeau, F. (2006). *The class* (L. Asher, Trans.). New York, NY: Seven Stories Press.

Bradshaw, P. (2009, February 26). Review of *The class*. *The Guardian*. Retrieved from http://www.theguardian.com/film/2009/feb/27/the-class-entre-les-murs

Brooks, R. (Director). (1995). *Blackboard jungle* [Motion picture]. United States: Metro-Goldwyn-Mayer.

Cantet, L. (Director). (2008). *The class* [DVD]. France: Haut et Court.

Dargis, M. (2008, September 25). Learning to be the future of France: Review of *The class*. *The New York Times*. Retrieved from http://www.nytimes.com/2008/09/26/movies/26clas.html

Denby, D. (2008, December 22). A better life: *Revolutionary road, Grand torino, The class*. *The New Yorker*. Retrieved from http://www.newyorker.com/magazine/2008/12/22/a-better-life-2

Ebert, R. (2009, February 4). Review of *The class*. *Roger Ebert.com*. Retrieved from http://www.rogerebert.com/reviews/the-class-2009

Frank, A. (1993). *Anne Frank: The diary of a young girl* (B. M. Mooyaart, Trans.). New York, NY: Bantam. (Original work published 1947)

Gueye, A. (2008). The color of unworthiness: Understanding blacks in France and the French visual media through Laurent Cantet's *The class*. *Transition*, 102, 158–171.

Milon, P. (2009, January 23). Review of *The class*. *Entertainment Weekly*. Retrieved from http://www.ew.com/article/2009/01/23/class

Plato. (2004). *The republic* (C. D. C. Reeve, Trans.). Indianapolis, IN: Hackett Publishing Company. (Original work published 380 BCE)

Simon, D. (Creator). (2008). *The wire: Season 4* [DVD]. New York, NY: Warner Home Video (Firm), HBO Video.

Weir, P. (Director). (1989). *Dead poets society* [Motion picture]. United States: Touchstone Pictures.

Wilson, E. (2009, February 25). *The class* spotlights a teacher's learning curve. *Edutopia*. Retrieved from http://www.edutopia.org/at-risk-students-film-class

Yang, K. H. K. (2009). Reading urban education through *The class*: Between Paris and Montreal. *Changing English*, *16*(2), 333–346.

· 6 ·

"I CAN'T TEACH YOU THAT OTHER STUFF"

Incorporating Biopics about Education into the Classroom

Occasionally, I teach a graduate seminar on secondary school curriculum, a course designed to provide a critical analysis of the content, organization, and evaluation of the secondary school curriculum. Specifically, we focus on 1) the relationship between education and culture; 2) race, class, gender, and curriculum; 3) curriculum in a postmodern society; and 4) accountability, globalization, and education (Hendry, 2011). During this course, we read three teacher memoirs and watch a film/television show that is either based on one of those memoirs or connected to the author's story. Those pairings include:

1. Michelle Rhee's *Radical: Fighting to Put Students First* (2013) paired with the documentary *Waiting for Superman* (Guggenheim, 2010). In her memoir, Rhee explores her journey through education, beginning as a Teach for America teacher and ending with her creation of the nonprofit organization Students First. In the documentary, Rhee's term as the chancellor of Washington, DC, public schools is highlighted.
2. Tony Danza's *I'd like to Apologize to Every Teacher I've Ever Had: My Year as a Rookie Teacher at Northeast High* (2012) paired with A&E's reality television show *Teach: Tony Danza* (Greif & Reed, 2010). In the show, actor Tony Danza teaches high school English at a school in Philadelphia, PA. In his memoir, he addresses his experiences with the show and what he learned about teaching.

3. Heather Kirn Lanier's *Teaching in the Terrordome: Two Years in West Baltimore with Teach for America* (2012) paired with scenes from the 4th season of *The Wire*. In her memoir, Lanier reflects on her two years teaching English language arts at a high school as part of the Teach for America program. The Baltimore high school at which Lanier taught was referred to as the Terrordome in the nonfiction book *The Corner: A Year in the Life of an Inner-city Neighborhood* (Simon & Burns, 1998), written by the pair who would go on to create the HBO series *The Wire*. Season four of *The Wire* focuses on a public school in Baltimore.

When we discuss each pair, I'm frequently impressed when my students pull out their cell phones and/or laptops and "fact check" the shows and memoirs. They are appalled by what Danza's television show leaves out and intrigued by the backlash from his students found on social media. Their attitudes toward Rhee become further complicated when they pair her narrative with the excerpts they see of her on *Waiting for Superman*, and they doubt the swift gains she made in her students' test scores at her first teaching position. They wonder about the absence of Lanier's reflections on race and ethnicity in her teaching assignment in the first part of her memoir, a subject that is addressed more directly on-screen in *The Wire*. Listening to those discussions that resulted from their skepticism led me to wonder what might be gained when educators and their students approach these memoirs as historical artifacts and examine them within the larger sociological context in which they take place. Inserting these and other texts into conversation invites questions and encourages students' explorations of the various ways the profession is represented in fictional and nonfictional texts.

When a colleague and I studied my students' responses to these pairings in their final course papers, we found that when the students' own stories become entangled with the narratives of the teachers they read about and saw on the screen, those connections inspired them to action (for example, to become better teachers or to fight the bureaucracy they faced each day) as a result of both their trust of some and a distrust of others of the authors' claims (Ramsey & Bach, 2013). We concluded that the teacher could act as mediator in these discussions to help readers navigate the contradictions that may be found in these narratives.

Biopics such as *Lean on Me* (Avildsen, 1989), *Dangerous Minds* (Smith, 1995), and *Freedom Writers* (LaGravenese, 2007) arguably garner the most attention by scholars who write about school films, but they are not usually treated as a separate genre from other non-biopic teacher films. As discussed in Chapters 4 and 5, those who research school films and television shows argue that the representations in most school films perpetuate the myth of the teacher as hero and the narrative of good and bad teachers (Ayers, 2001; Bulman, 2015; Dalton, 2010). Others, like McCarthy (1998), Henke (2008), and Chennault (2006) weave educational policy, authors' commentaries, and stories from the media in with their analyses of films, and conclude that films like *Lean on Me* and *Dangerous Minds* become ideological texts that incorporate distorted representations of schools. Although educational scholars note that some school films are based on memoirs and true stories, they go on to interpret them as they do other fictional films that are not based on actual teachers' stories. This decision is probably because the narratives of biopics mirror those of non-biographical movies featuring teachers. However, when viewed as more than just part of the "Hollywood curriculum" (Dalton, 2010), and instead as a larger part of educational discourse, analyses of biopics can reveal the intersections of educational policy, teachers' motives, representations of students, and cinematic structures.

Given the potential for these intersections, how should educators approach this genre in their courses? What happens when audiences learn that these stories are based on actual teachers and their students? What makes a teacher's story worthy of being memorialized in film, especially since during the process of adapting a story for the screen, the result comes to resemble the stories of so many other cinematic teachers? Does that make all teacher films, biopics or not, fabrications? Do these characters become just conglomerations of teachers that the writers and/or directors of the films want to see? In this chapter, I outline the questions raised by scholars who research biopics and suggest that educators use these questions as a way to teach biopics about teachers. I then go on to examine how instructors from communication studies, sociology, and teacher education incorporate school biopics into their courses. Finally, I offer two approaches to teaching biopics that reflect the conventions of the biopic genre.

The Teacher Biopic

As discussed in Chapter 4, biopics are generally described as films that feature important historical figures. They are often regarded as less respectable than other film genres (Rosenstone, 2007) and are dismissed for their tendency to praise or demonize a subject. They have come and gone in popularity; Custen predicted their demise in 1992, and Henke in 2008 suggested that the teacher biopic would die with *Dangerous Minds*. Both were wrong. In the years since *Dangerous Minds*, several notable biopics have joined the ranks, including *Freedom Writers* (LaGravenese, 2007), and *Won't Back Down* (Barnz, 2012).

One of the most notable, lengthy examinations of biopics is Custen's (1992) book *Bio/pics: How Hollywood Constructed Public History*. There, Custen defines a biopic as "a biographical film that depicts the life of an historical person, past or present" (p. 5). He finds the genre significant because the biopic is "the product of an organized culture of production" that shaped and was shaped by the public audience and together "create[d] public history" (p. 3). In other words, there is a close relationship between the public, production, and history that shapes audience's experiences with the genre. In his analysis of 271 biopics produced between 1927 and 1960, Custen coded each film according to the answers to these questions:

- What professions were featured?
- What was the gender of the main character?
- How much of their lives were portrayed?
- What studio produced the film?
- What was the social class of the subject?

Five of the films he considered featured the education profession, and all five biopics featured female teachers.

Like Custen's book, *Bio-pics: A Life in Pictures* (Cheshire, 2015) organizes biopics by the professions represented in them, including musicians, athletes, and politicians. Cheshire acknowledges the nuances in the genre and, for her study, dismisses the "inspired by the life of" films that starred a fabricated persona, such as Dracula, and films in which characters' names have been changed but the films remain "as thinly veiled bio-pics" (p. 5). In other words, she defines biopics for the purposes of her project as:

> ones where real names have been used, ones where the filmmakers have made a conscious choice to tell the story of a known person, and where audiences arriving at a cinema would have previous knowledge or expectation of what they are likely to see. If the subject is new to them, they would be able to leave safe in the knowledge that further research could be undertaken to determine the veracity of the film. (p. 6)

As with documentaries and reality television, it is this last characteristic that separates this genre from the other representations of teachers in films and television shows. Of course, audiences might not be aware of Escalante before they see *Stand and Deliver* (Menendez, 1988), but they are able to look up his story after they watch the film. They might even choose to watch and/or read a few interviews with Escalante, or perhaps visit the Garfield High School website to see if the AP Calculus program is still in place (I did all of these after watching the film). These comparisons can be quite revealing. For example, Bulman (2015) notes, "The movie *Dangerous Minds* provides a particularly revealing opportunity to analyze Hollywood's lesson plan and compare it to reality" (p. 50). He goes on to outline what aspects of the memoir the film manipulates to fit Hollywood's lesson plan. Cheshire explains that she organized her book into chapters that focused on particular subgenres because she found this grouping enriched classroom discussions by giving students a way to examine how similar concepts and figures were taken up in different films; it also led to some observations that could not have been made when just looking at the genre as a whole.

Part of the genre's longevity can be attributed to its ability to reflect contemporary attitudes and interests by focusing on a particular aspect of a subject's life. Bingman (2010) argues that the biopic is a "genuine, dynamic genre and an important one. The biopic narrates, exhibits, and celebrates the life of a subject in order to demonstrate, investigate, or question his or her importance in the world" (p. 10). In other words, by choosing to tell a person's tale from different angles, a figure could be presented in a sympathetic way or in a way that elicits anger from audiences. We find a good example of this flexibility in Cheshire's (2015) work, when she outlines how different aspects of figures' lives are left in screen adaptations and how those aspects are treated. However, in the genre of biopics about teachers, rarely are the characters' extreme behaviors, experiences, and feelings retained for the screen adaptations. Braithwaite's difficulties as a black man and his biracial relationship are glossed over (Clavell, 1967); Johnson's overtly hostile, almost violent, encounters with her students are left out (Smith, 1995); and Marin's objectification of his students merely hinted at (Cantet, 2008).

As explored in Chapter 4, scholars who focus on biopics tend to write about figures who already possess a degree of historical notoriety or infamy; they often overlook biopics about teachers. A notable exception is Cheshire (2015), who looks at two notable films featuring university faculty (*A Beautiful Mind* [Howard, 2001] and *Kinsey* [Condon, 2004]). Instead, teacher biopics such as *Freedom Writers* (LaGravenese, 2007) and *To Sir, With Love* (Clavell, 1967) are often discussed and taught alongside *Dead Poets Society*

(Weir, 1989) and *Bad Teacher* (Kasdan, 2011). Why? Perhaps because their narratives resemble each other: the fictional and the source story follow the same formula—a chronological recreation of a teacher-hero who enters a difficult teaching situation with an unsupportive administration and community, works hard and gets to know his/her students, and triumphs over adversity as the students learn to love and succeed in that teacher's subject area, if not all of school.

Much important work has been written about school films, their roles in perpetuating myths about teachers, and their influence in shaping the public's views of teachers. However, if we teach those films that are based on original teacher stories as biopics, then our hypothesizing about how Hollywood reworks representations of race, class, and gender can be compared with how others who report these stories (whether the teachers themselves or the media) depict race, class, and gender. As Bulman (2015) notes, "If Hollywood regularly distorts true stories of urban schools to conform to a generic formula, we need to ask why the formula is more culturally compelling than reality" (p. 50). His answer is that the formula appeals to "compassionate conservatives" who believe in the power of those teachers who can encourage their students to make good decisions and work hard. It is hardly a coincidence, then, that these are the stories that are published in memoirs and picked up by news media.

When considering a lesson or a unit on biopics that feature teachers, it is important to begin with a discussion of not only what makes a film a biopic, but also what questions scholars of biopics consider in their own work. Questions teachers and students might consider before analyzing biopics include some of the following:

1. What is a biopic?
2. What makes them lasting?
3. What makes someone a worthy subject for a biopic?
4. How is the culture and historical context portrayed in the film?
5. What does this film have to say about education?

The answers to these questions can constitute a way to structure conversations about the purpose of examining biopics about teachers. Is the educational objective to enact a close study of one influential biopic? Is it to enrich students' understanding of a particular educational reform or policy through its depiction in a biopic? Is it to uncover lasting trends in biopics and identify how they fit into what Bulman (2015) calls the Hollywood lesson plan and

Dalton (2010) refers to as the Hollywood curriculum? Given their basis in a story told by an actual teacher, biopics offer entry points into larger conversations about education that fictional films may not as easily provide. And those representations can hold more power in directing conversations about education. For example, while we may not be able to produce a number of teachers like John Keating from *Dead Poets Society* (Weir, 1989), Gruwell from *Freedom Writers* (LaGravenese, 2007) has gone on to share her approach to teaching through her curriculum and Johnson (Smith, 1995) through her pedagogy books. The implication is that it is possible to achieve success through the adoption of a curricular or pedagogical approach.

Potential Lenses for Teaching the School Film

Communication Studies

Communication studies is a field that examines how messages are communicated, from face-to-face conversations to social media. Mary Dalton, who teaches communication studies courses that focus mainly on media studies, is one of the most-cited and recognized scholars of school films. One of Dalton's contributions to the fields of communication studies, film studies, and certainly educational studies is her book, *The Hollywood Curriculum: Teachers in the Movies* (2010). There, she examines over 100 school films and finds that most of the teachers in these films fall into one of the following categories and share certain characteristics: the good teacher, the bad teacher, the female teacher, the gay teacher, and the school administrator. She also examines how students and teachers are positioned in relation to each other and to the institutions they occupy. She frames much of her argument using Fiske's (1989) notion of "leaky boundaries," in which real life and fictional depictions overlap and influence one another. Her readings of these films form what she calls "the Hollywood curriculum"—in other words, what Hollywood teaches audiences about schools.

Dalton's approach to teaching school films reflects this framework and focuses on the intersectionality of race, gender, sexuality, and social class in films including *Blackboard Jungle* (Brooks, 1955), *Conrack* (Ritt, 1972), and *High School High* (Bochner, 1996). In a course she designed titled Critical Media Studies: Education and Popular Culture, Dalton encourages students to analyze school films according to the major patterns found within the genre. In addition to the good/bad teacher trope, students may choose to explore a number of other themes, including race, gender, social class, sexuality, abuse of power, administrators, and students and schooling. Dalton hopes students will gain "an understanding of critical media theory, genre theory, critical pedagogy, and intersectionality." As the culminating project for the course, she asks students to create an anthology of their own essays about teachers in the movies. Through the construction of an anthology, students learn about copyright, formatting, indexing, and following style guidelines—all factors inherent in putting together a collection for publication (Dalton, 2015). In this course syllabus, Dalton's focus on the elements that created the Hollywood curriculum and its leaky boundaries also helps uncover the outliers—the films that lie outside of the audience's expectations.

Sociology

According to Robert Bulman (2015), sociologists do not often study film. Instead, "sociological research observes people in social interaction, tracks patterns of social inequality, investigates the working of social institutions, seeks to understand the process of social change, and studies the distribution of power in society" (p. 1). Bulman has long studied the genre of school film. His original book and its revised version, *Hollywood Goes to High School*, is an extensive examination of the genre through a sociological lens as he categorizes and critiques 177 films by specific cultural concepts, including individualism, elitism, and conformity. Like Dalton (2010), he points out similarities found in the genre, but his focus is on the socioeconomic status of the school. For example, if the school is an urban one, then the film will most likely be about the teacher; if the school is suburban, then the plot will center on the students. He briefly dwells on the implications of some of these films being based on "true stories" and what that might mean for these representations. For example, he treats *Dangerous Minds* (Johnson, 1995) as an updated version of *Blackboard Jungle* (Brooks, 1955) and outlines the uncannily similar characteristics between the two films while also acknowledging the differences between the film and Johnson's memoir.

In his own courses, Bulman pairs these films with sociological texts, such as Kozol's *Savage Inequalities* (1991), which is an examination of the inequities between urban and suburban schools. An important addition to the second edition of his book is his primer on how to research the genre from a social science perspective. His steps include choosing a research question, conducting a literature review, forming a hypothesis, identifying the variables, deciding which films to include, taking detailed notes to use as data, analyzing that data, building an argument, and using theory to explain the findings (Bulman, 2015, Appendix A). His guide is extremely clear and concise and a good place to start for those interested in conducting a study not only about school films, but films in general.

In step two, conducting a literature review, Bulman encourages students to also examine literature that is tangentially related to their research question to help "frame your research project and make sense of the findings" (p. 143). For example, if researchers are looking at reasons why students drop out of school in school films, they might consider educational research that considers the same topic. In the case of my work on *Napoleon Dynamite*, for instance, I considered studies on school "nerds" (Bach, 2006). Bringing films into contact with educational literature can challenge representations found in both approaches to understanding schooling and education.

Education

Like communication and sociology, the field of education covers many different aspects, including the study of how and what gets taught in formal and information settings. A third well-established scholar in the field of education who has written about and taught school films for many years is James Trier. In his syllabus, Trier defines education in popular culture as "teachers, students, principals, other educators, and the everyday processes of schooling" (2012, p. 1). Trier's extensive work analyzes these films and television shows, often from a teacher's perspective. In fact, he occasionally incorporates the experiences of his students who are teachers or will become teachers into his examination of these texts. Some of the assignments in his course, "Exploring Representations of Education in Popular Culture" include:

- **Analyze Two or More Films within a Subgenre of School Films.** In this assignment, students analyze two or more "subgenres" of school films, which Trier (2012) identifies as "inner-city," "suburban," "private," "sports," "supernatural," and "sci-fi."
- **Make a "Detournement" and Write an Explanatory Paper.** Trier (2007) explains the concept of a *detournement* as a challenge to dominant media. In this assignment, students would both make the detournement media text and write a paper explaining it. An example might be to take a scene from a biopic and intersperse it with excerpts from

the original text. This assignment asks students to consider how media manipulate images for public consumption.

- **Perform a "Short Circuit" Reading.** In this assignment, Trier pulls from Slavoj Žižek's (2006) definition of a "short circuit" reading. Trier (2015) writes in his course syllabus, "Oversimplified, this paper/project idea calls for analyzing one or more school films or episodes from a television series (like *The Wire*) in terms of some theory or *concept*—say, a social, psychoanalytical, or psychological theory or concept" (pp. 5–6).

Trier's approaches are interdisciplinary as he pulls from literary theory, philosophy, and film studies. He asks his student to make sense of what they see on screen and what those representations mean for their profession, but also he seeks to enable his students to challenge those images as a way of reclaiming their profession.

Two Additional Ways to Teach the School Biopic

Teaching the school film from the perspectives of communication studies, sociology, and education can help fashion a framework for teaching biopics. While all of the approaches in this section share characteristics for examining texts found in cultural studies, film and television studies, and new historicism, they are not meant to faithfully reflect one field over another. For instance, one need not be an expert in educational theory to grapple with multiple texts concerning a particular narrative. With that in mind, I'd like to offer two approaches to teaching biopics in the classroom.

Biopics lend themselves to being read both at a close level and at a distance as part of a larger examination of educational reform and policy. While one could certainly offer a special topics class that examines just biopics, I think we can incorporate this perspective into broader courses and enrich classroom conversation about the role of teachers in films and in society by simply rethinking how we define and consider these films with our students. Both of the approaches I offer here are interchangeable, but one approach probably complements the objectives of a particular discipline. Ultimately, they both focus on the structure used to create the narrative, interrogate the representations of schools, students, and teachers, and explore the role these texts play in shaping the public's perception of the profession.

Reading with Memoirs/Biographies

As discussed in Chapter 4, when putting a memoir or biography alongside the film adaptation (or vice versa), it becomes clear what aspects transfer to the screen, are manipulated for the screen, or are fabricated for the screen. In this approach, students either read and then watch the film adaptations of these teachers' stories, or they watch and then read. A film like *Stand and Deliver* (Menendez, 1988) might be framed by reading archival newspaper stories on Garfield's success, then reading an interview with the director/writers/producers/actors, and finally watching the film. The unit/lesson could end with students discussing Mathews's (1988) text, especially the last chapter in which he outlines his ideas for educational reform based on his experience with Escalante. A similar approach could be taken for *Dangerous Minds* (Smith, 1995), *To Sir, With Love* (Clavell, 1967), and *Freedom Writers* (LaGravenese, 2007). In doing so, there is less focus on representations of teachers and films and more on the larger questions of biopics, including how subjects are chosen for them and what is manipulated from the original story for the screen.

This approach is informed by some general guidelines: students read source texts while watching the film adaptations and consider differences and similarities in their narrative structure; they examine how schools, teachers, students, and administrators are represented; and they consider what role these stories play in the field of education. Following this approach also allows students to consider the role teacher memoirs play in the production of these films, the ways such narratives are altered for the screen, and the consequences of doing so.

Watching While Pulling in Media Stories and Educational Research

> Few real-life educators and/or educational researchers would point to any of these histrionic teachers as exemplary classroom instructors. Nonetheless, what the actors teaching on the silver screen do with students Delpit (1995) dubs "other people's children" is seen as just fine—as long as no one in the real world tries to do the same things with the children whom most of the nation's educators view as "their own."
>
> —Ladson-Billings (1998, p. 255)

Another way to teach biopics is to juxtapose them with stories about education from the media and the field of education. In the quote that opens this section, Ladson-Billings refers to the film *Dangerous Minds* (Smith, 1995) as a way of pointing out how these films neglect the assessment of students; instead of teachers *teaching* dangerous minds (the students), they are instead teaching *during* dangerous times (increased scrutiny and testing). Giroux (2001) advocates that educators approach these films seriously with their students and read them as political texts.

Another way of approaching these films is to pull in media stories that may or may not be related to the story portrayed on screen. In this way, stories are extended and connected to educational trends, perhaps to the time in which the films are set or as a comparison to the context of contemporary discourse. What kind of feedback, for example, would we have given to Marin from *The Class*? How does the feedback and mentorship Braithwaite receives in *To Sir, With Love* (Clavell, 1967) line up with what Bill Gates (2013) says about teachers in his TED Talk:

> We all need people who will give us feedback. That's how we improve. Unfortunately, there's one group of people who get almost no systematic feedback to help them do their jobs better, and these people have one of the most important jobs in the world. I'm talking about teachers. … Today, districts are revamping the way they evaluate teachers, but we still give them almost no feedback that actually helps them improve their practice. Our teachers deserve better. The system we have today isn't fair to them. It's not fair to students, and it's putting America's global leadership at risk. So today I want to talk about how we can help all teachers get the tools for improvement they want and deserve.

How are teachers evaluated? And, does any of that transfer to the screen? What feedback would we give Braithwaite (*To Sir, With Love*) or Johnson (*Dangerous Minds*) or Gruwell (*Freedom Writers*)?

Chennault (2006) suggests that teacher educators use school films with their students to discuss the various layers of meaning presented by a film or how these films are representations of the larger cultural context in which they exist. In the midst of preparing our preservice teachers for a career riddled with test preparation, direct instruction, comprehensive curricula and literacy standards, not to mention important issues of race, class, and gender, teacher educators do and should turn to film as one way to discuss what it means to be a teacher.

In response to films set in urban schools, Grant (2002) suggests asking students:

1. What exactly do urban teachers and students do in the films? What aspects of their lives are glossed over or omitted?

2. What kinds of people do you see living in the urban environments of these films? What kinds of people are missing?
3. What violence do you see in the films? How does this aspect of urban education compare and/or contrast with actual statistics and with reports in the media?
4. What are the physical, social, psychological, emotional, and cognitive consequences of centuries of poverty and racism in the films? How are these issues addressed in the films?

To that I would add:

5. How does this adaptation compare with the source stories for these adaptations? How do decisions such as the one to change the racial makeup of LouAnne Johnson's students change her as a teacher (or not)?

Conclusion

Dangerous Minds (1995), above all other biopics, seems to have garnered the most attention by those who teach school films. And, while scholars notice how Johnson's memoir has been adapted for the screen and how those alterations speak to Hollywood's style for creating biopics, and while this pairing serves as an easy entry point into understanding the school film biopic, there are many other pairings with films and memoirs that might be more nuanced or interesting to consider.

Finally, scholars who write about school films should consider how their analysis intersects with a text depending on the author's perspective and source material. Do biopics have a responsibility to portray a teacher's story more faithfully than the original stories (which may or may not be actual representations of the true story)? By examining these films as biopics, the potential for breaking open the teacher as savior myth becomes more readily available than when the narrative is dismissed as solely being fabricated for the screen. The truth is, these teachers portray themselves (or are portrayed) in these source texts as super teachers who enter this profession, meet with hardships, try to reach their students, and meet some form of success. When educational theorists juxtapose these narratives with current educational reform and use them as a starting point for discussing the consequences of faculty becoming targets or outcasts at their schools for their efforts and how these representations shortchange students, they blur the lines between reality and fiction and provide the seeds for real conversations. This boundary is perhaps most noticeable in the genre of reality television, which forms the subject of the third and final section of this book.

References

Avildsen, J. G. (Director). (1989). *Lean on me* [Motion picture]. United States: Warner Brothers.

Ayers, W. (2001). A teacher ain't nothin' but a hero: Teachers and teaching in film. In P. B. Joseph & G. E. Burnaford (Eds.), *Images of schoolteachers in twentieth-century America* (2nd ed., pp. 147–156). New York, NY: St. Martin's Press.

Bach, J. (2006). From nerds to Napoleons: Thwarting archetypical expectations in high school films. *Journal of Curriculum Theorizing, 22*(2): 73–86.

Barnz, D. (Director). (2012). *Won't back down* [Motion picture]. United States: Walden Media.

Bingham, D. (2010). *Whose lives are they anyway? The biopic as contemporary film genre*. New Brunswick, NJ: Rutgers University Press.

Bochner, H. (Director). (1996). *High school high* [Motion picture]. United States: TriStar Pictures.

Brooks, R. (Director). (1955). *Blackboard jungle* [Motion picture]. United States: Metro Goldwyn Mayer.

Bulman, R. C. (2015). *Hollywood goes to high school: Cinema, schools, and American culture* (2nd ed.). New York, NY: Worth Publishers.

Cantet, L. (Director). (2008). *The class*. [DVD]. Paris, France: Haut et Court.

Chennault, R. (2006). *Hollywood films about schools: Where race, politics, and education intersect*. New York, NY: Palgrave.

Cheshire, E. (2015). Bio-pics: A life in pictures. New York, NY: Wallflower Press.

Clavell, J. (Director & Producer). (1967). *To sir, with love* [Motion picture]. United States: Columbia Pictures.

Condon, B. (Director). (2004). *Kinsey*. [Motion picture]. United States: Fox Searchlight Pictures.

Custen, G. F. (1992). *Bio/pics: How Hollywood constructed public history*. New Brunswick, NJ: Rutgers University Press.

Dalton, M. (2010). *The Hollywood curriculum: Teachers in the movies* (2nd ed.). New York, NY: Peter Lang.

Dalton, M. (2015). *Course proposal for critical media studies: Education and popular culture*. Department of Communication Studies, Wake Forest University, Winston-Salem, NC. Unpublished.

Danza, T. (2012). *I'd like to apologize to every teacher I've ever had: My year as a rookie teacher at Northeast High*. New York, NY: Random House.

Delpit, L. (1995). *Other people's children: Cultural conflict in the classroom*. New York, NY: New Press.

Fiske, J. (1989). *Reading popular culture*. Boston, MA: Unwin Hyman.

Gates, B. (2013). *Teachers need real feedback* [Transcript]. TED. Retrieved from http://www.ted.com/talks/bill_gates_teachers_need_real_feedback/transcript?language=en

Giroux, H. A. (2001). Breaking into the movies: Pedagogy and the politics of film author(s). *JAC*, *21*, 583–598.

Grant, P. A. (2002). Using popular films to challenge preservice teachers' beliefs about teaching in urban schools. *Urban Education*, *37*, 77–95.

Greif, L., & Reed, A. (Producers). (2010). *Teach: Tony Danza* [Television series]. Philadelphia, PA: A&E.

Guggenheim, D. (Director). (2010). *Waiting for Superman* [Motion picture]. United States: Paramount.

Hendry, P. (2011). *Secondary school curriculum syllabus*. School of Education, Lousisiana State University, Baton Rouge, LA. Unpublished.

Henke, S. (2008). Dangerous minds: Constructing urban education between hope and despair. In S. Schramm-Pate & R. B. Jeffries (Eds.), *Grappling with diversity: Readings on civil rights pedagogy and critical multiculturalism* (pp. 97–115). Albany, NY: State University of New York Press.

Howard, R. (Director). (2001). *A beautiful mind.* [Motion picture]. United States: Universal Pictures.

Kasdan, J. (Director). (2011). *Bad teacher* [Motion picture]. United States: Columbia.

Kozol, J. (1991). *Savage inequalities: Children in America's schools*. New York, NY: Crown Publishers, Inc.

Ladson-Billings, G. (1998). Teaching in dangerous times: Culturally relevant approaches to teacher assessment. *Journal of Negro Education*, *67*, 255–267.

LaGravenese, R. (Director). (2007). *Freedom writers* [Motion picture]. United States: Paramount.

Lanier, H. K. (2012). *Teaching in the terrordome: Two years in West Baltimore with Teach for America*. Columbia, MO: University of Missouri Press.

Matthews, J. (1988). *Escalante: The best teacher in America.* New York, NY: Henry Holt.

McCarthy, C. (1998). Educating the American popular: Suburban resentment and the representation of the inner city in contemporary film and television. *Race, Ethnicity, and Education*, *1*, 31–48.

Menendez, R. (Director). (1988). *Stand and deliver* [Motion picture]. United States: Warner Bros.

Ramsey, S., & Bach, J. (2013, October). Teachers' stories: An examination of the role of teacher memoirs in a curriculum course. Paper presented at the meeting of the American Association of Teaching and Curriculum, Chicago, IL.

Rhee, M. (2013). *Radical: Fighting to put students first*. New York, NY: Harper.

Ritt, M. (Director). (1972). *Conrack* [Motion picture]. United States: Twentieth Century Fox.

Rosenstone, R. A. (2007). In praise of the biopic. In R. Francaviglia & J. Ronitzky (Eds.), *Lights, camera, history: Portraying the past in film* (pp. 11–29). College Station, TX: Texas A&M University Press.

Simon, D., & Burns, E. (1998). *The corner: A year in the life of an inner-city neighborhood*. New York, NY: Broadway Books.

Smith, J. N. (Director). (1995). *Dangerous minds* [Motion picture]. United States: Don Simpson/ Jerry Bruckheimer Films/Hollywood Pictures.

Trier, J. (2007). The spectacle and *detournement*. *Journal of Adolescent & Adult Literacy*, *51*, 274–278.

Trier, J. (2012). Seminar in educational studies: Exploring representations of education in popular culture. School of Education. University of North Carolina at Chapel Hill. Unpublished.

Weir, P. (Director). (1989). *Dead poets society* [Motion picture]. United States: Touchstone Pictures.

Žižek, S. (2006). *The parallax view*. Cambridge, MA: Massachusetts Institute of Technology.

SECTION III

REAL WORLDS: REALITY TELEVISION

· 7 ·

"AN ESSENTIAL INGREDIENT OF TRUST"

An Overview of the Pedagogical Aspects of Reality Television

> I think we need a new name for it [shows that use the conventions of a documentary but are not], a name that would contrast it not only with fiction, but with what we have been exposed to up until now on TV. Whatever that turns out to be, it will have to include an essential ingredient of trust.
>
> —Margaret Mead (1973, A63), *TV Guide*

It's hard not to find a channel today without at least one reality television show. Whether it's a look into the daily activities of housewives or into the competitive world of dance, reality television shows can provide an insider's view of professions and lifestyles and offer audiences ideas for improving their own lives. Reality television has gradually developed a distinct style and approach to content that brings together elements from documentaries, sitcoms, game shows, and soap operas. Documentaries and fictional films still dominate what audiences learn about education, since depictions of schools, teachers, and students have been largely spared from being captured on reality television shows. The genre of reality television, however, is a powerful pedagogical form that straddles the boundaries between entertaining and educating.

As the genre has developed, the names and definitions used to identify these shows have changed. Scholars have called them actual television, reality-based television, factual television, and reality television. Furthermore, reality television remains a difficult entity for those in television studies to define (Murray, 2009). Biltereyst (2004) offers a definition that focuses on content: "Most viewers and critics share the feeling that it refers to various factual television formats with a high reality claim, stressing the actions and emotions of real people (non-actors), often using a combination of 'authentic' (e.g. police, security or surveillance images) and staged images (e.g. fictionalized reconstructions, post-factum interviews)" (p. 117). Miller (2011) defines reality television by claiming it possesses three major components: it "documents actual events rather than fiction, features ordinary people rather than actors, and is typically unscripted rather than pre-written" (p. 136). Part of the problem is that a definition such as *an unscripted show that follows the lives of real people in real situations* does not cover the range of variations one might find. There are shows that feature celebrities, shows that create scenarios for participants (very often as contestants), and shows that involve on-screen makeovers.

The relationships that reality television forges with its audiences are also an important characteristic of the genre. (I'm going to refer only to American versions of these shows in this chapter, but there are versions of reality television in many other countries.) These relationships are often extremely strong and relevant to a show's direction as more and more shows seek to include audience participation through opportunities such as real-time voting on Lifetime's *Project Runway* or viewing a house's occupants on 24-hour Web cams on CBS's *Big Brother*. While reality television shows begin on television, they also employ the Internet and social media to interact with and sustain audiences who have come to recognize their potential roles in shaping a show's outcome. To individual viewers, reality television can be perceived as *real*, *not real*, or *almost real*, depending on the viewer's experiences.

Because reality television exists in the space of (re)constructed reality, audiences must learn new skills for interacting with a show's messages. As critics and scholars continue to explore audience members' fascination and engagement with reality shows, it becomes clear that these shows can and do reveal a lot about issues studied in media and cultural studies. Reality television continues to garner attention from those in education who are asking questions that overlap with other fields, such as media and cultural studies. These questions include *How can we educate reality television audiences to watch these shows without internalizing the potential stereotypes they reinforce?* and *Given the popularity of these shows, are there lessons for educators?*

While reality television shows tend to stay out of school buildings, children and adolescents are still frequently featured. Consider the wide variety of shows that have already appeared and the roles children have played on them. They can be framed as family members, even burgeoning stars, as in *Dance Moms*, a show in which young adolescent girls compete in dance competitions. They can be contestants, as in the case of *Kid Nation* where a group of children ran their own town and competed for gold stars worth $20,000. They can be found in and around schools, as in *Made*, a show where teenagers transform themselves. They can be identified as subjects whose lives need improving, as in Jamie Oliver's *Food Nation*, which was an attempt to improve school lunches in public schools. They can be selected to represent their own generation, societies, and cultures, as in *My Super Sweet Sixteen*, a show that filmed teenagers planning and attending their sixteenth birthday parties, or *NYC Prep*, in which cameras followed a small group of students who attended elite private schools in New York City. And yet within this vast array of formats and contexts, scholars have pointed out the ways reality television educates (Pozner, 2010; Leistyna, 2009) and how it can be used in education (Kuhn-Wilken, Zimmerman, Matheson, Banning, & Pepin, 2012; Miller, 2011). Some scholars, myself included, have even recommended that the genre's format serves as a pedagogical model (Bach, 2008; Eckenrode, 2008). In truth, the genre is only beginning to insert itself into the body of film and television shows that depict schools and schooling.

The question I want to take up is *Is the public ready for what* really *occurs in the classroom?* In this chapter, I first provide an overview of reality television and explain how it blurs the codes found in fictional and nonfictional cinematic texts. I then examine how pedagogy helps to make sense of how reality television shows teach through their use of content and structure. Finally, I outline the educative aspects found in several shows' representations of youth. Taken together, these discussions form the basis of what I call reality television pedagogy.

How Audiences Learned to Recognize Reality Television

Before turning to what audiences are learning about children and adolescents and whether the public is ready, or interested, to see reality television shows set in schools, we need to understand how the genre's codes, relationships with audiences, representation of content, and structure work together to educate audiences and how audiences have learned to recognize and read reality television. Most viewers of reality television today are able to recognize and understand how the genre manipulates cinematic styles, codes, formats, and content of other genres. Corner (2002) argues that those in society familiar with reality television live in a postdocumentary culture, one in which viewers recognize and accept the conventions from the documentary genre that have been incorporated into reality television.

In his essay, "Performing the Real: Documentary Diversions," Corner (2002) contrasts the purposes of documentaries and reality television shows in order to describe his concept of a postdocumentary culture. He identifies four potential functions of the documentary: propaganda and publicity; journalistic inquiry and exposition; an attempt to bring to light alternative viewpoints of popular narratives; and finally, diversion (p. 260). Reality television, Corner argues, has been influenced by the fourth function. By associating reality television with diversion, it becomes less about educating and more about entertaining—a stance that enables the genre to reconstruct the truth (usually done at the editing stage) for an audience's enjoyment. Continuing with this argument, Corner considers how the diversionary function enables reality shows' audiences to recognize and understand that what they are viewing might look like a documentary, but it is not.

Audiences have learned to read the codes that comprise reality television shows; in turn, identifying those codes helps them reconcile and sort out the intersections of reality television with other forms. Reality television capitalizes on three aspects that allow it to claim that it entertains and informs: first, it borrows aspects from documentaries that lend the genre an air of authority; second, reality television maintains a "performative, playful element"; and third, the way audiences make sense of what's on the screen has undergone a shift. Corner describes audiences' viewings as "at once more cynical and more comic, a mood in which versions of performance cut through questions of sincerity and authenticity" (p. 266). This movement does not mean the end for the documentary, concludes Corner, but instead serves as an explanation of how the genre's "practice, forms, and functions" have been relocated (p. 266). His arguments reflect the precarious balance between information and entertainment that some reality television shows attempt to straddle.

In fact, reality television does seem to rely on representing reality as a way of distinguishing itself from the strict constructs found in other television genres. It appeals to audiences in a way sitcoms, news shows, and soap operas do not through the notion that if it is real, it must be true. And, it is a genre that has come to be modified for channels that are primarily known for either fictional or nonfictional content. Television networks have scrambled to create reality television shows that match their channels' missions (e.g., the History Channel, Lifetime, and Bravo) because these programs are not only popular, but also cheaper to produce.

Murray and Ouellette (2009) describe reality television "as an unabashedly commercial genre united less by aesthetic rules or certainties than by the fusion of popular entertainment with a self-conscious claim to the discourse of the real" (p. 3). Their description of the tension between the real and not real aspects that are negotiated by reality television indicates that reality television exists largely for commercial purposes and that commercialism and entertainment go together. Like Corner (2002), Murray and Ouellette (2009) contend that reality television's focus on entertainment overshadows its potential to also inform. According to Murray and Ouellette, audiences are not so much interested in whether the real is captured, but rather in the spaces between "reality and fiction." They write, "[W]hat results is an unstable text that encourages viewers to test their own notions of the real, the ordinary, and the intimate against the representation in front of them" (p. 8). This inquiry forms the basis of the public's fascination with what they see on the screen(s) in front of them. Is it really real?

This question has existed since the very beginnings of reality television, given that it brings together various types of shows, such as game shows, documentaries, and soap operas. Most scholars agree that reality television as we have come to know it began with the airing of PBS's *An American Family*. Filmed in 1971 and airing in 1973, this show featured the Louds, an upper-middle-class California family, and captured nearly every aspect of their lives. Ultimately, 216 days of their lives were filmed and edited into 12 one-hour episodes that aired on PBS (Ruoff, 2002). Two narratives from that show became noteworthy and were picked up by the press: first, the storyline that built up to the Louds' impending divorce and, second, the representation of their son, Lance, as a gay man living in New York. Although the show was filmed in documentary style, the footage was arranged in such a way as to construct narratives, primarily the demise of the Louds' marriage. In fact, Margaret Mead, in reaction to the airing of the PBS show, wrote in *TV Guide*, "It is, I believe … a new way in which people can learn to look at life, by seeing the life of others as interpreted by the camera" (A61). From the beginning, Mead sensed the pedagogical potential of this new form to teach audiences about the ways people live in powerful ways. And, those lessons might change the way they see their worlds.

Mead's reaction to *An American Family* calls attention to two fundamental components of reality television: first, the way the genre *captures* reality and, second, the way it *represents* reality. Therefore, it is important to examine reality television's roots in the documentary format, both in purpose and style—even in the choice of filmmakers and television channel (Murray, 2009)—in order to understand the relevance of its departure from documentaries and appropriation of other forms, such as the sitcom, which usually contain a narrative arc across the season as well as within each episode.

Following *An American Family*, new shows continued to surface that are now generally categorized under the reality genre. The early 1990s came with the next big leap in reality television. Slocum credits "*The Real World* [with moving] the format ahead by staging an environment in which 'reality' could occur" (n.d., ¶5). Shows like *Big Brother* (based on a show from the Netherlands with the same name) and *Survivor* (based on a Swedish show) took this premise of "staging an environment" and inserting contestants (house members and castaways) into a house/remote location in order to create reality competitions that have, to date, endured 16 and 29 seasons, respectively.

Placing cast members in carefully chosen or created environments is just another example of how reality television departs from other forms of documentaries and factual television, and audiences are aware of these artifices. Even young audiences learn to focus on the real and not real in reality television and learn to read these shows through an understanding of how form and content work together to signify real and not real (Fitch, Huston, & Wright, 1993). In her analysis of the effects of reality television shows on children, Neapolitan (1993) examines how the formal features of these shows pull from factual and fictional texts in a way that blurs reality for them. Those formal features include using a voiceover in a factual text, while a fictional one would use voice characterizations, sound effects, and music. This negotiation between form and content continues for older, more seasoned, viewers as well. In their study of adult reality television consumers, Rose and Wood (2005) describe this experience as a paradox in which viewers negotiate various forms of authenticity. In the end, they find that those viewers who can successfully negotiate these boundaries are the ones who wind up enjoying these shows. Specifically, they define and name those paradoxes as *situation*, which includes the location and context of a show; *identification*, which includes the connections viewers make with characters;

and *production*, which includes the decisions producers make on what to air and how (Rose & Wood, 2005).

Negotiating Education and Entertainment: Reality Television Pedagogy

Various branches of pedagogy (the study of the practice and methods of teaching) consider the role culture plays in learning. Those who study cultural pedagogy, however, examine how learning extends into lessons not only about teaching content but also about teaching identity construction. According to Giroux and Simon (1988):

> Pedagogy is a deliberate attempt to influence how and what knowledge and identities are produced within and among particular sets of social relations. It can be understood as a practice through which people are incited to acquire a particular "moral character." (p. 12)

Giroux and Simon's definition shifts the focus of pedagogy from traditional and identifiable educational settings to all settings that engage strategies for "acquiring" an identity. This means that in order to understand the full educative process, researchers must examine several factors, including the educational practices located in popular culture that facilitate learning as well as the components of popular culture that attract audiences. In particular, scholars like Giroux (1998) consider how children become facets of popular media and targets for corporations. If we want to understand how learning occurs across settings, educators must study not only the media texts that young people consume, but the commercial products developed to capitalize (literally) on that consumption. So, for instance, if we want to understand the complex interactions between children and *Sesame Street*, we would need to include discussion of how the child draws on his/her Sesame Street toys and games, as well as on actual episodes of the television show, in order to get close to a full understanding of how *Sesame Street* educates and for what purposes.

One thorough examination of how corporations employ pedagogical strategies can be found in *Kinderculture* (Kincheloe & Steinberg, 2004), a collection of essays that examines children's cultural lives from Barbies to McDonald's through the lens of "cultural pedagogy." Cultural pedagogy, according to Steinberg (2011) "refers to the idea that education takes place in a variety of social sites including but not limited to schooling" (p. 17). Those efforts are often linked to capitalistic endeavors that perpetuate and promote certain behaviors.

Giroux (2004) critiques those relationships found in culture. He posits that culture "deploys" power through "representation, consumption, and distribution." Culture and its products "[exercise] a powerful pedagogical force over how people think of themselves and their relationship to others" (p. 62). Giroux (2009) argues that educators need to focus on how learning also takes place outside of schools and what that learning looks like given "the broader educational force of culture in the new age of media technology, multimedia, and computer-based information and communication networks" (p. 89). Popular culture, he explains with coauthors Silberman-Keller, Bekerman, and Burbules (2008), like school, "introduces learners to particular ways of life, and their mutual study and critique problematize both the ways of life under discussion and what it would mean to address such issues through a pedagogy in which popular culture becomes central to the very task of learning itself" (p. 3). That concept helps illuminate not only how television shows appropriate strategies that are often associated with formal school settings for the sake of increasing audiences and/or customers, but also how they can be appropriated by educators and students. For Giroux (1998), those in education who seek to understand how pedagogy operates in spaces outside of schools do so, in part, to understand how the world of media culture can create a situation in which "formal education and entertainment collapse into each other" (p. 253).

Those lessons are often caught up in issues of power, agency, discourse, democracy, and social transformation—issues that are also of interest to those who conduct work in television studies. The notion of citizenship, for example, is a topic that appears in both fields, albeit in slightly different ways. According to Sandlin, O'Malley, and Burdick (2011), the concept of public pedagogy, which is the study of how learning occurs outside of formal school settings, first appeared in 1894 as a way to describe "citizenship education within and beyond schools" (p. 339), indicating the concept of civic engagement.

In *The Uses of Television*, Hartley (2002) associates the act of watching television with the notion of citizenship. He asks, "Does television teach citizenship? How does it? How should it?" He is not necessarily interested in the medium by itself; he states, "Once again, the issue is not television itself (as a social institution or onscreen discourse), but the relations among the populations it serves: how these populations can be known, reached, taught; turned into citizens" (p. 157). Here, Hartley's term includes an approach to citizenship that includes consumerism. For Hartley, uncovering the relationships among media, audiences, and producers are important areas to examine in order to address these questions. Likewise, those who engage with public pedagogy seek to understand how concepts are taught as opposed to heralding or demonizing public entities and corporations. Examinations conducted by those in media, cultural, and educational studies conclude that watching television can be a way of turning audiences into citizens—instructing them on what to buy or how to live or how others live.

I have resisted applying the term *public pedagogy* to the genre of reality television because, first, those in media studies have long talked about the ways television teaches without using the term and, second, because I agree with Sandlin, O'Malley, & Burdick (2011), who contend that everything public could be considered pedagogical; however, the concept seems to be a useful way to discuss how and on what the genre educates. Reality television, it can be argued, "introduce[s] learners to particular ways of life" and, through various means, invites audiences to critique those representations. Some forms of reality television are indeed forms of pedagogy—what Burdick and Sandlin (2013) identify as engaging in the transfer form of public pedagogy, as when shows portray the process one can follow to become a good singer, partner, or home buyer. The lessons are not always clearly defined. Reality television teaches its lessons in the spaces between the real and not real as audiences learn to identify the structure, codes, and content that characterize this genre.

Reality television pedagogy is a pedagogy that blurs the real and not real, applies to formal and informal educational settings, and incorporates multiple approaches to learning. Therefore, the term *reality television pedagogy* covers the many strategies for using and examining reality television in experiences of learning. That learning can encompass content as well as skills. In their examination of how reality shows reinvented television, Ouellette and Hay (2008) note that reality television is educational in the sense that viewers are exposed to "guidelines for living that [they] are called upon to learn and follow" (p. 2). They identify the pedagogical lessons in these shows as more worthwhile than educational programs:

> The concrete skills, interpersonal advice, problem-solving techniques, step-by-step demonstrations, intimate feedback, motivational support mechanisms, and suggestions for everyday application offered by reality television are undoubtedly more useful to strategies of governing through self and lifestyle than educational programs of the past. (p. 3)

But, for others, the lessons on which reality television chooses to educate audiences are the wrong ones, or at least incomplete ones. Leistyna (2009) advocates for a more critical approach to watching reality television, one informed by critical media literacy. For Leistyna, shows like *Miami Ink* (set in a tattoo parlor) and *Deadliest Catch* (a show that focuses on the dangerous season of fishing in the Bering Sea) fail to capture the larger economic picture of these professions. He hopes viewers create a means of watching these shows that will allow them to make meaning of what they are seeing on their screens. In this way, reality television misses an opportunity to educate because it educates in partial ways that are dictated by its simultaneous entertainment and commercial purposes. We will revisit this pedagogical concept in Chapter 9, but it is clear that reality television is viewed by some as overtly educational and by others as not educational enough—a sentiment that reflects once again its hybrid roots in nonfictional and fictional forms.

Examining the genre through a pedagogical lens reveals a complex educational relationship between producers, cast members, viewers, social media, and filming techniques. That relationship depends on viewers navigating those components in order to make meaning of what they are seeing on their screens. Critics of reality television point out the gaps in what audiences learn through their watching these shows (Pozner, 2010; Leistyna, 2009; Ouellette & Hay, 2008). Considering these strong arguments on how television may be serving as a pedagogical agent, educators should be concerned with what is being taught, who is being taught, and who is teaching—questions the field of curriculum theory continues to ask (Pinar, Reynolds, Slattery, & Taubman, 1995/2008). Therefore, we should also be concerned with what messages these shows send that *they* claim reflect reality—the day-to-day experiences of the characters—and those that are constructed to fit into the genre of reality television. If scholars figure out how reality television functions to communicate meanings by examining shows that individuals inhabit, sometimes even on a daily basis, then they can teach students how to navigate those meanings. According to a recent headline in my local paper, "The Biggest Lessons: Pennington Study of TV's *The Biggest Loser* Finds Metabolism Might Be Taking a Heavy Hit," researchers are here to help in that endeavor by sorting out how effective one show's approach to weight loss really is (Peveto, 2014). Studies like these focus on the lessons that these shows teach and interrogate in important ways the reality of those messages.

In this next section, I examine several reality television shows that focus on children and adolescents in settings outside of school. These shows illustrate how relationships among the shows, audiences, and critics shape contemporary experiences of watching reality television. This complex interaction that spans multiple forms of media is one of the ways reality television operates in a pedagogical way. The complex, multimedia interactions around reality television also raise ethical concerns about whether the genre is appropriate for a show set in a school.

How Audiences Learn from Reality Television

Reality television pedagogy is concerned with how audiences learn to negotiate the genre itself by focusing on the boundaries between the real and not real. An essential component to that relationship is the way reality television shows include audience participation. Reality television promotes a sense of citizenship where viewers are encouraged to participate in the direction a show takes. (We will see in the next chapter what can happen to a show that provides limited space for that role.) As discussed earlier, Corner (2002) outlines the aspects of a postdocumentary culture that enable audiences to recognize shows that fall into the reality television genre; part of that relationship includes interactive opportunities such as voting for contestants, 24-hour Web cams, and on-screen commentary. Those interactions are also found in venues that are not directly related to a show or its website and social media efforts. Viewers and critics interact with and about shows on blogs, YouTube fan channels, and, in extreme examples, by visiting actual locations and interfering with the filming efforts (Wilson, 2004). As technology continues to advance, makers of television shows and viewers are able to interact in new ways.

In fact, the technological advancements that have occurred alongside the growth of reality television also reveal what audiences are learning from reality television. Hartley & Fiske (2003) contend that "Post-broadcast forms of television [which include satellite and cable means of delivery], especially those featuring interactive and user-choice options, and the popular dissemination of gaming, digital cameras, editing software and the like, have facilitated the beginnings of television as an autonomous means of interactive communication spread widely among ordinary populations" (p. xvi). This convergence is why, according to Jenkins (2003), "rather than talking about interactive technologies, we [scholars] should document the interactions that occur amongst media consumers, between media consumers and media texts, and between media consumers and media producers" in order to understand how these new technologies "demand more active modes of spectatorship"

(¶3). These interactions about reality television shows can become public as audience members react to programs that feature children and adolescents online through social media or websites.

These interactions provide ways for viewers to insert themselves not only into the shows themselves, but also into conversations about them. Hartley notes in *Television Truths* (2008) that because television watching is "widespread, well-liked, and regulated into the ordinary routines and relationships of daily life … everyone in the audience is also both an *expert* on TV and a *critic*" who understands the workings of the medium (p. 2). The increased incorporation of the Internet, social media, and podcasts *within* reality television shows as well as *outside* of the shows enables viewers and critics to review and comment on shows in the same way with almost the same level of expertise, even though their knowledge of a subject may be minimal. Viewers and their opinions are validated by their increased participation in the direction a show takes as well as through the online interactions with fans. These various forms of interaction are not found to this extent in other television forms.

Reality television, from its inception, has been able to form a special relationship with audiences. It uses the ability to intersect real and not real modes of representation with timely topics that reflect society's issues in ways that set it apart from other forms of factual television. Notably, creator Craig Gilbert's idea for *An American Family* stemmed from his interest in representing the "vast changes that were occurring in American society" in the late 1960s and early 1970s (Ruoff, 2002, p. 12). Consequently, the March 12, 1973, cover of *Newsweek* featured a picture of the Louds with the headline, "The Broken Family." The story within, "The Broken Family: Divorce U.S. Style," is a commentary on how divorces have changed throughout the decades. In this feature, there are comments and themes that can still be found in critics' words today, such as the making of ordinary people into celebrities and the construction of narratives to focus on the dramatic. As a case in point, when asked why he didn't ask the cameras to leave when his wife asked for a divorce, Bill Loud responded, "But we had gotten used to it [the camera crew]" (Ruoff, 2002, p. 49). Within this narrative, the Loud children were viewed as participants in their parents' divorce, and readers could make connections between the "real" children mentioned in the story about divorce and the Loud children whose parents' divorce became the "story" of a television show.

The Loud children and the ways audiences and the media commented on them resemble much of the commentary still associated with children's and adolescents' appearances in contemporary reality television shows. Young people have appeared in all types of reality televisions shows, from competitions to makeovers, but those approaches tend to fall under one of three categories that comprise reality television pedagogy. First, there are shows designed to "teach" children—about good nutrition, succeeding in life, making lifestyle changes—and children and adolescents are usually the main characters in these shows. Then, there are shows designed to teach audiences about children and parenting; here, children and adolescents tend to play minor roles, as these shows focus on the adults in their lives. Finally, there are shows that border on voyeuristic, providing insights into particular subcultures, most notably the Housewives franchise that follows wealthy families in Orange County, California; New Jersey; and Atlanta. Children and adolescents tend to play an even smaller role in these shows and often only appear in plot lines associated with their parents and caregivers. Whatever their role, large or small, there are important implications for using children as contestants, as representatives of a particular setting, or as supporting cast members; these implications can be traced through the interactions among critics, audience members, and those who make and appear in these shows.

Children as Contestants: *Kid Nation*

What is it about the representation of children and adolescents in reality television shows that concerns critics and viewers? Examining the responses to the reality television shows *Kid Nation*, *NYC Prep*, *Dance Moms*, and *Bring It* might be a good place to start in order to examine what audiences learn from reality television and why this genre might not be a good fit for exploring what goes on in schools. In 2007, Columbia Broadcasting System (CBS) prepared to air a show in which a group of children between the ages of 8 and 15 inhabited an abandoned mining town and would become responsible for the day-to-day activities that would enable to the town to run. They would also compete for cash prizes and the chance to get better jobs. This show was called *Kid Nation*. In the scene that opened the show, a yellow school bus traveled down a dusty road in the middle of a desert in New Mexico. In a voiceover, the host, Jonathan Karsh, explained that the 40 kids on the bus were about to inhabit a failed mining town called Bonanza for the next 40 days. But that wasn't all. He further explained that this town would contain no adults, and it would be up to the children to run the town, feed and care for themselves by completing jobs, and participate in a challenge held every few days to determine the social class to which they would belong. The clip ended with the host showing the four council members a gold star worth $20,000 that would be awarded to a deserving kid at the town meeting held every three days.

Even before the show aired, there were concerns over the children's physical and psychological well-being. For example, in an interview with National Public Radio, *Kid Nation* producer Tom Foreman responded to the notion that the show might become something straight out of William Golding's *Lord of the Flies*: "There are cameramen there. There are producers there. There is a medic there in case something goes wrong. There is a child psychologist there in case they need them. Those people are there" (Masters, 2007). There was also very little freedom given to the children to create their own system of government. A structured class was imposed on them that reinforced notions of capitalism and meritocracy—a system that scholars pointed out inhibited the children from producing anything truly transformational had they been offered more freedom (Meloy, 2009; Leistyna, 2008; Goodman, 2007/2008). In addition to concerns for the children's safety, viewers were also concerned with the potential working conditions to which they would be subjected.

The *LA Times* reported that there were allegations of child abuse and labor law violations:

> A complaint charging "abuse and neglect" by the mother of a 12-year-old girl who was burned in the face while cooking was made public last week. New Mexico Atty. Gen. Gary King said he will investigate whether producers lawfully kept state inspectors, who wanted to review work permits for the children, from the site. CBS lawyers maintain that no work permits were needed because the children were "participating," and not working, during the filming of the program. (Fernandez, 2007)

CBS's interesting use of the word "participating" as opposed to "working" raises important questions for reality television shows set in schools. Given the location of a setting in which students are supposed to be doing the work of learning, where would lines be drawn? How much time during school would be taken for interviews with the producers or waiting for camera equipment to work? From the concerns over child labor laws to the remote setting, it is doubtful that audiences would ever give up their concerns for the children's welfare. For several reasons, *Kid Nation*'s second season never commenced.

Teenagers as Housewives: *NYC Prep*

One solution to the problems with a competition-like show might be to move the cameras from a staged setting to a setting determined by the teenagers themselves, which constituted the premise of *NYC Prep*. Several critics' reactions to shows featuring children and adolescents reflect the ethical and moral implications of including them in reality television shows, especially those that could potentially perpetuate stereotypes. Bravo's *NYC Prep*, for example, attempted to capitalize on fictional representations of wealthy teenagers who attended elite schools and appeared to live privileged lives. The show's stars loosely resembled the group of characters found in the popular novel series *Gossip Girl* and the subsequent television show based on the books. Airing for one season in 2009, *NYC Prep* featured a group of New York prep students as they socialized, organized and attended charity events, and shopped. Arguing that America has become increasingly obsessed with youth culture and the financially upper-class elite, Meloy (2009) reflects that:

> Like *Kid Nation*, a growing number of contemporary reality television programs highlight a social class system that entails mobility—the ability to change social positions rapidly with ease—and exclusivity—the perception of having obtained privileges available to a select few. Such a contradictory paradox feeds the desire of a changing American public and offers vicarious access to a social system that privileges consumption over labor. (¶2)

NYC Prep promised to offer an insider's view of the privileged youth of New York's elite; however, gaining access to them proved to be a challenge for the producers (Bosman, 2009). Before, during, and after the production of *NYC Prep*, administrators at several elite private schools cautioned parents and students against agreeing to be part of the show, thereby illustrating the status of the genre in the eyes of potential employers and donors; these stakeholders were acutely aware of the genre's ability to manipulate representations of those who appear on reality television shows. Stephen H. Spahn, the chancellor of the Dwight School, stated in an interview with the *New York Times*, "We always counsel our students to avoid such opportunities, as they usually reflect wrong-headed stereotypes" (Bosman, 2009). In this article as well as others, the students who decided to be part of the show were accused of not representing this population; their participation "contradicted an unspoken rule at many private schools: to be showy or prideful is not only culturally inappropriate, but also in supremely bad taste. To be showy or prideful on reality television appears to be even worse" (Bosman, 2009). In spite of the charity events the students organized and the other actions they took, critics focused on the exaggerated statements made by the participants, including their prowess with females or the money they spent.

While the producers claimed *NYC Prep* would provide insight into the extravagant world of adolescents who attended elite private schools, my viewings of the show suggest that it was, in fact, primarily an attempt to educate the public on the lifestyles of children of wealthy parents. In attempting to do so, it relied mainly on stock characters—the playboy, the gorgeous blond, the scheming brunette—found in fictional accounts. In a particularly scathing review of *NYC Prep* on the website A.V. Club, Tobias (2009) admits to having fallen a bit too much for the reality part of reality television. He writes, "Oops, there I go again talking about the characters on *NYC Prep* as if they weren't as processed as a line of Bratz dolls" (¶8). Shows like *NYC Prep* continued in the tradition of the Housewives series, a franchise on Bravo that follows the daily affairs of a group of women from various places around the country such as Orange County, California; New York; New Jersey; and Atlanta, Georgia. In fact, the Atlanta spin-off is one of [the only] series with a mainly African American cast, thereby predicting how networks might use the same format to increase race, class, and gender diversity in their lineups by taking a formula and moving it into another setting.

When Parents Are the Focus: *Dance Moms* and *Bring It*

Two Lifetime shows seek to educate and entertain audiences on the competitive world of dancing, and both follow a similar formula for each episode and season. *Dance Moms*, which has just entered its sixth season, focuses on dancers between the ages of 8 and 13 and their moms from the Abby Lee Dance Company in Pittsburgh, Pennsylvania. *Bring It*, set in Jackson, Mississippi, is in its third season and focuses on the competitive world of hip hop majorette dancing. The girls in *Bring It* are between the ages of 7 and 17. Both shows share a similar structure for each episode: there is an announcement for that week's competition/event, an introduction to that week's conflict, preparation and travel to the competition, performances, awards, and aftermath. Both shows highlight competitive dancing, but they differ in that one features mainly white parents and children and the other focuses on African American parents and children.

The titles *Dance Moms* and *Bring It* suggest that the focus of the former will be on the moms and the latter on competition, but in both shows, moms garner as much attention as the children and the coaches. Both sets of moms are competitive and advocate for their daughters. They both get to ride the buses on the way to the competitions and stay in the prep room in order to help their daughters get ready. Nonetheless, the mothers are positioned differently, even in terms of physical space. Abby's studio is in a stand-alone building with a reception desk, while Miss D's studio is in a strip mall. The moms on *Dance Moms* sit on a sofa above the practice room and watch the events down below. They can talk to each other and are often beckoned into the dance space to hear Abby critique their daughters. The *Bring It* moms, until recently, stood, stand on the sidewalk outside of the studio and peer through the blinds. They are rarely allowed into the dance space and once, when they were brought in from the cold, they were quickly dismissed because one of them spoke during practice. Miss D explains that the studio is not a place where parents socialize and "eat your wings." For both shows, however, capturing the parents' conversations serves as the catalyst for much of the conflict. In *Dance Moms*, those conversations are fraught with tension as they argue over who should get a solo or who will be in the group performance. The *Bring It* moms can be seen teasing each other, participating in the dance competitions, and usually supporting each other's children. Also, the *Bring It* students pray together as a group before competition; the *Dance Mom* students do not.

The main characters in each show are the coaches, Abby Lee and Diana (affectionately called Miss D). They are loud, authoritative, and skilled. Miss D and Abby may not love the parents of their dancers (there's a lot of yelling and arguing with them), but they certainly claim to love their dancers. While the coaches differ in approach, they both want to win and insist their students work hard. It's all about competition.

In an interview with NPR, Lifetime's executive vice president and general manager Robert Sharenow shared his new vision for the channel. "My goal," he said, "… is to have our channel reflect … the true breadth of the American population better, and I think that means inviting a lot of different people into the tent" (Neely, 2014). The juxtaposition of these two shows (*Bring It* aired after *Dance Moms*) demonstrates that one of the channel's strategies is to take successful formulas and apply them to different settings. But, in their efforts to provide glimpses into different aspects of competitive dance, Lifetime implies a hierarchy of sorts in the dance world. One is a formal, competitive world, practiced in a stand-alone studio with moms seated comfortably on a sofa. The other is located in a strip mall where the moms are nearly shut out of practices. *Dance Moms*' performances take place on stages (with applause and cheering at the end of each number); *Bring It* performances take place in gymnasiums (with audiences cheering during numbers). While both dance worlds are legitimate professions, the differences in race and class, in the shows position the competitive world of dance found in *Dance Moms* as the more serious pursuit.

Competition, class structure, and criticism surround *Kid Nation*, *NYC Prep*, *Dance Moms*, and *Bring It*. They are examples of adult versions the gamedoc and the Housewives franchise reality television shows that have been adapted to star children. Whether they are educating children, as in *Kid Nation*, or educating audiences, as in the other three, their formulas would not transfer into the world of schools. While competition exists in schools and students are certainly criticized for their performances, these experiences may be too real. As we read in Chapter 1, those lessons are for the documentary to cover—a format that does not veer too far into the realm of entertainment but resides mainly in its purpose to educate and solve.

Showing Us the Real World

These lessons about lifestyle, class, and race are also reflected in the shows that feature adolescents, and many of those shows can be found on MTV. MTV was credited with the next big revolution in reality television with its airing of *Real World* in 1992 (Ouellette & Hay, 2008). This show brought together young adults from all over the country and moved them into a house for several months. It is currently in its 31st season and has long departed from its initial foray into important social topics, such as AIDS, sexual orientation, and racism; it now addresses topics such as "homophobia, sloppy hookups, and drug and alcohol addiction" (Pozner, 2010). However, there are several shows on MTV that feature adolescents that are popular among young people and worth mentioning briefly, if only because they convey the same life messages as shows that feature adults—hard work can move you into different social classes, makeovers are magical, and if you're outlandish, pregnant, or extremely popular, you, too, can appear on a reality television show. Those shows include:

1. MTV's *Made* follows students who undergo various forms of boot camp to lose weight, appear in a fashion show, or make the cheerleading team.
2. MTV's *My Sweet Sixteen* viewers watch teenagers and their families plan and attend lavish birthday parties.

3. MTV's *16 and Pregnant*, as well as sequels *Teen Mom* and *Teen Mom 2*, follow four teenage girls through their pregnancy and first years raising babies, juggling school, and navigating relationships.

Reality television pedagogy teaches audiences that just about anything can be turned into a game, that one path to stardom is through reality television, and that, given the trajectory of reality television, the more outrageous the show, the better. They may also come away with the impression that their interactions with shows position them as experts and that the shows are fodder for those in education looking for ways to enliven their lessons or relate to their students. Lifetime even continues the discussion of parenting through its site "Lifetime Moms," featuring recipes, new stories about parenting issues, and advice columns.

Reality television pedagogy mirrors the expectations that reality television must balance the need to entertain and the need to educate, but when it leans too far toward one category, it becomes fodder for criticism. Reality television also positions viewers as experts, since it provides a space for audiences to engage and comment on the form with confidence. Reality television pedagogy, like critical pedagogy, must remain concerned with who is represented (and who is not) in these shows and for what purposes.

Given the moral and legal boundaries and concerns viewers take up when it comes to children and adolescents, it's unlikely that we will see a show called *Graduator* in which students scramble to become the single graduate of a high school. But, although *NYC Prep* was unable to get into actual schools, there has been at least one reality show filmed almost entirely in a public school. In the next chapter, we pick up the question of "Is America ready to see what really happens in its schools?"

References

Bach, J. (2008). Project teach: Using reality tv shows to teach methods courses. *Curriculum and Teaching Dialogue*, *10*(1&2), 41–53.

Biltereyst, D. (2004). Media audiences and the game of controversy: On reality TV, moral panic, and controversial media stories. *Journal of Media Practice*, 5(1), 7–24.

Bosman, J. (2009). Who's afraid of "NYC Prep"? Retrieved from http://www.nytimes.com/2009/07/05/fashion/05nycprep.html?partner=rss&emc=rss&_r=0

The broken family: Divorce U.S. style. (1973, March). *Newsweek*, 47–56.

Burdick, J., & Sandlin, J. A. (2013). Learning, becoming, and the unknowable: Conceptions, mechanisms, and process in public pedagogy literature. *Curriculum Inquiry*, *43*, 142–177.

Corner, J. (2002). Performing the real: Documentary diversions. *Television New Media, 3*, 255–269.

Eckenrode, D. (2008). An "amazing race" through the library: Reality television meets problem-based learning. In D. Cook & R. Sittler (Eds.), *Practicing pedagogy for library instructors: 17 innovative strategies to improve student learning* (pp. 127–138). Chicago, IL: Association of College Research Libraries.

Fernandez, M. E. (2007, August 29). *Kid nation* puts Hollywood labor tension into sharp focus. *Los Angeles Times*. Retrieved from http://articles.latimes.com/2007/aug/29/entertainment/et-kidnation29

Fitch, M., Huston, A. C., & Wright, J. C. (1993). From television forms to genre schemata: Children's perceptions of television reality. In G. L. Berry & J. K. Asamen (Eds.), *Children & television: Images in a changing socio-cultural world* (pp. 38–52). Los Angeles, CA: Sage.

Giroux, H. (1998). Public pedagogy and rodent politics: Cultural studies and the challenge of Disney. *Arizona Journal of Hispanic Cultural Studies, 2*, 253–266.

Giroux, H. A. (2004). Cultural studies, public pedagogy, and the responsibility of intellectuals. *Communication and Critical/Cultural Studies, 1*, 59–79.

Giroux, H. (2009). Cultural studies, critical pedagogy, and the politics of higher education. In R. Hammer & D. Kellner (Eds.), *Media/cultural studies: Critical approaches* (pp. 88–106). New York, NY: Peter Lang.

Giroux, H. A., & Simon, R. I. (1988). Schooling, popular culture, and a pedagogy of possibility. *Journal of Education, 170*, 9–26.

Goodman, E. (2007/2008). *Kid nation. Rethinking Schools Online, 22*(2). Retrieved from http://www.rethinkingschools.org/archive/22_02/kid222.shtml

Hartley, J. (2002). *Uses of television*. London, UK: Routledge.

Hartley, J. (2003). Reading television after 25 years: A new forward by John Hartley. In J. Fiske & J. Hartley (Eds.), Reading television (pp. ix–xxii) (2nd ed.). New York, NY: Routledge.

Hartley, J. (2008). *Television truths: Forms of knowledge in popular culture*. Malden, MA: Blackwell.

Jenkins, H. (2003). Interactive audiences? The "collective intelligence" of media fans. Retrieved from http://labweb.education.wisc.edu/steinkuehler/curric606/readings/Jenkins2002.pdf

Kuhn-Wilken, E., Zimmerman, T. S., Matheson, J. L., Banning, J. H., & Pepin, J. (2012). *Supernanny*'s solutions for families: An ethnographic content analysis of parenting messages on reality television. *Journal of Feminist Family Therapy, 24*, 316–339.

Leistyna, P. (2009). Social class and entertainment television: What's so real about reality television? In R. Hammer & D. Kellner (Eds.), *Media/cultural studies: Critical approaches* (pp. 337–359). New York, NY: Peter Lang.

Masters, K. (2007). *Kid nation* raises controversy ahead of air. Retrieved from http://www.npr.org/templates/story/story.php?storyId=12476751

Mead, M. (1973, January 6). As significant as the invention of drama or the novel. *TV Guide*, A61–63.

Meloy, M. (2009). From *Kid nation* to caste nation: Mobility, privilege, and the paradox of class on reality television. *Americana: The Journal of Popular Culture (1900–present)*, 8(1).

Retrieved from http://www.americanpopularculture.com/journal/articles/spring_2009/meloy.htm

Miller, sj. (2011). Demythologizing reality TV: Critical implications as a new literacy. *International Journal of Critical Pedagogy*, 3(3), 135–152.

Murray, S. (2009). "I think we need a new name for it": The meeting of documentary and reality TV. In S. Murray & L. Ouellette (Eds.), *Reality TV: Remaking television culture* (pp. 65–81). New York, NY: New York University Press.

Murray, S., & Ouellette, L. (2009). *Reality TV: Remaking television culture*. New York, NY: New York University Press.

Neapolitan, D. M. (1993). *An analysis of the formal features of "reality-based" television programs* (ERIC Report ED 360063). Retrieved from https://archive.org/details/ERIC_ED360063

Neely, P. (2014). Hoping to reach a wider audience, Lifetime breaks out of familiar formula. Retrieved from http://www.npr.org/blogs/codeswitch/2014/07/26/335422000/hoping-to-reach-a-wider-audience-lifetime-breaks-out-of-familiar-formula

Ouellette, L., & Hay, J. (2008). *Better living through reality TV*. Malden, MA: Blackwell.

Peveto, K. (2014, January 25). The biggest lessons: Pennington study of TV's *The biggest loser* finds metabolism might be taking heavy hit. *The Advocate*. Retrieved from http://theadvocate.com/news/acadiana/10660846-123/the-biggest-lessons-pennington-study

Pinar, W. F., Reynolds, W. M., Slattery, P., & Taubman, P. M. (Eds.). (1995/2008). *Understanding curriculum: An introduction to the study of historical and contemporary curriculum discourses*. New York, NY: Peter Lang.

Pozner, J. L. (2010). *Reality bites back: The troubling truth about guilty pleasure TV*. Berkeley, CA: Seal Press.

Rose, R. L., & Wood, S. L. (2005). Paradox and the consumption of authenticity through reality television. *Journal of Consumer Research*, *32*, 284–296.

Ruoff, J. (2002). An American Family: A *televised life*. Minneapolis, MN: University of Minnesota Press.

Sandlin, J. A., O'Malley, M. P., & Burdick, J. (2011). Mapping the complexity of public pedagogy scholarship: 1894–2010. *Review of Educational Research*, *81*, 338–375.

Silberman-Keller, D., Bekerman, Z., Giroux, H. A., & Burbules, N. C. (2008). Introduction. In D. Silberman-Keller, Z. Bekerman, H. A. Giroux, & N. C. Burbules (Eds.), *Mirror images: Popular culture and education* (pp. 1–8). New York, NY: Peter Lang.

Slocum, C. (n.d.). The real history of reality TV, or, how Alan Funt won the cold war. Writers' Guild of America, West. Retrieved from http://www.wga.org/organizesub.aspx?id=1099

Steinberg, S. (2011). Kinderculture: Mediating, simulacralizing, and pathologizing the new childhood. In J. Kincheloe, & S. Steinberg, (Eds.). *Kinderculture: The corporate construction of childhood* (pp. 1–53). Boulder, CO: Westview.

Tobias, S. (2009, June 23). *NYC prep*. Retrieved from http://www.avclub.com/tvclub/nyc-prep-29589

Wilson, P. (2004). Jamming *Big Brother*: Webcasting, audience intervention, and narrative activism. In S. Murray & L. Ouellette (Eds.), *Reality TV: Remaking television culture* (pp. 65–81). New York, NY: New York University Press.

· 8 ·

"ARE YOU HERE TO TELL A STORY?"

An Analysis of One Reality Television Show about Teaching

On October 1, 2010, a short-lived reality television series featuring a celebrity teaching a tenth grade English class in a public high school premiered on the cable channel Arts & Entertainment (A&E). That celebrity teacher was Tony Danza, best known for his roles in the sitcoms *Taxi* and *Who's the Boss?* A few months before the show *Teach: Tony Danza* (Greif & Reed, 2010) aired, a promotional advertisement ran on A&E. The promo opens with a first-person camera shot of someone walking down a school hallway and entering a classroom. As the students look up to see who has entered their classroom, Danza speaks in a voiceover: "Everybody gets nervous on their first day of school, and I'm no different. It's hard being the good guy. You know, where I come from I'm pretty popular, but that's not going to help me here." The camera then focuses on Danza, dressed in a button down shirt with a tie, standing behind a desk in front of a chalkboard. Some of the students are smiling, while others look incredulous. As he announces, "I'm Mr. Danza. I'm your English teacher," the words "It's not a role, it's reality" appear on the screen. For the first time, a reality television show was about to demonstrate to America what was happening in one of its schools.

This chapter provides an analysis of *Teach: Tony Danza* in an effort to understand how a reality show featuring a questionably qualified celebrity teacher was unable to capture the common narratives found in films and television shows set in schools, a failing that essentially led to its being canceled. As noted in the previous chapter, the field of television studies lends insight into how audiences are able to watch and interact with a reality television show on teaching in a way that may inform their own thinking about the profession. The expectations and form of reality television, like the documentary and biopic, ultimately cannot represent the reality of the teaching profession in a way that promotes a better understanding of the challenges schools face or in a way that sustains a large audience.

Somewhere between Real and Not Real: *Teach: Tony Danza*

How did Tony Danza wind up teaching high school English for a reality television show? It's a question he's been asked often. In the show's opening credits, in interviews, and in his memoir based on his experiences during and after the show, Danza reveals that, as he neared his 60s, he began to wonder about the "what ifs" in his life, including his original plan to become a teacher. (Danza actually earned a degree to teach history.) Inspired by President Obama's call to service and a Teach for America documentary, Danza mentioned to his friend, producer Leslie Greif, that he was thinking about taking up teaching. Greif replied, "What a great idea for a television show." After several meetings, A&E took an interest in the idea and began looking for a willing school. They finally found one, and Danza moved there and began teaching one English class of 26 students.

Teach's seven one-hour episodes cover Danza's journey in teaching inside and outside of the classroom. Each episode is set primarily in Northeast High School (NEHS), a public high school in Philadelphia with approximately 3,400 students who speak 57 different languages. Danza and his students share their classroom with David Cohn, an instructional coach who observes Danza and provides him with one-on-one feedback about his teaching. (One of the school's requirements for allowing Danza to teach was the presence of a teacher in the classroom.) Also present, of course, were the camera crew, other teachers, administrators, and students in and around the school. Although Danza only teaches one tenth grade English class, he appears to remain on campus all day and participates in a number of extracurricular activities, including several fundraisers, various team practices, and a disproportionate amount of time walking through the hallways. Outside of NEHS, he records his thoughts in Web diaries (monologues delivered in front of a Web camera), and the camera crew follows him through his daily activities.

The show's portrayal of Danza's daily experiences as an English teacher sparked a wave of conversation about teaching on online discussion boards (including A&E's), radio programs, and interview talk shows. These conversations and A&E's use of the show's companion website put the education profession under public scrutiny in ways rarely seen. In addition, *Teach: Tony Danza* was produced around the same time as a number of documentaries about education, including *Waiting for Superman* (Guggenheim, 2010) and *The Lottery* (Sackler, 2010). The discourse at that time championed the need for great teachers in every classroom, the potential of alternative teacher certification programs, and the rise of charter schools to help counteract the failings of public schools, especially those in urban areas. The show promised not only entertainment from an actor best known for his comedic, yet heartfelt, roles, but also an inside look into the "troubled" urban school. In addition, working within the docu-soap format meant that each week the show would have to establish and deliver a complete storyline filled with conflict and resolution. And it would have to work within the recognizable elements of the reality television show drama.

Teach's audiences probably had certain expectations for a reality show set in a high school with a celebrity teacher, but what were they? They probably did not expect the intensity found in previous school films and television shows set in schools, and they most likely weren't expecting the drama, competition, and shocking scenes promised by reality shows, so what did they expect? What promised to make it interesting was watching Danza struggle as a teacher, but if he had struggled, the students would have suffered—an unacceptable outcome. So the issue becomes *Why did Danza agree to a reality television show rather than a documentary?* The answer may lie in what reality television promises—real events packaged into stories—and a way for the actor to get back on television. Even though the producers went to their usual strategies, recording hours of footage, arranging it into storylines, and incorporating audiences through companion websites, *Teach* ultimately could not attract a large enough audience.

One of the reasons for the lack of ratings may be the way the codes of reality television failed to transfer into an actual school setting that focused on teaching and learning. As discussed in Chapter 7, most reality television viewers live in Corner's (2002) postdocumentary era and can recognize the codes and elements on which reality television relies. *Teach* encourages viewers to ask new questions about representations of schools on the screen. According to Kompare (2004), "The key question for reality TV, now and for the foreseeable future, is not *whether* its reality is produced but *how* it is articulated with existing codes and expectations" (p. 112, emphasis in original). While *Teach* incorporates the codes of reality television, it fails to escape the mundane workings of a classroom, especially when the school did not live up to audience's expectations of the narrative found in films and other media. It might be that the show was *too* real. In this chapter, I explore the origins of the show and the critics' reaction. Then I move to an examination of how *Teach: Tony Danza* takes up different elements of reality television in each episode and attempts to use them.

Origins of and Reactions to the Show

Teach: Tony Danza raised important questions about reality television's presence in schools. While not the first show to be filmed in a school setting (for example, PBS's *American High* [Cutler, 2000]) and some episodes of MTV's *Made* [Kusbit, 2002] were set in schools), it is the first show to capture the workings inside of a classroom, showing what lessons look like, how students interact, and how the teachers manage students. Television critics were initially skeptical but supportive of the show's use of the reality television format to feature the teaching efforts of an actor. McNamara (2010) of the *LA Times* reflects that, "It would be easy to dismiss A&E's new reality show *Teach: Tony Danza* as the vanity project of a faded TV actor. But it would be wrong. Not inaccurate, perhaps, but wrong" (¶1). To support his claims of Danza's sincerity, McNamara references the many scenes in which Danza shares his fears and frustrations with teaching, often in the early morning hours to a Web camera, and his increasing acknowledgement that this profession is not about him-as-expert but about his students. The *New York Times*' Stanley (2010) describes the show's premise more succinctly: "It sounds like a joke" (¶4). Like McNamara, Stanley goes on to defend the show for its attempts to portray the profession accurately. However, critics like Stuever (2010) from the *Washington Post* likened Danza to those in the public who feel confident that they know what goes on in public schools:

> Those of us who haven't darkened the doors of a public school lately nevertheless feel qualified to editorialize at length about perceived failures therein, based on test scores and what we think we know. Add to this all the buzz about a new, pro-charter-school documentary called *Waiting for Superman*, and our culture can often appear to be engaged in a spate of teacher-bashing. Somehow, everyone could be a better teacher except those who've devoted their lives to it. (¶4)

What made the show worth watching, according to Stuever, were the students and the other teachers. He points out how "The school's principal, assistant principal, and other faculty members attempt to disabuse [Danza] of the fantasy that he's starring in a real-life version of *Stand and Deliver*" (¶7). But Danza's real motives for teaching are further complicated by the genre of reality television. No matter how genuine his reasons are, viewers, the school's administrators, his colleagues, and his students would wonder if he agreed to do the show for financial and professional reasons. As one of his colleagues asked him, are you here to teach, or "to tell a story?"

Critics were also quick to anticipate how the reality television genre might manipulate aspects of the show. In her story about *Teach*, *LA Times* reporter Graham (2010) recounts the genesis of the show—the conversation Danza had with Greif. Danza shared with Greif his desire to take up President Obama's call to service and try teaching: "The friend, now a *Teach* producer, thought Danza might go one step further. Graham quotes Greif's memory of the conversation that followed. Greif remembers saying, 'Tony, it would actually make a fascinating show if we chronicled a genuine journey of what it's like to be a teacher'" (¶43). Graham continues, "What if a show was honest about a big, complicated urban public school, they wondered. What if it inspired other baby boomers to join the teaching ranks?" (¶44). But Danza, too, was worried about the show's influence on his students' education, as he tells them:

> I know you kids signed up for this … but you didn't sign away your 10th grade," he said. "It's very important that you learn, you know, [*Of*] *Mice and Men* and the elements of plot and the who, what and why if someone's a hero, or a flawed hero and *Mockingbird* and *Julius Caesar*, it's important that you learn that. And just because we're doing a TV show, that doesn't excuse us. We can't make a game out of this. (¶47)

Reporters and reviewers were also worried about the impact of the show's representation of NEHS's students. In his column, "*Teach: Tony Danza* on A&E: A Sensitive Teacher and a Fine, Rare Look at High School Reality," Storm (2010) understands the possible skepticism of audiences, "given the mind-numbing degradation of most reality shows" (¶14). He continues, "One newspaper columnist last year cautioned Philadelphia officials not 'to pimp' our kids' education to an unemployed sitcom actor who wants to kick-start his stalled career on the backs of students who'll be distracted by cameras and microphones" (¶15).

Classroom teachers also gave their opinions on A&E's decision to use a celebrity to teach a group of students under the conventions of a reality television show. Retired teacher and guest blogger for *The Notebook*, Pincus (2010) predicted that students would not passively allow themselves to be misrepresented or manipulated by a celebrity teacher in a reality show. She writes:

> The most enlightening segments (something I hope will continue in future episodes) are the small group discussions the students have after class, in which they smartly deconstruct Danza's teaching. They know. After all, they've had ten years of practice reading (and shaping!) their teachers. They are very aware of the ways in which their actions can impact the kinds of choices Danza will make in the future. And we get to listen to them plot. (¶20)

High school teacher/blogger Thomas (2011) also notes that the show "reveals to non-educators what happens after the bell rings. This is a truth that the general public needs to know. It is a vital insight for anyone discussing school reform" (¶5). But it seems as if, from the get-go, reality television could never be expected to represent all of the realities of the classroom. Given the public's experience with the genre, would *Teach* even stand a chance of showing some of the truth? Or was Danza and Greif's idea about selling the profession a more reasonable outcome for the genre than revealing reality?

How the Show Blurs Codes from Fictional and Nonfictional Texts about Teachers

According to Kompare (2004), reality television blurs codes from fictional and nonfictional sources. In his discussion of *The Osbournes* (Harding, 2002), Kompare points out how this show and *An American Family* (Gilbert, 1973) not only drew from different genres, but also interacted with audience's notions of "the family." *Teach* enacts a similar approach, only it pulls from the rich Hollywood narrative that Dalton (2010) argues has shaped audience's expectations of teachers, especially teachers in urban schools. *Teach*'s debut episode attempted to construct a narrative found in school films, such as *Lean on Me* (Avildsen, 1989): the teacher, the sports team, or the school itself begins as an underdog intent on overcoming a big obstacle.

The show positions Danza as someone interested in teaching to contribute to the well-being of reluctant students in need of a good teacher. In the debut episode, titled "Back to School," Danza sits in an auditorium with several other new teachers and listens to the facilitator claim that there are only three groups of people who are forced to be places they don't want to be:

those in prisons, asylums, and schools. In the break-out session that follows (which only aired on the website as a video extra), the new teachers are asked to draw a picture of the journey that brought them to NEHS. "You're going to illustrate your life's journey that brought you to Northeast today," instructs the facilitator.

Danza draws a series of three images: a pair of boxing gloves with the word "Brooklyn" written over it, a clapperboard with the word "Hollywood" over it, and a picture of himself with an arm around a student and the word "Northeast" over it. He tells his partner for the session about the third image: "And so here I am at Northeast High, a teacher with his imaginary arm—because I don't think you're allowed to touch the kids—around a student. … My hope is that I will, you know, be able to have some effect." His intention seems to be to become a teacher who cares for his students and their futures.

In his first meeting onscreen with his new principal, Ms. Carroll, Danza tells her that one of his reasons for becoming a teacher and capturing the experience on camera is to "show what's going on in urban education." She says that one of the reasons she agreed to the show was that she "felt his sincerity." She then warns Danza: "If this doesn't work, you're out of here." The show deliberately sets up and reinforces the message that Danza is new, he doesn't have a lot of preparation, the kids don't want to be in school, and the principal is poised to remove him from the classroom immediately if he does not do a good job.

Danza's first few lessons appear to be mediocre. He talks for almost the entire period, gives his students their homework assignment after the bell rings, and alienates some of them with his insistence that they use hand sanitizer upon entering and exiting his classroom. (He tells them he's protecting them against the swine flu, but they think he thinks "Kids are gross.") When he collects their first homework assignment, he asks students to volunteer to read their personal experience stories out loud. There are no volunteers, and the show inserts cricket noises used as non-diegetic sound effects to emphasize Danza's "failure" to motivate his students to share their stories. He finally offers to read a student's story. Several stories later, he's not only performing his students' stories but also identifying the parts of the story for them. Finally, one of the football players, Daniel, asks if they can read their own stories, and Danza realizes his mistake. He gets a quick talk from Cohn after class who advises him to "Let the kids have a chance to give an answer," and Danza seems to get it. But before he's able to hone his teaching skills, Danza must report to the boys' locker room to serve as an assistant coach for the football team.

The decision to have Danza coach football may seem odd. Given Danza's background, it would have seemed more appropriate for him to work with a group who could benefit from his experience—drama or dance or boxing. Instead, he finds himself being introduced by the head football coach to the team, who says, "I preach to you all of the time. Sometimes you have to hear it from someone else. This man, he's an actor, a showman, blah, blah, blah, and guess what? He's helping us out this year as a teacher, and he's helping us out as an assistant coach. Listen to what he has to say." He then asks Danza to give an impromptu talk. Danza rambles on for several minutes as the football players try to pay attention. Afterward, some of them confess, "I didn't hear nothing," and "He talks a lot." The head coach tells Danza that he was surprised at him for not asking the players to speak and says, "We need to hear their stories." Danza seems baffled and reflects, "I didn't even understand what [the head coach] was trying to say. He was saying I gave a bad speech. I know that." Later in the episode, he shares his frustration with his friend who is also a former teacher: "I can make them laugh, but can I make them learn? … At the end of the semester, there has to be some learning. I don't know if I'm up to this."

At the football game, Danza speaks to parents—a lot of them. One parent asks him, "What kinds of tools and knowledge are you bringing to the classroom?" Meanwhile, the football team is losing the game, and the coach tells his team "You gotta start playing football." Principal Carroll tells Danza during the game, "You have to build relationships." At the end of the week, after the football team loses, the team, like Danza, is challenged to go home and spend the weekend thinking about their performances and come back Monday to try again. It is a narrative common to school films featuring football games. One almost hopes for a montage of Danza training for his next lesson.

Teach complicates two ingrained traditions in school films and television shows—the representation of schools with diverse populations and the alternatively certified teachers who find themselves teaching in them. Indeed, Danza possesses many of the qualities found in the cinematic teacher-protagonists who teach in schools with diverse populations. He is an outsider, alternatively certified, and questionably qualified, similar to the teachers found in biopics such as Erin Gruwell from *Freedom Writers* (LaGravenese, 2007), LouAnne Johnson from *Dangerous Minds* (Smith,

1995), and Mark Thackeray from *To Sir, With Love* (Clavell, 1967). In this first episode, *Teach* attempts to pull from these films' depictions of urban school students, who are often represented as needing someone to come in and save them from the other teachers and administrators who underestimate their abilities (Bulman, 2004; Dalton, 2010). Danza's students don't appear to need saving; there are no schoolwide problems to overcome, such as low test scores or roaming gangs of students. At this point, the focus is on Danza, and we hope to see him either transform into a great teacher, get fired, or quit.

Involving *Teach*'s Audience through Its Website

Reality television incorporates its companion websites as well as various forms of social media, such as Facebook and Twitter, as a means to involve its audiences in ways documentaries and biopics traditionally do not. Whether audiences are watching what is going on in the *Big Brother* House (de Mol, 2000), voting for their favorite singer on *American Idol* (Fuller, 2002), or posing questions to a Bravo host to ask the "Housewives," reality television exploits social media to keep audiences engaged with shows before, during, and after an episode airs. Interactions with a reality television show through its website or through social media platforms are integral not only to including the audience, but also to helping producers reimagine the ways particular events can be represented on a show. As Hill (2005) notes, factual television "includes television programmes with interactive elements, such as voting, and related websites or mobile content. The interactive and multiplatform elements of various factual television programmes are part of the story of the restyling of factuality" (p. 5). A&E attempted to direct *Teach*'s viewers to its companion website for the show as a way for them to continue their interaction with Danza's journey and engage in conversations about education.

The show's website featured many traditional symbols associated with schooling (the channel has taken down its site for *Teach*). The background for each page was a blackboard with eraser streaks across it and various chalk doodles of a sun and stars. In the center of the screen, a piece of chalk scribbled across the board to lead the eye to several shots of Danza in a tie and button-down shirt, his "uniform" during most of the show. At the bottom of the page was the image of a sheet of torn notebook paper with the show's description written on it and several more photographs of Danza cut out and "stuck" onto the site with strips of clear tape. Throughout the airing of the show, A&E updated the *Teach* pages to allow viewers to post comments on that week's episode. After the season ended, fans could click on four additional links: "Grading Mr. Danza," in which Danza's onscreen students assigned him letter grades for his teaching; "Watch Video," where viewers could watch unaired clips from the show; "Photo Gallery," where viewers could see pictures from the show; and "Yearbook," where there were photographs of those involved in the show and extra information about them. Additional tabs at the top of the page offered links to "Photos," "Exclusives," "Discuss," and "Shop."

But these elements were somewhat basic, and the website lacked many of the sensational, more interactive components of previous companion websites, such as real-time video footage (*Big Brother*) or interviews with that week's winner (*Project Runway*). *Teach*'s website's features resembled school-like experiences, conjuring up images of classrooms, grades, and tests. This approach meant that the overall online experience failed to give viewers any real agency in the show. They could not vote for their favorite lesson, determine what Danza should teach next, or read students' real-time Tweets during the airing of an episode. Instead, *Teach*'s online interactions restyled Danza's role as the teacher by positioning his students and viewers as experts, granting them a space to comment not only on issues related to his teaching performance, but also on larger conversations about education in the United States.

The only meaningful place for fans to contribute was on the show's discussion boards. In 1997, Levy, writing about fan culture, introduced the concept of collective intelligence among fans, which depends on "knowledge [becoming] available to all members of a community" (quoted in Jenkins, 2006, p. 136). This availability, according to Levy, might expand a community's productive capacity in part because there is a broad range of expertise on which to draw. The inception of the Internet and its consequent use by fans, he argued, enabled fans to share knowledge more quickly, making fandom "much more effective as a platform for consumer activism" (p. 136).

By continuing *Teach*'s narrative from television to the Internet in the form of discussion boards, A&E created a "horizontal integration" that encouraged fans of the show to become "more active spectators" (Jenkins, 2006, p. 147). This horizontal movement introduced new voices into the show's narrative while destabilizing Danza's control of that narrative. Viewers who chose to visit the discussion boards inserted themselves into Danza's narrative by referring to their own experiences and commenting on the show's representation of teachers, school, and education. For example, fans were able to call upon the realities of teaching in ways that the show did not by referring to their own experiences with being students, with having children who attended school, and with teaching themselves.

In the second episode, "Tested," *Teach* capitalizes on the role a show's companion website can play. In this episode, Danza teaches John Steinbeck's novel *Of Mice and Men* (1937), which he gleefully explains "isn't even in the curriculum." He is shown once again performing for the class by reading the novel aloud to them and nearly dancing down the hallway on the way to give his first quiz. He soon learns after grading those quizzes that there is a large difference in the comprehension levels of his students.

As he realizes the different levels of learners he has in his classroom, he shares his belief that if his students just try, they'll succeed, a narrative commonly found in biopics such as *Stand and Deliver* and *Lean on Me*. Standing by this belief, he refuses to let three students go to the resource room, a place where they can get assistance, and tells them to try their best taking the test in his classroom. Cohn confronts Danza after class, confirms that he did refuse to let those students take their test in the resource room, and then takes their tests from Danza, presumably escorting those students to the resource room with the tests. Danza responds in a Web diary entry, "So I'm in hot water because I wanted the kids to try a little harder." The next several scenes show Danza talking to various administrators and participating in a team meeting where he was advised of the serious legalities involved in not letting Individualized Educational Plan (IEP) students use the resource room. At the end of the episode, viewers are invited to view Tony's test on the A&E website, which was posted as a PDF file (see Fig. 8.1 for a page of the test).

After each airing of an episode of *Teach*, the moderator of A&E's discussion boards, aetv_rita (2010), would invite viewers to comment on an issue explored in that evening's show. For example, the posts to the discussion board titled, "Take the *Of Mice and Men* test from episode 2 'Tested'—Talk about it here," demonstrate the direction many of the discussion posts took during the show. As of March 17, 2011, this discussion strand had 44 posts by 39 contributors (it has since closed to new posts and has been removed from the website). The conversation among the posters to the "test" thread turned from comments on Danza's test to the topics of tracking (sorting students into

Section 4: Figurative Language (3 points each, 18 points total)

1. "The shade climbed up the hills towards the top." Circle one.
   a. Personification b. Simile c. Onomatopoeia d. Hyperbole

2. "The night sky was a black velvet blanket." Circle one.
   a. Personification b. Metaphor c. Simile d. Onomatopoeia

3. Give an example of irony in *Of Mice and Men*.

____

____

____

4. Buzz is an example of ______________________. Fill in the blank.
5. Give the definition of satire:

____

____

6. Foreshadowing is a hint or suggestion of something that will happen later in the story. What might be foreshadowed by the scene where George warns Lennie that Curly's wife is a troublemaker?

____

____

____

____

Of Mice and Men

Section 5: The Book: Multiple Choice (3 points each, 24 points total)

1. What is the name of the town from which George and Lennie are fleeing at the beginning of the book?
   a. Weed b. Soledad c. Salinas d. Sacramento

2. Which of the following best describes the setting of this book?
   a. 1920s New York
   b. 1980s Utah
   c. 1940s New Mexico
   d. 1930s California

Figure 8.1. A page from Tony Danza's *Of Mice and Men* test (aetv_rita, 2010).

different classes according to their academic ability) and inclusion (the practice of including students with special needs into classrooms).

In A&E's Web space, the viewers became the expert commentators; they were able to share their experiences of Danza's show and their own experiences with school and have those experiences affirmed or contested by other viewers. *Teach*'s website, by posting Danza's test and inviting viewers to comment on it and other educational issues, positions them as expert commentators. Since there was no interactivity with what they saw on the screen each week, however, they remained passive ones.

Exhibiting Professional Behavior: A&E's Choice of Celebrity Teacher

While many reality shows make celebrities out of "ordinary" people, those shows that focus on existing celebrities represent a number of decisions influenced by the performer's past career. As demonstrated earlier in the discussion of *Teach*'s reviews, A&E's choice of Danza brings about several assumptions regarding the type of teacher he will portray on the screen. In his discussion of how reality television makes "calculated choices" in choosing its celebrities, Kompare (2004) writes, "Reality genre has shifted even more toward self-conscious performance (that is, exhibition), rather than the revelation of 'natural behavior'" (p. 106).

In the third episode, "Just Say No," Danza continues to learn that "exhibition" is detrimental to his students' learning and that being a celebrity teacher means he must choose among various professional obligations. The episode opens with Danza singing the national anthem at a Phillies baseball game, which serves as a reminder of his celebrity status and that he does have fans. (Several of Danza's students in the first episode admit to being unaware of his body of work.) After he finishes singing, he jokes to the camera that he's going to stay at the game, instead of getting ready for his class the next day.

This opening scene highlights the growing number of invitations his celebrity status garners and serves as an introduction to a series of requests that comes in the next few scenes. He is still working with the football team. He is also asked to serve as the guest speaker at senior pin night, even though he doesn't teach seniors. He reveals that he had a prior commitment to perform his live act at Atlantic City before beginning the filming of *Teach*. And then comes the request to organize a charity show for the mayor's wife's organization. Danza has less than one week to prepare, and NEHS students need to be involved. "I have a problem saying no," he confesses and accepts all requests.

At this point in the season, it appears that Danza has only been teaching for a few weeks, and he is beginning to identify which of his students need additional attention. For example, one of his students, Algernon, isn't completing his homework and has been getting into trouble in other classes. When Danza begins to interrogate Algernon about his study habits during class, Cohn cautions him not to push Algernon too much. But Danza tries to encourage Algernon to take school seriously. He tells him, "They're dying to pick kids out of this environment." In the end, Danza persists in an effort to get Algernon to submit a paper so he doesn't fail his class and Algernon does at the very last minute. It's exhausting watching Danza follow up with Algernon, and the attention he is able to give him is not something a teacher with a full roster of classes might be able to give to one student.

As the episode progresses, some of the more seasoned teachers begin to sense Danza's tendency to over-commit and visit him to offer advice, but his schedule gets even busier. He has a football game on the same day as the mayor's wife's charity performance. In an effort to emphasize just how stretched Danza is, the cameras go back and forth with shots of his celebrating a win with the football team and then the assistant principal, Ms. Denaples, waiting for him to show up to the mayor's performance. After those two successful endeavors, Danza has just one obligation left outside of his classroom, so the next scenes are of his October 10 Atlantic City show. The whirlwind week has taken its toll on Danza, and he makes a decision to dedicate himself to his primary role, that of a teacher. The next day, Danza quits the football team and most of his extracurricular activities. He decides to concentrate on his job.

Once again, the show decided to focus on a common conflict that teachers face, both on screen and off—balancing multiple roles and having to decide whether to prioritize teaching. Danza gives up his extracurricular activities, the ones that highlight his celebrity status, in favor of meeting the challenges of the classroom, where his celebrity status and related behavior are far less important. Danza learns that the outrageous classroom "performances" and the buffoonery from his previous roles have no place in the classroom, and the audience sees a far less entertaining but far more sincere attempt at teaching. Without the outrageous antics that made shows like *The Osbournes* and *Celebrity Rehab* popular, audiences see Danza's "natural behavior" as opposed to a "self-conscious performance" (Kompare, 2004, p. 106). But here's the problem: that does not make for interesting reality television.

Distorting Time to Create School-Like Narratives

Like many other reality television shows that document the lived experiences of an individual or a group, *Teach* cuts and splices its footage for the purposes of constructing 45-minute stories. Events that may have taken place over several weeks may seem to occur over a shorter period of time (usually a week of school in *Teach*). Producers mix and match chronologically recorded scenes out of order so as to increase the drama of what happens in a single episode. While *Teach* appears to unfold along with the school year (there are shots of the date on bulletin boards and mentions by administrators at faculty meetings to enable the audience to keep track of the passage of time), each episode contains a complete storyline for a particular issue Danza encounters as a teacher. Kompare (2004) writes about reality television's approach to repackaging storylines into recognizable narratives. In his discussion of *The Osbournes*, he describes how "[t]he producers were able to structure the episodes using familiar generic codes: problems are introduced, conflicts play out, and the end of the episode reaches a mild resolution" (p. 108). The juxtaposition of several scenes from *Teach*'s episodes "Homesick" and "Solidarity" seem to imply that they were intentionally assembled out of order and out of context in order to create the expected narrative format.

For the most part, Danza's students are well behaved, and the most distracting classroom behaviors they exhibit—the ones that frustrate him the most—are those that might seem nearly inconsequential to the veteran teacher. Take, for example, an interview Danza had with NPR and his thoughts on teaching and student behavior:

> There are moments of extreme joy and there are moments of extreme desperation—and self-doubt and just emotional ... sometimes, Armageddon. It's thrilling, and yet it's, you know, you look down and you're working your tail off trying to make them see some value in *Of Mice and Men*, for instance, and you look down and you see somebody making origami ... It kind of breaks your heart. (Raz & Danza, 2009)

Throughout the show, Danza slowly learns that teaching is not a performance. But in "Homesick," a narrative is constructed with Eric Choi, the student who makes origami figures. He is introduced as an apathetic student who, after being confronted with one of his paper creations, confesses that he is not interested in "Mr. Danza's off-topic topics." This comment is emphasized with a montage of Danza speaking about the cars he owns and the Broadway shows he's been in. Then there are multiple shots of Eric folding paper and slouching in his desk.

When Danza gives Eric back the test that he failed, Danza tells him, "I have to call home." Eric cries at this piece of information, and the audience is not surprised, as they know Eric's parents have high expectations for their son's academic performance. Eric shared this information with the class on the first day. The show repeats that scene just in case the audience does not remember. Danza meets with Eric's father and, with the help of a bilingual counselor, tries to convey to him that Eric needs to read more. Eric plays a special role in Danza's journey by personifying the reality that Danza's "entertaining" teaching style is not really contributing to his students' education. This storyline represents a turning point in Danza's approach to teaching.

The episode also attempts to draw a parallel between Eric's and Danza's performances in the classroom. After another mediocre lesson, Danza tells Cohn about his problems engaging Eric and Eric's comments about Danza's teaching. Cohn is surprised to learn that "quiet Eric" shared his opinion and tries to convince Danza to stop treating teaching as he would an acting gig. He tells Danza, "When you're flustered, you talk more," and he encourages him not to think "What am I going to do?" but rather "What are the kids going to do?" Danza decides to try to do less talking; he puts students into groups so they can write their own myths. Danza goes first and raps his myth, and then encourages students to be creative and incorporate the elements they have learned as part of their unit. Eric and Ben, who was also shown being uninterested in Danza's class, perform their myth as a creative skit, and the show attempts to reinforce the notion that the best lessons are those that are student-centered. This is a lesson audiences rarely see in school films and television shows because teachers played by Robin Williams and Michelle Pfeiffer often steal the shot with their teaching performances. Danza is pleased with his students' presentations and realizes "getting them to teach themselves" is a perfect way to get students engaged. It has taken him four episodes to unlock the secret of teaching.

In the fifth episode, the show's team uses archived footage to undermine Danza's own words as part of the story's narrative. "Solidarity" is set in early November and deals with both student conflict and the enforcement of a new schoolwide uniform policy. The episode is an examination of how solidarity with one's students can be a good thing, but solidarity with one's peers can lead to trouble.

The episode opens with a scene in a locker room where Danza and several students have congregated around a boxing bag. Danza reveals that he's going to try to bond with some of his students through boxing. In the next scene, the camera captures a group of students running down a hallway, and Danza learns that his student, Howard, just "got jumped" by a group of students, one of whom took his iPod. Howard tells the story to Danza, who seems distracted at the time and doesn't really ask any questions about the situation. The tension between the boys escalates when Howard's friend, Matt, tries to intervene on his behalf. Danza attends a series of mediations between Howard and the boy who took his iPod to help resolve their conflict. During one of those meetings, he asks Howard, "Why didn't you tell me?" The episode then repeats the scene where Howard did try to tell Danza that someone had stolen his iPod. As with "Homesick," "Solidarity" attempts to emphasize the importance of listening to one's students.

"Solidarity" also focuses on the implementation of a new school uniform policy and attempts to construct a storyline in which one of Danza's lessons may have instigated a student's act of defiance to the new policy. In an effort to empathize with his students' dismay about the new uniforms, Danza excitedly tells them he's been wearing a uniform since the beginning of the year (button down shirt, dress pants, and tie). Then he pulls out a NEHS tie and tells them, "We're all in [this] together." But a student points out he's not in *their* uniform.

Meanwhile, Danza continues to teach and find ways of connecting his content to his students' lives. One of his lessons begins with a journal assignment in which students consider the benefit of an authoritarian government, and Danza discusses the act of protesting with his students. This scene may have been an effort to set up a possible motive for Matt P.'s reaction to the new uniform policy, which begins with a shot of Monte and Matt P. walking to school and arguing about uniforms. Matt P. seems to be upset at the school's effort to make them dress as if they attended a parochial or charter school. In an effort to exercise some autonomy, Matt P. wears the wrong shoes on purpose and is kept outside of the metal detectors at the entrance of the school. He finally puts on the "approved" style of shoes and goes through the metal detector. He later confesses that he was trying to make some sort of point before putting on the correct shoes that he had in his school bag the entire time. As his ID is scanned, he hands Assistant Principal Denaples a paper bag with a dog biscuit inside and tells her, "Thanks for putting up with my trouble." Denaples is furious and has to explain to Danza the significance of the gesture: "Like you're a bitch." A puzzled Danza responds, "In my day, we gave them apples," and wonders how he arrived at a point "where students under their breath compare [teachers and administrators] to dogs." Denaples responds, "You haven't been in schools." Danza convinces Matt P. to write Denaples an apology letter, capping off another successful learning experience packaged into a week's episode, though it might have taken longer.

In this way, reality television, especially in a school setting, is likely to deviate from the way time is traditionally represented in the genre of school films. Unlike such films, for which the narratives of gradual growth and success traditionally require a chronological telling, reality television needs to manipulate time to create dramatic episodes with brief but complete narratives. As Kavka and West (2004) point out, reality television "reorders time, distilling it into socially recognizable units which are reiterable" (p. 139). Through repeated viewing of this type of format, audiences may slowly adjust their need for a chronological frame when engaging with this format and become willing to accept that what may have taken weeks to build up and then be resolved can be represented in 45 minutes. But, once again, audiences are also familiar with the rhythms of an actual, full class period, so perhaps they yearn for the details that would help them to make sense of classroom decisions portrayed on screen. If they are not there, then the nebulous connections break down.

Supporting Roles or Leading Roles?

As *Teach*'s episodes continue, Danza's students and their stories become more prominent than the story of his learning to teach. Previously, children have appeared on reality television as contestants or in supporting roles (*Kid Nation*, *The Biggest Loser*). With the genesis of such shows as Bravo's *NYC Prep* and Lifetime's *Dance Moms*, children continue to be featured prominently, but often have little to no agency in their representations. Danza's students, however, are given a bit more agency in the show through their monologues with the camera and conversations caught on camera without teachers or administrators present. As the show continues, Danza's students' lives begin to form the basis of the show's plot, but they never have the chance to achieve the celebrity status children in other reality television shows achieve, mainly because doing so would mean interfering with the very basics of education. Instead, their stories unfold as if the audience were Danza, and we watch him sort through evidence to make sense of his students' behavior.

The episode "To Cheat or Not to Cheat" opens with a series of interactions between Danza and various administrators. The episode revolves around two sets of friends: Stephanie and Illeana and Matt and Howard. When Stephanie and Illeana refuse to share their worksheets with each other one day during class, Danza sets out to determine why they are no longer friends. It turns out the two girls began arguing when Stephanie started hanging out with Crystal and Illeana started dating Eric. The story of their unraveling friendship unfolds in front of the camera as they each reflect on its demise, and Danza offers some fatherly advice. There are tears from the girls, a suspected spitting incident, and assessments of the relationship from other friends. However, it is the second storyline that demonstrates how the show manipulates students' actions into a storyline while still making space for their side of the story.

The second storyline in this episode deals with Howard and Matt, the pair Danza tried to help in "Homesick." Howard returns to school after an absence and needs to make up a test on *Julius Caesar*. Danza sends him to take his test in the hallway so he can go over the test with the other students in the classroom. Howard admits to not being ready for the test: "Shakespeare test, how you gonna study Shakespeare?" In the scenes that follow, the camera in the classroom zooms in on Matt, who pulls his phone out of his pocket. (The audience even gets to hear the sound of the text notification.) In the hallway, the cameras show Howard texting and then receiving a text. For the next few shots, the cameras move from hallway to classroom, from Matt's phone to Howard's phone, clearly suggesting that the boys are indeed texting each other about the test as Danza goes over the answers.

Danza finally catches Matt texting and tells him to put the phone away. He suspects their cheating and reports it to Cohn, who tells him that he can't do anything about it because he didn't see it. Danza says he is not going to show Howard and Matt the tape, but rather make them admit to cheating. He meets with them and asks them to give a presentation on Act III as evidence that they read and understood the play. After their meeting, Howard says, "I don't know how he caught me." Later in the hallway, they reveal on camera that they did cheat, and Matt asks Howard, "Didn't you see the cameras?" Howard says he felt they were too far away.

Howard then tells Matt that he can get them out of the assignment. Howard tells his classmates that Danza has accused him of cheating, thus positioning himself as the victim. He then confronts Danza and tells him, "If you think I cheated, give me a zero on the test," thereby calling Danza's bluff. After listening to Howard (who earlier in the series had difficulty with reading the assigned material) praise study guides and Danza's improved teaching as the reasons for his high score, Danza compromises and asks for a 20-word summary of the acts covered on the test. Danza wonders, "Did I get through to him? I don't think so."

Episode seven, "Teacher's Pet," focuses on Danza's relationships with three students—Algernon, Chloe, and Johnny. His interactions with Algernon are a continuation of their relationship in episode three, supporting Cohn's prediction that it is going to take some time for Danza to gain Algernon's respect. Danza has just finished teaching *Julius Caesar* and announces that the next lesson will be on how to write a five-paragraph essay. The topic is, "Who was responsible for Julius Caesar's death?" Danza also mentions that the marking period is about to end and this grade will play a large part in determining the grades on their report cards. After collecting their essays, Danza is disappointed by their lack of quality and gives his students an opportunity to rewrite them. Eventually, 21 out of 26 students resubmit their essays. Upset by the fact that all of his students didn't turn in revised essays, Danza tracks down each remaining student, even pulling some of them out of class, to collect the missing essays. Eventually, he has all of them but Algernon's. Without the grade for this essay, Algernon will fail his English class.

Algernon confesses to the camera that Danza's giving him so many chances is not helping him understand the consequences of turning in work late. Danza's other students know that he's giving Algernon extra chances and view his behavior as unfair to the rest of them who turned in their work. Frustrated in part by the attention and second chances Danza seems to give some of his students and her participation grade (a grade based on students' engaging in class discussion and work; some teachers use this as a way for rewarding students for their good behavior), Chloe tries to get transferred out of his class. As a result, Principal Carroll tries to tell Danza that he is not connecting with all of his students: "Kids don't want to be invisible." She explains that he needs to work on his relationship with a few kids. Danza doesn't seem to see a problem.

Meanwhile, Danza has been watching a group of students wandering the hallways and tries his best to convince one of them, Johnny, to stay out of trouble and start going to class. Danza's efforts, which involve speaking with Johnny's teachers and negotiating arrangements, work for a while, but his mentee soon finds himself in court for joy riding. Danza offers to help Johnny catch up with schoolwork and speak on his behalf to his teachers. He also tries to talk to Johnny and his group of friends about self-discipline and how it is a choice. He wonders, "Can we make a dent in a kid like that?" and confesses, "I see something in him that reminds me of me." In the end, Algernon passes, Johnny doesn't.

Danza's students do not achieve the celebrity status that many other reality television stars do. As Holmes (2004) notes, *Big Brother*'s contestants are greeted by fans when they leave the house; shows like *Dance Moms* and *American Idol* have reunion shows and audiences. *Teach* just has the cameras and a group of students whose antics are deemed by the producers to be worth camera time. Perhaps these camera-worthy moments are, as Hill (2005) describes, those "moment[s] of authenticity when real people are 'really' themselves in an unreal environment" (p. 324).

Conclusion

Whether he's teaching his students the rudiments of boxing (reminiscent of Michelle Pfeiffer in *Dangerous Minds*) or trying to help a student who is not in his class finish the school year (again, another approach found in several films, including *To Sir, With Love* [Clavell, 1967]) Danza clings to his belief that if he can just convince these students to "get smart early," they will be successful in life. The irony is that Danza became successful and remains so in his own life without "[getting] smart early." Nonetheless, Danza seems to enter the classroom determined to impart this wisdom even as he demonstrates both its attraction and its limitations.

A couple of years after finishing his year at Northeast, Danza wrote a memoir about his experience, *I'd Like to Apologize to Every Teacher I've Ever Had: My Year as a Rookie Teacher at Northeast High School* (2012).

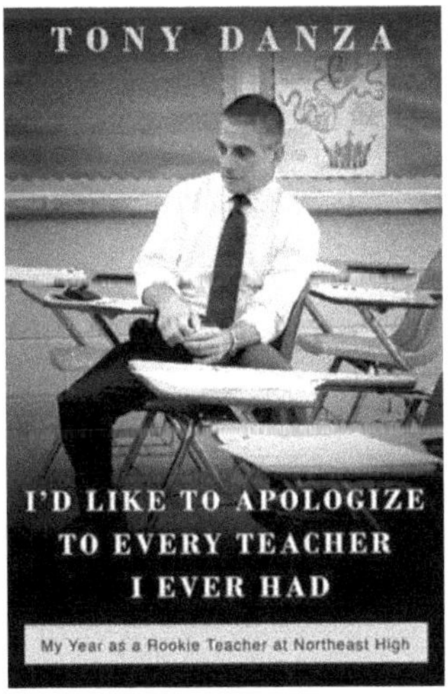

Figure 8.2. The cover for Danza's memoir of his experiences at Northeast High School. Source: Danza, T. *I'd Like to Apologize to Every Teacher I've Ever Had: My Year as a Rookie Teacher at Northeast High School*. New York: Penguin Random House. 2013. Reprinted by permission of Penguin Random House LLC. All rights reserved.

In this book, Danza attempts to address the gaps left in his television show—namely, how the idea for the show began, how the cameras and producers regarded what was going on in the classroom, and how this experience opened his eyes to the realities of teaching. But Danza's book, taken with the number of interviews, blogs, and online commentaries mentioned in this chapter, makes us, as readers, question once again the sincerity and skill Danza brought (or didn't bring) to the classroom. Reality television, coupled with the interactive and ongoing role of social media in extending conversations about a series no longer on television, gives rise to its own subculture and builds its own avenues of audience engagement.

In the end, a show that relied on the conventions of the reality television genre could not manipulate the teaching profession into something marketable, popular, and profitable. Airing on Friday nights, the show opened with 937,000 viewers and had fallen to 606,000 in one of the last episodes, causing the channel to cut the season two weeks short by airing the last two episodes back-to-back (Futon Critic, 2010). If anything, *Teach* demonstrates how rarely those exciting teachable moments in the classroom can be packaged for the screen. Even Danza's most successful lesson, the presentation of original myths, transferred poorly to the screen.

Without the blocking and scripting that accompanies the feature film or sitcom, without careful editing and background music—elements generally not used in reality television—the audience feels too much like students watching their peers giving a presentation. And perhaps that is the problem. Maybe Danza's show reminds us of our actual high school experiences, rather than the imagined ones we have come to expect.

References

aetv_rita. (2010). Take the *Mice and Men* test from episode 2 tested! Talk about it here! Retrieved from http://community.aetv.com/service/displayDiscussionThreads.kickAction?as=119137&w=327039&d=591819&ac=new

Avildsen, J. G. (Director). (1989). *Lean on me*. [DVD]. United States: Warner Brothers.

Bulman, R. (2004). *Hollywood goes to high school: Cinema, schools, and American culture*. New York, NY: Worth.

Clavell, J. (Director). (1967). *To sir, with love* [Motion picture]. United Kingdom: Columbia Pictures.

Corner, J. (2002). Performing the real: Documentary diversions. *Television & New Media*, 3, 255–269.

Cutler, R. J. (Director). *American high* [Television series]. Los Angeles, CA: Actual Reality Pictures.

Dalton, M. (2010). *The Hollywood curriculum: Teachers in the movies* (2nd ed.). New York, NY: Peter Lang.

Danza, T. (2012). *I'd like to apologize to every teacher I ever had*. New York, NY: Random House.
de Mol, J. (Creator). (2000). *Big brother* [Television series]. New York, NY: Columbia Broadcasting System.
Fuller, S. (Creator). (2002). *American idol* [Television series]. Los Angeles, CA: Fox Network.
Futon Critic Staff. (2010). Exclusive: A&E to wrap *Teach: Tony Danza* early. Retrieved from http://www.thefutoncritic.com/news/2010/10/22/exclusive-aande-to-wrap-teach-tony-danza-early-205015/8937/#hXkIs2UuGJYYjhpf.99
Gilbert, C. (Director). (1973). *An American family* [Television series]. New York, NY: WNET.
Graham, K. A. (2010). Tony Danza goes back to school. *LA Times*. Retrieved from http://articles.latimes.com/2010/mar/31/entertainment/la-et-danza31-2010mar31
Greif, L., & Reed, A. (Producers). (2010). *Teach: Tony Danza* [Television series]. Philadelphia, PA: A&E.
Guggenheim, D. (Director). (2010). *Waiting for Superman* [DVD]. United States: Paramount.
Harding, C. B. (Director). (2002). *The Osbournes*. [Television series]. United States: MTV.
Hill, A. (2005). *Reality TV: Audiences and popular factual television*. Abingdon/New York: Routledge.
Holmes, S. (2004). All you've got to worry about is the task, having a cup of tea, and doing a bit of sunbathing: Approaching celebrity in *Big brother*. In S. Holmes & D. Jermyn (Eds.), *Understanding reality television* (pp. 111–135). London, UK: Routledge.
Jenkins, H. (2006). *Fans, bloggers, and gamers: Exploring participatory culture*. New York, NY: New York University Press.
Kavka, M., & West, A. (2004). Temporalities of the real: Conceptualising time in reality television. In S. Holmes & D. Jermyn (Eds.), *Understanding reality television* (pp. 136–153). London, UK: Routledge.
Kompare, D. (2004) The Osbournes as "An American family." In S. Murray & L. Ouellette (Eds.), *Reality TV: Remaking television culture* (pp. 97–116). New York, NY: New York University Press.
Kusbit, B. (Director). (2002). *Made* [Television series]. Darlinghurst, AU: One Louder Entertainment.
LaGravenese, R. (Director). (2007). *Freedom writers* [DVD]. United States: Paramount.
McNamara, M. (2010, October 1). Television review: *Teach: Tony Danza* on A&E. *Los Angeles Times*. Retrieved from http://articles.latimes.com/2010/oct/01/entertainment/la-et-danza-review-20101001
Pincus, M. (2010). Teach, Tony Danza, teach. *The Notebook*. Retrieved from http://thenotebook.org/blog/102956/teach-tony-danza-teach
Raz, G. (Interviewer) & Danza, T. (Interviewee). (2009). Tony Danza shows high school students who's boss [Interview transcript]. Retrieved from http://www.npr.org/templates/story/story.php?storyId=113166330
Sackler, M. (Director). (2010). *The lottery* [Motion picture]. United States: Great Curve Films.
Smith, J. N. (Director). (1995). *Dangerous minds* [DVD]. United States: Don Simpson/Jerry Bruckheimer Films/Hollywood Pictures.

Stanley, A. (2010, September 30). Television review: *Teach: Tony Danza. New York Times.* Retrieved from http://tv.nytimes.com/2010/10/01/arts/television/01teach.html?_r=1&ref=tonydanza

Steinbeck, J. (1937). *Of mice and men.* New York, NY: Covici, Friede, Inc.

Stuever, H. (2010). Tony Danza teaches English in real Philadelphia high school in A&E TV show. *Washington Post.* Retrieved from http://www.washingtonpost.com/wp-dyn/content/article/2010/09/30/AR2010093006430.html

Storm, J. (2010). *Teach: Tony Danza* on A&E: A sensitive teacher and a fine, rare look at high school reality. *The Inquirer.* Retrieved from http://articles.philly.com/2010-09-30/news/24978237_1_english-teacher-tony-danza-reality-show-premieres

Thomas, J. E. (2011, January 5). *Teach: Tony Danza* captures classroom reality. Teaching Tolerance: A Project of the Southern Law Center. Retrieved from http://www.tolerance.org/blog/teach-tony-danza-captures-classroom-reality

· 9 ·

"MAKE IT WORK"

Incorporating Reality Television into the Classroom

At the end of each spring semester, my preservice teachers are finishing their student teaching internships and are anxious for practical lessons that will help prepare them for their first teaching jobs. Given their desire, I took some time several years ago to construct a lesson I thought they might find useful. I asked them to envision what materials they felt they would need to outfit their new classrooms. How would they collect and store student work? Did they have a favorite type of pen they liked to use while grading? I asked students to put together a shopping list, complete with prices, and bring it to class. My plan was to discuss the high cost of supplies and the minimal budget their schools might give them to set up their classrooms. A lesson I thought would be relevant and engaging soon became tedious as each student rattled off a long list with prices. It was difficult for us to picture some of the supplies students referenced without actually having a photo, and we often spent time searching for images of them on the classroom computer. I was ready to drop the lesson altogether until I was inspired by reality television to make over my lesson.

Project Runway, a favorite show of mine, challenges contestants to create outfits for actual clients; they have one to two days to design, create, and show their outfits. At the end of the episode, a panel of judges determines which designer's outfit is the winner and which designer is "out"—or eliminated from the show. During most episodes, the designers visit a New York fabric store,

Mood, where the contestants purchase fabric and sewing supplies for their creations. One semester, while watching the show, I was reminded of a comment Madeleine Grumet had made at a recent conference. After admitting she had been neglecting her personal reading and instead watching *Project Runway*, she posed the question to the audience, "What if we taught curriculum courses in a style like *Project Runway*?" Educators, she said, could issue semester-long challenges in which students would tackle real-world issues that schools face. I thought, "Why can't I take a similar approach?"

So I modified my lesson based on a typical challenge found in an episode of *Project Runway*. We now take a field trip that helps make this abstract lesson more concrete. Our challenge takes place at our local office supply store (I make arrangements with the store's manager ahead of time) and includes the following directions:

***Project Runway*—Office Depot Challenge**

For this challenge, you and your team have (a hypothetical) $50 and 30 minutes to "buy" a paper management system for your new classroom. You need to make sure you have supplies for the following:

1. A way to collect, keep, and pass back papers.
2. A set up for late work.
3. A way to organize and grade student work.
4. Anything else you think is essential.

You will be judged on how well you keep within your budget, the ease of your system (both for you *and* your students), and the validity of your explanation to the rest of the class about your choices.

In groups of 2–3, students grab carts and "go shopping," placing in their carts the items they would use in their classroom and keeping a running tally of how much money they spend. At the end of the 30 minutes, we meet in the office furniture area, and they share how and why they spent the money. While students replace the items on the shelves, the judges (usually a colleague and a former student) and I deliberate. Then we announce the top two teams and award them gift cards. It's a lot of fun and a great way to end the semester. Asking students to synthesize aspects of teaching, including the simple act of touching actual products and seeing actual prices, can be quite eye opening for them.

Given the popularity of reality television among our students, these shows can be an attractive form of popular culture to incorporate into the classroom. Reality television shows serve not only as material for students and teachers to deconstruct and analyze, but also as a way to teach content. In Chapter 7, I introduced the concept of reality television pedagogy, an approach to education that hovers between the genre's educational and entertainment purposes; I also introduced the ways the genre's form and structure can create learning experiences that position viewers as experts. Those educators who incorporate reality television pedagogy into their courses look to these shows as a way of creating a sense of real-world application and engagement with their course material.

Engaging in reality television pedagogy can result in successful learning experiences if the educators and students involved are able to negotiate the real and not real aspects that viewers do while watching these shows. Examining the scholarship on reality television pedagogy reveals that educators tend to incorporate reality television into their courses in one of three ways: as a means of engaging in forms of media literacy, as a way to present related course content to their students, and as a model for designing lessons. In this chapter, I will examine each of these three approaches as well as discuss what makes them successful examples of reality television pedagogy.

A Disclaimer

Before I examine the practices of educators who incorporate reality television into their courses, I would like to state that I do understand (as do our students, according to Corner, 2002) the insidious nature of reality television with its tendencies to focus on extreme human behavior, to manipulate reality, to promote consumerism, and to capitalize on voyeurism. It often creates a highly competitive atmosphere and edits storylines to highlight the best and worst of people. I addressed many of those concerns in my earlier work with a team of fourth grade teachers (Bach, 2011) who attempted to navigate these issues with their own students. In point of fact, reality television pedagogy is not for everyone. However, one of the reasons that educators bring television into their classrooms is because of its ability to educate in an entertaining fashion. As Hartley (1999) explains, "one of the main attractions of TV is that it is not like formal education" (p. 41) because it exists outside of "scholastic compulsion, tedium, control, and conformism" (p. 41). That being said, simply showing a reality television show to break the tedium is *not* reality television pedagogy—or even pedagogy, for that matter.

Pedagogical models based on reality television also serve as a form of *hidden curriculum*, an educational theory that argues that alongside the stated lessons in school, there are unstated lessons students are expected to learn.

Those lessons are mainly related to social behavior, such as the lessons that following instructions and raising hands to answer questions can contribute to success in school. Ouellette and Hay (2008) make a similar observation about television. They argue that television teaches social behavior and that reality television, in particular, teaches those lessons through sport and play:

> To the extent that TV educates about the proper forms of belonging, of managing differences, and of participation by citizens in various spheres of life, this education occurs as play or sporting task in the current regime of TV. Learning, mastering, and performing the "rules of the game" is tantamount to successful performances of membership and citizenship. (Ouellette and Hay, 2008, p. 174)

Those lessons come in handy for participating in shows like *Survivor* and *Project Runway* where one's ability to stay on the show depends on one's ability to get along, cause a controversy, or anticipate what the judges want to see. But some of those lessons also transfer to the classroom, especially when success involves working in groups, coming up with creative ideas, and pleasing the teacher.

When educators adopt elements of reality television pedagogy into their courses, they engage in what Hartley (1999) describes as "DIY [do-it-yourself] citizenship." He argues that although television teaches, we can't be sure what they are teaching. According to Hartley, viewers go on to use these shows "who knows how, by populations whose purposes and actions are outside of the pedagogic relations used by TV" (p. 47). What happens when educators, then, bring television into a setting noted for its "compulsion, tedium, control, and conformism"? Negotiating television's entertainment and educational purposes becomes extremely important in reality television pedagogy.

Consider the danger in using reality television as a gimmick to revise a traditional lesson into something "fun." For example, Tony Danza used an *American Idol* format, a show in which singers compete to win a recording contract, as a way to inspire his students to read poems of their choice in front of the class—a twist on the traditional recitation of a memorized poem assignment found in many English language arts classrooms. He awarded prizes: the winner won a flip camera; second place won eight dollars. After this experience, Danza (2012) reflects in his memoir, "For the prizes, the kids go crazy. For the purpose of memorizing poetry, not so much" (p. 149). This simple, yet profound, observation should serve as a warning for those educators looking for gimmicks to encourage student learning. While reality television can serve as a motivating factor, it cannot successfully improve lessons that already lack a connection to the world outside of the classroom. Furthermore, reality television does not always help students connect on a deeper level with course content.

Reality Television Pedagogy as Media Literacy

Hartley (1999) argues that scholars should be concerned not only with the intentions of a particular show but also with what happens to its audiences after they view it. What have they learned, and what are they doing with those lessons? Media literacy is an educational approach that seeks to enable viewers to ask those questions of themselves. Publications on incorporating reality television into the classroom have found this to be a popular approach, especially for use with nonprint texts, and the pedagogical strategies that make up the field apply particularly well to reality television. The Center for Media Literacy (2011) associates the benefits of media literacy with more than just reading and interpreting texts. It claims that media literacy is

> a 21st-century approach to education. It provides a framework to access, analyze, evaluate, create, and participate with messages in a variety of forms—from print to video to the Internet. Media literacy builds an understanding of the role of media in society as well as essential skills of inquiry and self-expression necessary for citizens of a democracy.

Media literacy is not just about teaching how to interpret and use the messages we receive via various media. According to Considine, Horton, and Moorman (2009), "Media literacy requires teaching about media—the language it uses along with its narrative, codes, and conventions" (p. 474). Closely related to media literacy is *critical media literacy*, in which viewers interrogate the medium, questioning its motives and representations. As Kellner and Share (2005) explain, "Critical media literacy involves cultivating skills in analyzing media codes and conventions, abilities to criticize stereotypes, dominant values, and ideologies, and competencies to interpret the multiple meanings and messages generated by media texts" (p. 372). Critical media literacy, then, enables viewers to read and engage with texts in order to understand the larger implications of their role in society as well as their potential influences on audiences' perceptions of the worlds (re)presented in them.

Humanities and social sciences educators, especially those in English departments, are embracing the potential of treating the offerings of reality television as texts to read, critique, and research. For example, Miller (2011) designed a freshman composition course he titled "Big Brother Recycled" that focused on the origin and many reappropriations of the phrase "big brother" throughout various cultural artifacts. As a culminating assignment, students were asked to view at least eight hours of reality television and create a project that addressed several topics related to the course's content. Students could chose to:

- integrate a reflection on issues of race, class, gender, sexual orientation, gender expression, national origin, ability, and/or religion;
- reflect on your role as the viewer and consumer of the show as it relates to course content (readings, theories, and discussions);
- reflect on how this show perpetuates myths or leads to a new way of considering humans and the media;
- reflect on and explain who you would/n't recommend this show to;
- reflect on and share what you learned about yourself in this process;
- ponder the ethics involved in viewing/spying/consuming that which is not yours. (p. 142)

While Miller ran into difficulties with members of his department, who were initially skeptical about his use of reality television in a "reading class" (p. 144), his students analyzed how shows perpetuated and challenged stereotypes, how the genre distorts reality, and how the shows interact with audiences. And perhaps as an unexpected consequence, Miller's department now engages in conversations about the use of New Literacies, a field that focuses on the interactivity of multiple forms of texts in which users consume and produce works and how that approach might be used in future courses.

Likewise, Pozner (2010) considers the potential pedagogies of reality television inside and outside of the classroom. In particular, she believes that viewers need to learn how to interrogate the representations of women in reality television. As a teacher of women's and gender studies courses in addition to many media literacy workshops, she focuses on issues of race, class, and gender in shows such as *The Surreal Life* (a show similar to *The Real World* that features "former" celebrities living together in a mansion), *America's Next Top Model*, and *Flavor of Love* (a dating show in which women compete to date rapper Flavor Flav). In Pozner's book, *Reality Bites Back* (2010), she has an entire chapter dedicated to media literacy, "Fun with Media Literacy! Drinking Games, Deconstruction Guides, and Other Critical Thinking Tools." Careful to acknowledge that when playing a drinking game during *America's Next Top Model*, there is a fine line between drinking when "the bitch they hate gets eliminated" and when "a very thin girl is called fat, calls herself ugly, or says she needs to eat less," Pozner hopes media literacy will help viewers not only understand the implications of these representations but also do something to challenge them.

Aware of the complications of appropriating students' cultural texts, she calls for educators, parents, and siblings to "create a safe space that allows kids to investigate and decode media for themselves. Don't lecture; listen and ask questions. You may be the expert in life experience, but kids are the experts in the media that surround them" (p. 309). This concept is important for those educators who are critical of reality television and might not have considered or surveyed their students for their personal tastes in entertainment. Choice, discussion, and conversation should characterize media literacy approaches that incorporate reality television pedagogy.

Reality Television Pedagogy as Content

Reality television shows, especially those created for educational channels whose original purpose was to produce nonfictional content (such as the History Channel, the Learning Channel, and Animal Planet), can be used to complement a course's subject matter. Currently, there are shows about fishing in the Bering Sea, raising children, decorating homes, interacting with drug and alcohol abusers, and, as we discussed in the previous chapter, teaching high school students. While these shows cannot and do not attempt to "teach" viewers how they can go about fishing, parenting, and teaching, they do provide valuable glimpses into professions, and this exposure has been shown to increase students' understanding of those particular fields (Bach & Weinstein, 2014; Kuhn-Wilken, Zimmerman, Matheson, Banning, & Pepin, 2012). Educators and students might watch an episode or even clips from a particular show and "fill in the blanks" of what's missing in these representations. Or they might watch an episode as a way to introduce a course topic. Approached with the notion that what they are seeing is not the entire picture, but rather a snapshot, can enrich the learning of a course's content.

Reality television provides a way of applying course content to ready-made scenarios. One example can be found in the book *Cinemeducation* (Alexandar, Lenahan, & Pavlov, 2012), which is a collection of essays that examine ways film and television shows might enhance the education and training of those entering the healthcare delivery system. In the chapter "Too

Reel for Comfort: Reality TV," Lenahan (2012) categorizes and describes various reality television shows that deal with health-related issues. She points out that some of these shows influence the public's knowledge about particular health conditions and may influence audience members to seek a particular treatment from their health care provider. She then offers critical questions and scenarios medical educators might use with their students to discuss topics such as ethical issues in medical care, substance use, and obesity and eating disorders. Like Lenahan, educators who are using reality television shows to teach their students about their profession do so by interrogating and critiquing representations of professionals found in shows.

Another strategy educators have undertaken with reality television is using it as content material for their courses. With the large number of shows on particular professions (medicine, parenting, real estate), educators have a wide variety of shows to watch and discuss with their students. For instance, in their examination of the reality television show *Supernanny*, Kuhn-Wilken et al. (2012) identified the particular parenting practices emphasized throughout the series and mapped them onto current knowledge about effective parenting. *Supernanny* is a show where a family who has children who misbehave reach out to the producers requesting help. If chosen, the show will send out Jo Frost, a British nanny, who comes to help the family learn how to work together. On the first day, Jo watches the family and then gives them her assessment of their dynamics. She then spends the next day or so with the family, coaching them on parenting techniques before leaving them on their own for a few days to practice them. Those days are filmed so Jo can review them. Jo then returns, debriefs the family on their performance, and offers a few more pieces of advice before leaving. Usually, family members find their relationships tremendously improved as they become confident in their newly gained skills and knowledge.

In particular, those educators who focus on the media's representations of families must confront the issue of how reality television can distort perceptions and/or influence behaviors related to raising children. For example, Kuhn-Wilken et al. (2012) reach several conclusions based on their experiences using this show with their students. Those conclusions can serve as recommendations for educators considering using reality television to discuss course content and professional skills. The researchers reflect on what they learned through this experience as well by summarizing how different educators in different professions might use reality television:

- By understanding the manner in which the mass media may be shaping parents' efforts or understandings, a practitioner is more aware of what information is available or invisible, and can shape interventions accordingly.
- Focusing on parenting messages in the media is also an effective way for therapists to build rapport or deepen conversations with families. The familiarity of television may provide a sense of safety, which could make discussions easier for newer clients.
- Practitioners may also choose to incorporate *Supernanny* clips or episodes into homework assignments by asking clients to rehearse how they would respond to the behaviors portrayed on *Supernanny* episodes. ... Practitioners and clients could view clips of the show together in a session depicted as a learning tool for change. (p. 334)

The idea of clients and practitioners watching episodes together is intriguing as it positions both parties as experts who know how to view these shows through their shared understanding of the genre. Kuhn et al.'s findings support my own, with colleague Weinstein (Bach & Weinstein, 2014) in our study conducted with preservice teachers who watched episodes of *Teach: Tony Danza*. We found that there were certain aspects of the genre that, when focused on, enriched our discussions of the teaching profession. We also found that whether one watches these shows as insiders or outsiders can result in different interpretations or understandings of what it means to be a parent, nanny, teacher, or student. Both of our approaches highlight how these conversations can lead to a better understanding of how media might shape audiences' perceptions of certain professions.

Reality Television Pedagogy as Lesson Template

A third approach available to reality television pedagogy educators is to adapt a lesson to the structure of a gamedoc. Gamedocs, a combination of soap operas and game shows, create scenarios in which "ordinary" people compete for prizes, usually against each other. One such forerunner in this genre is *Survivor*, which originated in Sweden and subsequently inspired a similar show in America with the same name. In this show, two teams are taken to a remote location and expected to survive with limited food supplies and/or equipment. Every few days, the teams compete in a challenge and the losing team must send a team member home. The final member, or sole survivor, wins one million dollars.

This show's template—which consists of a theme/gimmick, teams, challenges, voting, dismissal, and reward—serves as an unlikely model for classroom practice. Furthermore, as in the case of Danza's *American Idol* contest, it can result in an undesirable learning experience in which students focus more on the format than on the teacher's actual objective—learning. John Dewey's educational philosophies can serve as a guide for helping to bridge this gap between entertainment and education in reality television pedagogy. In *Experience and Education*, Dewey (1938/1998) criticizes schools for being removed from society, that is, being isolated from that for which it hopes to prepare students. For Dewey, "the belief that all genuine education comes about through experience does not mean that all experiences are genuinely or equally educative" (1938/1998, p. 13). He argues that education should not be based on an either/or situation and that the gap between the subject matter and teacher, on the one hand, and experience, on the other, can be reconciled. For those seeking to use reality television as a pedagogical model, Dewey's philosophies can help sort out the dos and don'ts of such an approach.

This approach differs from the previous two in that the show's structure lends itself to being a potential pedagogical model, rather than a text to critique and/or deconstruct. If an educator decides to adapt a pedagogical strategy based on the structure of a gamedoc, students, teachers, and any outside participants (e.g., judges or clients) need to remain within the boundaries between the real and the not real. In other words, just as audiences negotiate reality television shows, so too must educators and their students negotiate this dichotomy in the classroom. On the one hand, they must recognize the positive real aspects of the show (by real, I mean that which exists outside of the classroom, such as those who are practicing in a profession or spaces outside of the confines of the classroom), especially the role the mentors/judges can play in critiquing the contestants'/students' products. On the other hand, they must also accept the subjectivity and the artificiality that comes with constructing a challenge that brings together a format from television with the necessary content of a course. Learning does become a game, but it's a game in which students must remember not to lose the focus on content and educators adjust to assessing student learning in unconventional manners.

Gamedocs possess educational components that some have adapted to the classroom. For example, Eckenrode (2008) uses the format of the CBS show *Amazing Race* to introduce her students to the various resources in a library. Take the *Project Runway* activity that I used to open this chapter. This type of show begins with a challenge (often with a real client); sometimes contestants work on their own, sometimes in teams, to complete that challenge. They are then given or expected to gather the materials needed to complete the challenge. A work session ensues, and contestants often receive mentorship from current practitioners in the field during this portion of the show. A panel of expert judges evaluates the final products, selects one designer as that week's winner, and often presents an additional prize, perhaps the production and sale of the winning design. Of course, contestants must leave the show if their product receives the lowest scores, and the entire set-up encourages fierce competition (and occasionally some unethical behavior), but, as I argued in Chapter 1, the experience contains what most documentaries support—educational experiences that are relevant to students.

In another episode from *Project Runway*, "All Dolled Up" (third episode from the second season), contestants received the challenge to create a life-sized outfit for Barbie's My Scene Line. The contestants took a field trip to a toy store to receive their challenge so they could look at actual dolls and their marketing (and, presumably, to get some advertising for the sponsors). This approach can be likened to what Dewey would call a purpose that involves observation, significance, idea, plan, and project. "A genuine purpose" according to Dewey, "always starts with an impulse. Obstruction of the immediate execution of an impulse converts it into a desire … A purpose is an endview" (1938/1998, p. 78). This show's purpose works because students have a desire in this field—an interest in designing clothes. The show works because it merges its own need to produce a show with the contestants' desires to succeed in the featured profession.

These challenges are successful also because they incorporate elements of what Dewey considers to be an essential part of study. According to Dewey (1938/1998), "Anything which can be called a study, whether arithmetic, history, geography, or one of the natural sciences, must be derived from materials which at the outset fall within the scope of ordinary life experience" (pp. 86–87). For Dewey, the contact with new experiences and materials in one's environment is an important factor in learning. However, merely introducing new experiences and materials into the process is not enough. He writes, "It is also essential that the new objects and events be related intellectually to those of earlier experiences, and this means that there be some advance made in conscious articulation of facts and ideas" (p. 90). In other words, learners are at different levels in their study, in part because of their previous experiences; educational opportunities should allow them to begin at their current level and then exhibit advancement. In *Project Runway*, this means contestants who have experience working with certain types of fabric might be challenged to work with this material in new and more challenging ways. Often, the show will add additional components to a challenge that stretches the contestants even further. In the Barbie show, for example, they were asked to make a mini-version of their outfit for a doll. Those contestants who push themselves to take risks are often those who are rewarded.

Personal advancement of one's knowledge and skills through feedback is another hallmark of gamedocs and is an invaluable component in Dewey's tenets. According to Dewey, the educator has two responsibilities to learners and their growth: first, to make sure that the problems they encounter are within the realm of their experience and abilities; two, that the problem instills a desire to acquire new knowledge and skills. In *Project Runway*, Tim Gunn serves as the contestants' mentor and gives ongoing feedback throughout the challenge. His approach is to offer contestants an alternative perspective, and his comments are an attempt to get them to see something in their work that they might not see. His mantra "Make it work" often results in substantial growth in the contestants' skills and thinking processes. Contestants also receive group and individual feedback after the episode's runway show from a panel of expert judges, which frequently includes supermodel and host Heidi Klum, fashion designer Michael Kors, magazine editor Nina Garcia, and, for the Barbie episode, a guest judge from Mattel. The feedback is often accompanied by "real-life" consequences. In this case, the reward for the best work in this challenge had his outfit manufactured and sold as part of the Barbie clothing line. The designer of the lowest scoring outfit was sent home.

Of course, gamedocs contradict several of Dewey's tenets of democratic education: they are exclusionary to begin with—one must audition and/or apply to appear on them. Contestants often receive feedback in the form of harsh comments before being told "You're out," or "Go and pack your knives," or "You're no longer in the running to become America's next top model." The negative feedback, dismissal from the group, and potential embarrassment in front of an audience can lead to what Dewey (1936/1998) warns as a "mis-educative" experience that "has the effect of arresting or distorting the growth of further experience" (p. 13). But the disregard for the way one evaluates a contestant calls into question the real motives of shows like *Project Runway*. Are they really intended to improve a designer's skills? Or are they looking to find the best designers? Perhaps they are meant merely to entertain. Would these shows bother with providing support and feedback if they didn't want to merge the entertainment with the education?

Reality Television Pedagogy for the Educator

The way these shows represent feedback through the guise of judging can also offer educators ways to improve their practice. In reality shows, contestants are often mentored and evaluated by the show's experts who are either judges or advisors. These experts do differ in their approaches to delivering feedback, ranging from overly negative criticism to carefully crafted constructive criticism, which they usually offer at the very end of an episode. Tyra Banks, for example, on *America's Next Top Model,* often employs an explosive style, whereas Heidi Klum on *Project Runway* attempts a quieter one.

Also imparting advice and wisdom and, indirectly, offering educators ideas for providing feedback in a more formative manner are the shows' mentors. The mentors of these shows are the ones who work with the contestants throughout the show and oversee and assist them during the actual competition. One such role model is *Project Runway*'s Tim Gunn whom law educator Higdon (2007) sees as offering critiques designed to help improve a student's ability to make more effective choices in the future (p. 173). Higdon turns to Gunn's model as a way to consider alternate ways of evaluating the work of his law students, and he encourages his peers to adopt the Tim Gunn model of giving feedback (unlike those approaches made popular on *American Idol*). Higdon identifies four principles of Gunn's approach: Gunn does not focus on the right or wrong of an outfit, but instead on the wearer's potential reaction; he encourages his mentees to consider how another designer might approach this work; he asks mentees about the thinking that went into their designs; and, finally, he does not use his critiques as an opportunity to belittle or patronize a young artist. In other words, role models for educators do not always have to be those who publish manuals or serve in traditional classroom settings.

Conclusion

Just as Dewey argues that education will only work if it combines traditional and progressive aspects, so, too, will reality television pedagogy only work if participants can dwell between the real and not real aspects of the genre and reconcile the entertainment with the educational purposes. The three pedagogical approaches I've mentioned in this chapter are successful because they attempt to apply course content to students' experiences with reality television as another enhancement to their educational journeys, much as Dewey suggests. They take into consideration students' potential stances on the genre and capitalize on that experience. And, they are entertaining.

As shown in these three chapters, reality television holds much promise for education by offering texts to analyze critically and to inspire. But, like all popular culture, it is ethereal and demands that we listen to our students to tell us when it's time to move on. It's quite possible that reality television, unlike documentaries and biopics, will one day no longer belong in the classroom.

References

Alexander, M., Lenahan, P., & Pavlov, A. (Eds.). (2012). *Cinemeducation: Using film and other visual media in graduate and medical education*. London, UK: Radcliffe Publishing.

Bach, J. (2011). How teachers negotiate the use of reality television in their pedagogy. *Pedagogies: An International Journal*, 6, 144–153.

Bach, J., & Weinstein, S. (2014). Who's the teacher? What Tony Danza taught us about English education. *English Education*, 46, 300–326.

Center for Media Literacy. (2011). Media literacy. Retrieved from http://www.medialit.org/media-literacy-definition-and-more

Considine, D., Horton, J., & Moorman, G. (2009). Teaching and reaching the millennial generation through media literacy. *Journal of Adolescent & Adult Literacy*, 52, 471–481.

Corner, J. (2002). Performing the real: Documentary diversions. *Television & New Media*, 3, 255–269.

Danza, T. (2012). *I'd like to apologize to every teacher I ever had*. New York, NY: Random House.

Dewey, J. (1938/1998). *Experience and education: The 60th anniversary edition*. West Lafayette, IN: Kappa Delta Pi.

Dewey, J., & Post, E. A. (1939). *Intelligence in the modern world: John Dewey's philosophy*. J. Ratner (Ed.). New York, NY: Modern Library.

Eckenrode, D. (2008). An "amazing race" through the library: Reality television meets problem-based learning. In D. Cook & R. L. Sittler (Eds.), *Practical pedagogy for library instructors: 17 innovative strategies to improve student learning* (pp. 127–138). Chicago: Association of College and Research Libraries.

Hartley, J. (1999). *Uses of television*. London, UK: Routledge.

Higdon, M. J. (2007). From Simon Cowell to Tim Gunn: What reality television can teach us about how to critique our students' work effectively. *Perspectives: Teaching Legal Research and Writing*, 15, 169–173.

Kellner, D., & Share, J. (2005). Toward critical media literacy: Core concepts, debates, organizations, and policy. *Discourse: Studies in the Cultural Politics of Education*, 26, 369–386.

Kuhn-Wilken, E., Zimmerman, T. S., Matheson, J. L., Banning, J. H., & Pepin, J. (2012). *Supernanny*'s solutions for families: An ethnographic content analysis of parenting messages on reality television. *Journal of Feminist Family Therapy*, 24, 316–339.

Lenahan, P. (2012). Too reel for comfort: Reality TV. In M. Alexander, P. Lenahan, & A. Pavlov (Eds.), *Cinemeducation: Using film and other visual media in graduate and medical education* (pp. 545–558). London, UK: Radcliffe Publishing.

Miller, sj. (2011). Demythologizing reality TV: Critical implications as a new literacy. *International Journal of Critical Pedagogy*, *3*(3), 135–152.

Ouellette, L., & Hay, J. (2008). *Better living through reality TV*. Madden, MA: Blackwell.

Pozner, J. L. (2010). *Reality bites back: The troubling truth about guilty pleasure TV*. Berkeley, CA: Seal Press.

minding the media

CRITICAL ISSUES
FOR LEARNING AND TEACHING

Shirley R. Steinberg
General Editor

Minding the Media is a book series specifically designed to address the needs of students and teachers in watching, comprehending, and using media. Books in the series use a wide range of educational settings to raise consciousness about media relations and realities and promote critical, creative alternatives to contemporary mainstream practices. *Minding the Media* seeks theoretical, technical, and practitioner perspectives as they relate to critical pedagogy and public education. Authors are invited to contribute volumes of up to 85,000 words to this series. Possible areas of interest as they connect to learning and teaching include:

- critical media literacy
- popular culture
- video games
- animation
- music
- media activism
- democratizing information systems
- using alternative media
- using the Web/internet
- interactive technologies
- blogs
- multi-media in the classroom
- media representations of race, class, gender, sexuality, disability, etc.
- media/communications studies methodologies
- semiotics
- watchdog journalism/investigative journalism
- visual culture: theater, art, photography
- radio, TV, newspapers, zines, film, documentary film, comic books
- public relations
- globalization and the media
- consumption/consumer culture
- advertising
- censorship
- audience reception

For additional information about this series or for the submission of manuscripts, please contact:

Shirley R. Steinberg
msgramsci@gmail.com

To order other books in this series, please contact our Customer Service Department:
(800) 770-LANG (within the U.S.)
(212) 647-7706 (outside the U.S.)
(212) 647-7707 FAX

Or browse online by series:
www.peterlang.com

www.ingramcontent.com/pod-product-compliance
Ingram Content Group UK Ltd.
Pitfield, Milton Keynes, MK11 3LW, UK
UKHW021015120926
8556IPUK00040B/1162

9 781433 129155